AIR TRAFFIC CONTROLLER TRAINING PROGRAM

Dr. James E. Turner
President/CEO
Aviation Education Systems, Inc.

New York   London   Toronto   Sydney   Tokyo   Singapore

We would like to thank the Federal Aviation Administration
for some of the materials used in this book.

Prentice Hall
15 Columbus Circle
New York, NY 10023

An Arco Book

Prentice Hall and colophons are
registered trademarks of Simon & Schuster, Inc.

Manufactured in the United States of America

1 2 3 4 5 6 7 8 9 10

Library of Congress Cataloging-in-Publication Data

Turner, James E., 1942-
    Air traffic controller training program / James E. Turner.
      p.   cm.
    "An Arco book"—T.p. verso.
    ISBN 0-13-019209-0 : $18.95
    1. Air traffic control—Study and teaching—United States.   2. Air
traffic control—Vocational guidance—United States.   I. Title.
TL725.3.T7T883   1991
629.136'6'02373—dc20   91-552
                                                            CIP

CONTENTS

PREFACE

It's been several years now since I decided to write the book that's now called *Air Traffic Controller Qualifying Test*. I'm proud that hundreds of Air Traffic Controllers attribute their success to having this book to help them with the entrance examination with the FAA.

That brings me to the reason behind the present volume. Learning to be an Air Traffic Controller has not really changed in the years since I started in the profession, and the pass/fail ratio at the FAA Academy in Oklahoma City has not greatly improved.

This book will give you a look at the FAA's course in Oklahoma City. It should eliminate the fears and apprehensions that you may have about the so-called "Zero Knowledge" curriculum. This book should allow you the opportunity of being one of the select few individuals who run the skies!

—Dr. James E. Turner

ACKNOWLEDGMENTS

I would like to thank my wife Donna and my children, J. Scott, Elizabeth, Ross and Dyanna for allowing me the time away from them to make this book possible.

I would also like to extend my thanks and appreciation to Katherine Zandides and David Myslenski for their hard work and dedication in helping me write this book.

FOREWORD

by J. Lynn Helms
Former FAA Administrator

This is not a book about flying. It is a book about a career. A career that is exciting and rewarding, one that has some characteristics that are unique in the American job market. I know of no other career where the employer will train you for the job, pay you while you are training, offer the opportunity for income some three times the national average in just a few years, and include an outstanding pension and retirement program. FAA Controllers have their own pay and retirement benefits program, which is superior to that of other government employees. Becoming an air traffic controller is an excellent opportunity for a secure future in a growing field. In my nearly fifty years in aviation I have never heard of a Controller being laid off for lack of work.

Since inception in the mid 1920s, airline traffic has steadily increased. In the last ten years, there has been an unprecedented growth, worldwide. Every forecast I have seen shows a continuing growth trend through the end of this century, with a corresponding demand for more Air Traffic Controllers.

The U.S. Government's aviation authority, the Federal Aviation Administration, announced in 1981 the creation of the National Airspace Systems Plan. This defined program of modernization would occur during the succeeding fifteen or more years, steadily bringing in new technology which became available in that time period. That new technology in the form of new automated equipment is now coming into the air traffic control system, offering a wonderful opportunity for young people to become "part of the best while using the best."

Becoming an air traffic controller requires only one thing of you: You must be prepared to WORK! College attendance is not required, and the field is open to all who qualify. ATC (Air Traffic Control) is not just a job, it is a career, a career respected around the world. I have literally traveled around the world (in one year alone I was in twenty-seven foreign countries) and in every country I found the job of ATC to be highly respected and well paid. Today, retired U.S. controllers are being offered positions in Australia, Canada, England, and other countries. Air traffic control is an international profession. Because English was adopted many years ago by the International Civil Aviation Organization as the official language for ATC, U.S. Controllers are in demand worldwide.

Dr. Turner has not tried to address these issues. Rather, he has specifically oriented this book to help you learn, to introduce you to the job and how it should be done. He brings to this book the experience and knowledge of some twenty years as an air traffic controller. The career that starts with this book will see the participant growing in a decade of greater advancement than at any other time in ATC history. Such advances include new satellite navigation, communication and reporting systems, new automated sector suites (work stations), new digital data communications systems that do not require voice for information exchange, new collision avoidance systems, new "dual mode" radars that can see weather and airplanes at the same time, new precision landing systems that will allow the airplane to land without the pilot touching the controls, and many others—all of these systems are now in the final stages of testing and will shortly be available for use.

I encourage you to think deeply and boldly about entering this career path. It is made up of outstanding professionals who have made the U.S. Air Traffic Control System the finest and safest in the world. You can be part of it. Good luck.

In the aviation world, to the people who know, there are only two groups that have mastered the skies. There are the pilots who move around in it, and there are the controllers, the ones who move them around in it.

The world of Air Traffic Control can never really be understood by anyone who has not had a chance to be part of it.

This book is dedicated to the select few who are given the chance to own the skies, the men and women who control the air traffic of the world.

> The heights by great men reached and kept,
> Were not attained by sudden flight.
> But they, while their companions slept,
> Were toiling upward in the night.

HENRY WADSWORTH LONGFELLOW

PART ONE

THE WORLD OF
AIR TRAFFIC CONTROL

The Job of the Air Traffic Controller

The federal government employs more than 24,000 air traffic controllers at airports, en route traffic control centers, and flight service stations throughout the nation. Air traffic controllers keep track of planes flying within their assigned area and make certain that they are safe distances apart.

AIRPORT CONTROLLERS

The main responsibility of airport tower or terminal controllers is to organize the flow of aircraft in and out of the airport. As a plane approaches an airport, the pilot radios ahead to inform the terminal of its presence. The controller in the radar room just beneath the control tower has a copy of the plane's flight plan and has already observed the plane on radar. If the way is clear, the controller directs the pilot to a runway; if the airport is busy, the controller fits the plane into a traffic pattern with other aircraft waiting to land. As the plane nears the runway, the pilot is asked to contact the tower. There, another controller, who is also watching the plane on radar, monitors the aircraft the last mile or so to the runway, delaying any departures that would interfere with the plane's landing. Once the plane has landed, a ground controller in the tower directs it along the taxiways to its assigned gate.

A similar procedure is used for departures. The ground controller directs the plane to the proper runway. The local controller then informs the pilot about conditions at the airport, such as the weather, speed and direction of wind, and visibility. The local controller also issues runway clearance for the pilot to take off. Once in the air, the plane is guided out of the airport's airspace by the departure controller.

EN ROUTE CONTROLLERS

After each plane departs, airport tower controllers notify en route controllers who will next take charge. There are 24 en route control centers located around the country, each employing 300 to 700 controllers, with more than 150 on duty during peak hours at the busier facilities. Airplanes generally fly along designated routes; each center is assigned a certain airspace containing many different routes. En route controllers work in teams of up to three members. Each team is responsible for a section of the center's airspace. A team, for example, might be responsible for all planes that are from 30 to 100 miles north of an airport and are flying at an altitude between 6,000 and 18,000 feet.

As a plane approaches a team's airspace, the radar controller accepts responsibility for the plane from the previous controlling unit. The controller also delegates responsibility for the plane to the next controlling unit when the plane leaves the team's airspace. The radar controller, who is the senior team member, observes the planes in the team's airspace on radar and communicates with the pilots when necessary. Radar controllers warn pilots about nearby planes, bad weather conditions, and other possible hazards. Two planes on a collision course will be directed around each other. If a pilot wants to change altitude in search of better flying conditions, the controller will check to determine that no other planes will be along the proposed path. As the flight progresses, the team responsible for the aircraft notifies the next team in charge. Through team coordination, the plane arrives safely at its destination.

FLIGHT SERVICE STATION CONTROLLERS

In addition to airport towers and en route centers, air traffic controllers also work in flight service stations operated at over 100 locations. These controllers provide pilots with information on the station's particular area, including terrain, preflight and inflight weather information, suggested routes, and other information important to the safety of a flight. Flight service station controllers assist pilots in emergency situations and participate in searches for missing or overdue aircraft.

The Selection Process

Competition for air traffic controller jobs is keen because the occupation's relatively high pay and liberal retirement program attract many more qualified applicants than the number of job openings.

THE WRITTEN TEST

Air traffic controller trainees are selected through the competitive Federal Civil Service system. Applicants must first pass a written test that measures their ability to learn the controller's duties. Arco's *Air Traffic Controller Qualifying Test* provides in-depth information on applying for the written test and full-length sample tests for practice.

Applications and test scores are kept on file at the Special Examining Unit (SEU), located at the FAA's Mike Monroney Aeronautical Center in Oklahoma City. As FAA regions have positions to fill, applications are requested from the SEU to review for employment consideration. The SEU sends those applications with the highest scores for that region, usually three applications for each opening. Eligible candidates who meet other pre-employment requirements may be selected for training.

PRE-EMPLOYMENT PROCESSING

Once a candidate has been referred to an FAA Regional Office, the pre-employment process begins. This process includes the completion of additional forms, a medical examination, a paper and pencil psychological test, an interview, and a background suitability/security investigation. Pre-employment processing normally takes from two to four months to complete. Once it is completed, candidates are considered with other eligibles for openings at the FAA Academy as they occur.

The Interview

Applicants will be asked to report for an interview at an air traffic facility near their home. The interviewer will look for evidence that the applicant possesses the personal characteristics required of a controller—motivation, practical intelligence, and ability to speak distinctly and concisely, to name a few.

Take a look at the evaluation forms that are to be filled out by your interviewer (Figures 1 and 2 on the following pages). They will help to boost your confidence by indicating what the interviewer is looking for. Remember, the interview is an important part of the pre-employment process and should be treated seriously. Dress appropriately, speak clearly, be prepared, and be confident—these are the traits that will make the right impression on your interviewer.

FIGURE 1.

JOB INFORMATION LIST
Air Traffic Control Specialist

NAME OF CANDIDATE

INSTRUCTIONS — This is a reminder of the information which should be covered in each interview. Tell applicant that he will later get much of the material referred to below in written form if he is appointed. Take care that covering this list doesn't use time needed for getting information from applicant.

"✓" each item as you cover it ↓

1. THE POSITION *(ATC specialties)*

2. THE BASIC PURPOSE *(Describe briefly)*

3. THE FAA *(The mission of, and relation to DOT)*

4. THE ORGANIZATION *(Regions, areas, facilities)*

5. OTHER FAA FUNCTIONS *(Design equipment, install and mainta_____ pilots, airports, airplanes; plan and establish airways, air navigation facilities; rese_____*

6. TYPES OF EQUIPMENT USED BY AIR TRAF_____ *(Most advanced communications, radar, d_____*

7. LOCATION OF WORK *(De_____ nd isolated locations of AT Facilities)*

8. JOB CONDITIONS *(Hours, rotat_____ ifts, overtime, short turnarounds, week-ends and holidays)*

9. CAREER CONDITIONAL APPOINTMENT *(Three years to "Career," first year probationary)*

10. STARTING GRADE AND SALARY *(Entrance grade)*

11. TRAINING *(At Academy in OKC, include per diem travel allowances etc.; on-the-job-training)*

12. PROMOTION *(Merit promotion systems; stress merit, not automatic)*

13. MOBILITY *(Working in different environments, i.e., different geographic locations and low to high activity)* RIGHT OF AGENCY TO ADMINISTRATIVELY REASSIGN

14. FEDERAL EMPLOYEE BENEFITS *(Retirement, annual and sick leave, health insurance, step increases, incentive awards, group life insurance)*

15. WITHDRAWAL PROCEDURES *(Academy, post-academy)*

FAA Form 3300-23 (10-70)

GPO 901-639
FAA AC 71-6211

FIGURE 2.

INTERVIEW RECORD AND EVALUATION FOR Air Traffic Control Specialist		LOCATION
NAME OF CANDIDATE	DATE OF BIRTH	DATE OF INTERVIEW
ADDRESS		TELEPHONE NUMBERS
RESTRICTIONS ON AVAILABILITY (e.g., location, grade level, date available)		OFFICE NO.
GRADE LEVEL APPLIED FOR GS–	CANDIDATE'S OPTION PREFERENCE ☐ STATION ☐ CENTER ☐ TOWER	HOME NO.

PART I – INTERVIEW AND EVALUATION

A – APPEARANCE ("X" applicable box(es))

1. ☐ IMMACULATE 2. ☐ NEAT 3. ☐ DISHEVELED 4. ☐ UNSHAVEN 5. ☐ UNCLEAN 6. ☐ SLOVENLY

7. ☐ OTHER (If "X," specify)

B – ORAL EXPRESSION (Write "Yes" or "No" as applicable in each box)

DICTION
1. ☐ DEFECTS OR DISTRACTION IN VOICE 2. ☐ CHOOSES WORDS PRECISELY 3. ☐ PRONOUNCES WORDS CORRECTLY
4. ☐ SPEAKS CLEARLY 5. ☐ SLURRS SPEECH 6. ☐ LISPS OR STAMMERS 7. ☐ HARD TO UNDERSTAND
8. ☐ OTHER (If "Yes," specify)

FLUENCY
9. ☐ VOCABULARY ADEQUATE 10. ☐ SENTENCE STRUCTURE CLEAR 12. ☐ QUESTIONABLE USE OF SLANG OR COLLOQUIALISMS
13. ☐ PRONOUNCES WORDS CORRECTLY 14. ☐ PRONOUNCES TOO RAPIDLY ☐ OTHER (If "Yes," specify)

UNDERSTANDING
16. ☐ MAKES HIMSELF UNDERSTOOD ORALLY ☐ UNDERSTANDS OTHERS EASILY 18. ☐ LISTENS TO WHAT OTHERS SAY
19. ☐ COMMENTS (If "Yes," explain)

SAMPLE

C – ATTITUDE ("X" applicable box(es))

1. ☐ ENTHUSIASTIC 2. ☐ FRIENDLY 3. ☐ QUIET 4. ☐ TALKATIVE 5. ☐ DISCOURTEOUS 6. ☐ ARGUMENTATIVE
7. ☐ CONFIDENT 8. ☐ CONFUSED 9. ☐ OTHER (If "X," specify)

D – STABILITY (Write "Yes" or "No" as applicable in each box)

1. ☐ GETS UPSET EASILY 2. ☐ SEEMS HIGHLY NERVOUS 3. ☐ LOOSES SELF-CONTROL READILY 4. ☐ APPEARS SELF POSSESSED
5. ☐ REACTS STRONGLY WHEN DISAGREED WITH 6. ☐ RELAXED 7. ☐ TENSE

E – PERCEPTION AND VITALITY (Write "Yes" or "No" as applicable in each box)

1. ☐ SLOW TO UNDERSTAND QUESTIONS 2. ☐ LETS HIS ATTENTION WANDER 3. ☐ IS OBJECTIVE
4. ☐ DISPLAYS SOUND JUDGMENT 5. ☐ SLOW TO RESPOND TO QUESTIONS 6. ☐ APPEARS ALERT AND ENERGETIC

F – MOTIVATION AND INTEREST (Write "Yes" or "No" as applicable in each box)

1. ☐ EXPRESSES A POSITIVE INTEREST IN AIR TRAFFIC CONTROL 2. ☐ REASONS FOR DESIRING THIS TYPE OF WORK ARE SOUND
3. ☐ EXPRESSES DESIRE FOR A CAREER THAT IS CONSISTENT WITH THE NEEDS OF AIR TRAFFIC CONTROL 4. ☐ SEEMS INTERESTED IN DOING A JOB WELL 5. ☐ EASILY DISCOURAGED
5. ☐ COMMENTS ON ANY OTHER OBSERVATIONS FELT SIGNIFICANT

FAA Form 3300-22 (10-70) SUPERSEDES FAA FORM 3300-19

FIGURE 2—CONTINUED

PART II - APPRAISAL

INSTRUCTIONS — Read the instructions below before completing evaluation.

    1. If you appraise the candidate as "Unacceptable", an objection to this candidate will be sent to the Civil Service Commission.

    2. If you appraise the candidate as "Below Average", an objection to this candidate may be sent to the Civil Service Commission.

    3. If your appraisal is "Unacceptable" or "Below Average", state your reasons.

APPRAISAL ("X" applicable box)

1. ☐ UNACCEPTABLE   2. ☐ BELOW AVERAGE   3. ☐ AVERAGE   4. ☐ ABOVE AVERAGE   5. ☐ EXCELLENT

REASONS FOR "UNACCEPTABLE" OR "BELOW AVERAGE" APPRAISAL

_____
_____
_____
_____
_____
_____
_____
_____
_____
_____
_____

INTERVIEW PANEL RECOMMENDATIONS

_____
_____
_____
_____
_____
_____

	SIGNATURE AND TITLE
PRINCIPAL INTERVIEWER ▶	
INTERVIEWER II ▶	
INTERVIEWER III ▶	

FAA AC 71-6312

The Medical Examination

Upon successful completion of your interview, you will be scheduled for a medical examination. The examination will include blood chemistries, an audiogram, and a psychological test.

All applicants for controller positions are required to provide a urine sample during the medical examination that will be screened for the presence of drugs. The drug screening will be repeated during your career as a controller.

Some of the medical requirements established by the Office of Personnel Management that you must meet are listed here as examples:

- Applicants for terminal and center specialist positions must demonstrate distant and near vision of $^{20}\!/_{20}$ or better in each eye separately. If glasses or contact lenses are required, refractive error in each eye separately that exceeds plus or minus 5.50 diopters of spherical equivalent or 3.00 diopters of cylinder is disqualifying.

- Applicants for flight service station specialist positions must demonstrate distant and near vision of $^{20}\!/_{20}$ or better in at least one eye. If glasses or contact lenses are required, a refractive error that exceeds plus or minus 8.00 diopters of spherical equivalent will necessitate an ophthalmological consultation.

- You must demonstrate normal color vision (without the use of x-chrome lenses).

- You must not have established medical history or clinical diagnosis of any of the following:

  1. Psychosis, neurosis.
  2. Substance dependence, including alcohol, narcotics, and nonnarcotic drugs.
  3. Any other mental or personality disorder that the Federal Air Surgeon considers a hazard to safety in the air traffic control system.
  4. Diabetes mellitus.
  5. Other organic, functional, or structural disease, defect, or limitation found by the Federal Air Surgeon to constitute a hazard to safety in the air traffic control system.

The FAA regional flight surgeon will review the results of the examination and military records, if applicable, to determine if you meet the ATCS medical requirements. If you do not meet these requirements, you will be notified as to the reason(s). The examinations are paid for by the FAA, but travel costs incurred in reporting to the examinations must be paid for by you. If you have a problem that requires further evaluation to determine your eligibility, you will have to pay all associated costs. Once employed as an air traffic control specialist, you will be required to pass an annual medical examination that will be paid for by the agency.

The Security (Suitability) Investigation

This investigation will include inquiries to former employers and/or educational institutions and a review of Federal Bureau of Investigation, military, and police files. If the investigation reveals any questionable information concerning your conduct, reliability, character, trustworthiness, or loyalty to the U.S. Government, you may be removed from consideration. Falsification of any information may remove you from consideration or, if discovered after appointment, may result in your separation from employment. It is sometimes difficult to answer certain questions (such as those concerning arrests), but this type of information may not be disqualifying, whereas intentionally failing to provide the information could be disqualifying.

THE HIRING PROCESS

Candidates who are selected for air traffic control specialist positions report directly to the FAA Academy at the Mike Monroney Center in Oklahoma City, Oklahoma. (See Figures 3 and 4, "Sample Notification of Selection" and "Travel Fact Sheet" on pages 12 through 17.) Employment processing and employee orientation will take place at the academy.

FIGURE 3. SAMPLE NOTIFICATION OF SELECTION

U.S. Department
of Transportation

**Federal Aviation
Administration**

Eastern Region

Federal Building
John F. Kennedy
International Airport
Jamaica, New York 11430

Dear:

This confirms your selection for the position of Air Traffic
Control Specialist (ACTS), GS-2152-7, Salary $17,824 per
annum, with the _____ Region. This is a career-condi-
tional appointment, effective October 23, 1985.

Your course number is 50120, and your _____ umber is 86001.
The class begins on October 23, 19_   _____ on January 21,
1986.

You are to report to the H_____ building Auditorium,
Mike Monroney Aeronautic_ ____ _500 S. MacArthur,
Oklahoma City, Oklaho_ ____ __ on October 23, 1985, for
entrance-on-duty p___

Your appointment _ _____ ugent upon a satisfactory medical
examination, recei_ __ satisfactory security clearance, and
satisfactory review of military medical records. You are
required to serve a 1-year probationary period beginning the
effective date of your appointment.

Your assignment at the FAA Academy will be for a 12- to 16-
week period. You will receive reimbursement for the
difference, if any, between travel expenses to the FAA
Academy and travel expenses to your facility assignment.
During this period at the Academy, you will be paid $38 per
day in living expenses in addition to your salary (see
enclosed travel fact sheet).

The screening process at the Academy is designed to evaluate
your potential as an Air Traffic Control Specialist. This
screening is conducted on a pass/fail basis, and you must
obtain a passing score of 70 or better to remain in the air
traffic control occupation (see enclosed fact sheet and
performance standards). We are currently experiencing a 30
percent to 40 percent failure rate during the screening
process at the Academy. For this reason, we strongly advise
that you incur no relocation expenses until you have satis-
factorily completed the screening process at the Academy. Any

FIGURE 3—CONTINUED

moving expenses incurred as a result of relocation to your permanent facility will be paid at your own expense. If possible, we encourage you to take a leave of absence from your position rather than terminating your present employment in case you do not complete the Academy screening program successfully.

Subsequent training received at your assigned facility will also be conducted on a pass/fail basis. Therefore, your failure to pass training requirements for, or to accept promotion to, higher graded ATCS positions may constitute grounds for your reassignment, demotion, or possible separation from the agency.

Individuals who complete the screen successfully will be assigned to either the en route or terminal option and to a facility within that option. Placement decisions will be based on organizational needs, the Aca___y screen performance, and an interview with the st____ ___o discuss personal preferences such as geograp____ ____on.

Regarding your career advanc__ ___ __nities, this agency follows a policy of promo____ ___nin when filling higher grade ATCS positions. ___ _____ opportunities for promotion are excell___ _____ promotions are by no means automatic. To ear____ ___must satisfy all Office of Personnel Manag___ ___ements and, in addition, meet exacting stand____ ____ning and proficiency established by the agency. In ____ ___g, you will receive one or more such noncompetitive p____tions. You should also expect to remain at your assigned facility for a substantial period of time, assuming satisfactory progression in the training program. Reassignments to other facilities or to other regions are never routine and are extremely rare for employees in a developmental status. Once you reach the full-performance level, you will then have the opportunity to bid on further advancement under the Merit Promotion Program. You will be required to compete with other employees for announced vacant positions.

In order that we may be assured that you have read and understood the information in this letter concerning the agency's policy on training requirements, promotion, and placement procedures, you must sign the statement at the end of this letter on the copy of this letter which I have enclosed, and return the signed copy in the franked envelope. This copy will then be placed in your Official Personnel Folder. The signed copy will indicate your acceptance of the position, as well as your acceptance of the conditions of your continued employment.

FIGURE 3—CONTINUED

If after your acceptance of this position you are unable to report to the Academy, please telephone and advise _____ _____ that you are no longer interested in the position.

It is a pleasure to welcome you to the Federal Aviation Administration. Good luck in your new career!

                                        Sincerely,

Enclosures

I have read the above letter, and, as stated in the letter, I understand that both the screening program at the FAA Academy and subsequent training received at the Academy or at my assigned facility are conducted on a pass/fail basis. Therefore, my failure to pass training requirements for, or to accept promotion to, higher graded ATCS positions may constitute grounds for my reassignment, demotion, or possible separation from the agency. I also understand the option and facility assignment policy and accept it as a condition of employment.

_____   _____
        Signature   Date

FIGURE 4. TRAVEL FACT SHEET

TRAVEL FACT SHEET

• New Federal employees are responsible for paying their own
  way to the first duty assignments. However, in reporting to
  the temporary training site in Oklahoma City, their first
  duty location, new air traffic controllers will be reimbursed
  for any cost of travel that <u>exceeds</u> the cost of travel from
  their homes directly to the first permanent duty assignment.

Examples:

```
                                                      Boston
                                                        •
                                  Chicago       New York
                                     •             •
                                                  D.C.
       Oakland                                     •
          •
                   Oklahoma City
                         •
       Los Angeles
           •
              Ft. Worth-Dallas
                     • •
                                                      Miami
                                                        •
```

a. New hire Jones lives in Miami but is being hired by Los
Angeles. He is entitled to reimbursement from <u>Miami to
Oklahoma City to Los Angeles "minus" Miami to Los Angeles =
nothing</u> (the distance is the same).

b. New hire Smith lives in Chicago and is hired by Boston.
She is entitled to <u>Chicago to Oklahoma City to Boston "minus"
Chicago to Boston = some money</u> (as the trip to Oklahoma City
and back is further).

c. New hire Gonzalez lives in Dallas and is hired by Fort
Worth. He is entitled to <u>Dallas to Oklahoma City to Ft.
Worth "minus" Dallas to Ft. Worth = most of the travel
expenses</u> (as Dallas and Ft. Worth are very close together).

FIGURE 4—CONTINUED

You are entitled to travel to Oklahoma City by commercial airline (coach class) or by Federal contract air service, if the contract airlines service the points of travel. If you travel by privately owned vehicle, you will receive payment of expenses not to exceed the cost of airfare either by commercial coachfare or contract air service fare, depending on what is available or the route used. In order for this comparison to be computed, you must maintain the following records: dates, times, mileage readings, and toll receipts (if in an automobile), hotel receipts, airline receipts, and taxi or airport limousine receipts for fares in excess of $15. Contact the Aeronautical Center's accounting office (telephone number (405) 686-2414 or, if available, FTS 749-2414) for information on making travel arrangements if you will be traveling to Oklahoma City by air, whether you will be traveling by commercial airline or by Federal contract air service.

- If you are unable to afford the airline ticket from your home to Oklahoma City (and would be entitled to have all or most of it paid), make reservations for the flight and call the accounting office in Oklahoma City (405) 686-2414 or FTS 749-2414) and provide the following:

  1. Date of flight
  2. Name of airline
  3. Flight number
  4. Your name, course number, and class number

  Your ticket will be prepaid in Oklahoma City to be picked up by you at your departure point. This should be done well in advance of your travel.

- If you decide to drive rather than fly to Oklahoma City, keep in mind that you will have only 1 day travel time after completing the Academy program to report to your assigned facility. Consequently, it will not be to your advantage to drive if the driving distance from Oklahoma City to your new facility exceeds 1 day.

- For the trip to Oklahoma City, you will be reimbursed for lodging and other expenses at a daily flat rate of $50.

- You will be reimbursed only for those travel/living expenses incurred from necessary travel. If you arrive in Oklahoma City early, the time between midnight of the day of your arrival and your designated reporting date will be at your own expense.

- While attending the Academy program, you will be paid a daily flat rate of $38 to help defray the cost of maintaining a temporary residence in Oklahoma City. The daily rate (or per diem) is in addition to your GS-7 salary. Per diem expenses

FIGURE 4—CONTINUED

are not authorized if your residence is within 25 miles of
the Academy.

● On your first day of the orientation at the FAA Academy, you
  will receive your official travel orders and a $1,000 check
  to help cover your en route travel expenses and the initial
  weeks of your temporary assignment in Oklahoma City.
  (Current FAA employees will receive $1,000 <u>minus</u> the advance
  already received from the employing region.) As you continue
  in the Academy program, you will receive two additional
  checks, one after 2 weeks at the Academy and the other
  approximately 2 months after your starting date.

  Obviously, it will be your responsibility to budget your per
  diem wisely; you will not be entitled to more living
  expenses than the $38 daily flat rate. Full reimbursement
  for the travel expenses to Oklahoma City may take additional
  time, since it is not paid in a predetermined amount.

● If you withdraw from the Academy program prior to the graded
  laboratory problems, your travel and transportation
  entitlements will cease at the time of withdrawal. Your
  transportation home will be at your own expense.

● If you withdraw at or beyond the graded laboratory problems
  portion of the Academy program or if you are involuntarily
  removed for nonsuccessful completion of any course, you will
  be reimbursed for appropriate travel and transportation
  expenses from Oklahoma City to your home, not to exceed the
  cost of travel to the permanent duty assignment.

● <u>All</u> students withdrawing or being separated from the Academy
  <u>must</u> be processed through the Aeronautical Center Travel
  Section <u>prior</u> to departure from the Academy.

● All expenses in connection with the movement of household
  goods or relocating your family to Oklahoma City or to your
  permanent duty location are your responsibility and at your
  expense. (Due to the intensity of the training program, it
  is not recommended that family members or pets accompany you
  to Oklahoma City.) While at the Academy, be sure to pick up
  a copy of the FAA employee pamphlet "Permanent Change of
  Station."

The FAA Academy

The FAA has developed and adopted a mandatory, centralized training program at the FAA Academy in Oklahoma City, Oklahoma. Under this program, all GS-7 employees must attend the FAA Academy for an 11- to 16-week screening and training program. As employment processing and employee orientation take place at the academy, newly hired air traffic controllers report directly to Oklahoma City rather than to the regional facilities where they will be working.

IMPORTANT: Academy screening and training are conducted on a pass/fail basis.

Your satisfactory completion of the screening/training program is based on a composite score determined from appropriately weighted evaluation instruments administered during the program. A passing score of 70 is required.

Failure to Complete the Program

In the event that you do not successfully complete training, you may be reassigned, demoted, or in most cases, separated from employment. Those employees who have transferred from other agencies or who have been reassigned from within the Department of Transportation or the FAA do not have any legal entitlement to the positions that they vacated to accept positions as air traffic controllers.

Progression to Full-Performance Level

Up to the full-performance level, ATCS promotions are based upon satisfactory completion of training prerequisites and regulatory requirements and are made without competition. After reaching the full-performance level, any subsequent promotions will be based on overall performance, as compared to the performance of other employees. Progression may require competition under the Merit Promotion Program, and opportunities for advancement will depend on the number of vacancies available, performance, and qualifications (as ranked against other competitors), and, in some cases, willingness to transfer to other locations.

TRAINING COURSES

Specific option training courses of the ATC developmental program are conducted at the academy or at the assigned field facility. Progression to the full performance level requires an extended developmental period (three to five years) with several levels of job-performance evaluation and demonstrated proficiency both in the working environment and as a result of standardized formal training.

Pass/fail screening occurs at the end of each training phase at the academy. Within each phase blocks of instruction have been identified for testing purposes. Your satisfactory completion of a phase is based on a composite score determined from appropriately weighted evaluation instruments administered during that phase. A passing score of 70 has been established for each phase. The following evaluation instruments are used in the various phases:

End-Of-Block Tests

These tests determine if you have accomplished the objectives of a designated portion of subject matter within a phase. They are multiple-choice in form, with answer sheets that lend themselves to computer analysis.

Comprehensive Phase Tests

These tests determine if you have retained the knowledge necessary to accomplish all the objectives for that phase. They are also multiple-choice with answer sheets that lend themselves to computer analysis.

Controller Skills Test (CST)

This test measures speed and accuracy in recognizing and correctly solving air traffic control problems. It requires judgments on spatial relationships and makes use of the knowledge and skills that have been acquired in the nonradar phase; it allows for application of the rules and procedures contained in the *Air Traffic Control Handbook* and other reference materials used in the nonradar phase. Since the test is one of application, no specific study is required. The multiple-choice items are presented in booklet form. Each section of the booklet must be completed within a given time.

Synthetic Area Chart Test

You are given a map of the synthetic control area depicting only the area boundaries and circles indicating VORs. You are required to complete the map and are graded on accuracy and completeness.

Lab Problems

The lab problems require you to apply knowledge taught in the classroom. Each graded problem is evaluated by a different instructor to ensure minimum subjectivity. A standard grading form is used by all instructors.

Instructor Assessment

Instructor assessment is used to evaluate the promise or potential that the student shows based solely on the student's performance on lab problems, but which takes into account the amount of training the student has assimilated up to that time. Separate assessments are made by each of the six instructors who grade your laboratory problems. These assessments are made during the laboratory portion of phase III.

PART TWO

AIR TRAFFIC CONTROL TRAINING COURSE CURRICULUM

CHAPTER I

Lessons 1–8

ORIENTATION AND OVERVIEW
FAR INTRODUCTION AND TERMINOLOGY
FAR AIRSPACE
AIRCRAFT IDENTIFICATION AND PERFORMANCE
MAP STUDY
NAVIGATION
RADIO AND INTERPHONE COMMUNICATION
PROPOSED FLIGHT PLANS AND FIX POSTING
ESTIMATING EN ROUTE FLIGHT PLANS
PROCESSING DEPARTURE FLIGHT PLANS
RECORDING CLEARANCE AND CONTROL INFORMATION

ORIENTATION AND OVERVIEW

The Screen is administered in four blocks of academic instruction, followed by a laboratory application segment consisting of simulated air traffic control problems. Your satisfactory completion is based on achieving a composite score of 70 or above. Your composite score will be determined from weighted academic tests, graded control problems, and a final Controller Skills Test (CST).

Objective

Given an orientation and overview of the Air Traffic Screen, you will be able to identify:

1. Academic subjects.

2. Laboratory organization, administration, and grading criteria.

3. Examination procedures (Block Tests, CCT, CST, Map Test).

4. Counseling responsibilities and procedures.

Academics

Listed below are the subject areas covered during the four blocks of academics and in the laboratory orientation, along with the respective tests and control problems.

BLOCK 1

Orientation and Overview, AT-2-1
FAR Introduction and Terminology, AT-2-3
FAR Airspace, AT-2-5
Aircraft Identification and Performance, AT-2-7
Map Study, AT-2-9
Navigation, AT-2-11
Radio and Interphone Communication, AT-2-13
Proposed Flight Plans and Fix Posting, AT-2-15
Estimating En Route Flight Plans, AT-2-17
Processing Departure Flight Plans, AT-2-19
Classroom Exercise
Recording Clearance Control Information, AT-2-121
Block 1 Review, AT-2-23
Block 1 Test

BLOCK 2

Forwarding Flight Plan and Control Information, AT-2-25
Aero Center Map Test
Forwarding Flight Plan and Control Information Rev., AT-2-27
General Control, AT-2-29
Board Management, AT-2-31
Block 2 Review, AT-2-33
Block 2 Test

BLOCK 3

Letters of Agreement, AT-2-35
Vertical Separation, AT-2-37
Lateral Separation, AT-2-39
    Classroom Laboratory Exercise
Longitudinal Separation, AT-2-41
    Classroom Laboratory Exercise
Block 3 Review, AT-2-43
Block 3 Test

BLOCK 4

IFR Flight Direction Altitude Assignment and Altimeter Setting, AT-2-45
IFR Clearance and Route Assignment, AT-2-47
Departure Procedures, AT-2-49
Arrival and Approach Procedures, AT-2-51
Holding Aircraft, AT-2-53
Initial Separation of Arrivals and Departures, AT-2-55
   Classroom Laboratory Exercise
Block 4 Review, AT-2-57
Block 4 Test

Recognizing Air Traffic Situations, AT-2-59
Practice Problems 1 and 2
Course Review, AT-2-61

Comprehensive Course Test

Practice Problems 3 and 4

LABORATORY ORIENTATION

Introduction to Laboratory and Laboratory Procedures, AT-2-63 (contained in the Student Reference Manual, ATM-2-2)

Controller Skills Test

LESSON 1
FAR TERMINOLOGY, AIRSPACE, AND PERFORMANCE CHARACTERISTICS OF SELECTED AIRCRAFT

To be an effective air traffic controller you must be able to communicate with pilots and controllers. To avoid confusion, you must familiarize yourself with standard words and phraseology. You must know and understand about airspace, and you must recognize aircraft and know their characteristics. This lesson provides that information and gives you a better understanding of the remaining lessons.

Objectives

You will be able to identify aviation terminology, uncontrolled, controlled, and special use airspace, and performance characteristics of selected aircraft, without references, and in accordance with Federal Aviation Regulations (FARS) Part 1, 71, 73, 75, the airman's information manual (AIM), and the 7110.65F.

Lesson Guide

A. Introduction to FARS

1. Rules and Regulations

Federal Aviation Regulations (FARS), establish/provide rules and regulations for all aircraft operating in the United States. They are issued by the FAA Administrator and were originally established to provide a system for air commerce.

2. Promote Safety of Flight

FARS give directions that promote safety of flight.

3. All Aircraft in the United States

FARS apply to all aircraft operating in the United States.

B. Definitions

1. Aircraft

A device used or intended to be used for flight in the air.

2. Air Carrier

A person who, by lease or other arrangement, engages in air transportation to include commercial air carriers, air ambulence, and aircraft carrying cargo.

3. Airport

An area of land or water that is intended to be used for landing and takeoff of aircraft and includes its buildings and facilities, if any.

4. Air Traffic

Aircraft operating in the air or on an airport surface, exclusive of loading ramps and parking areas.

5. Air Traffic Clearance

An authorization by Air Traffic Control, for the purpose of preventing collisions between known aircraft, for an aircraft to proceed under specified conditions within controlled airspace.

6. Air Traffic Control

A service operated by appropriate authority to promote the safe, orderly, and expeditious flow of air traffic.

7. I.F.R. Conditions

Weather conditions below the minimum for flight under visual flight rules.

8. V.F.R. Conditions

Weather conditions equal to or greater than minimums for flight under visual flight rules.

9. Flight Level

A level of constant atmospheric pressure related to a reference datum of 29.92 inches of mercury. Flight levels start at 18,000 feet mean sea level and are stated in three digits; i.e., "Flight Level Two Four Zero."

10. Shall

Used in imperative sense means a procedure is mandatory.

11. May

Means a procedure is optional.

C. Federal Airspace

1. Uncontrolled Airspace

That portion of airspace that has not been designated as continental control area, control area, control zone, terminal control area, or transition area.

   a. Vertical Limits

   Surface upwards to the base of overlying controlled airspace within the counterminous United States. Pilots assume all responsibility for flight in uncontrolled airspace.

2. Controlled Airspace

Consists of those areas designated as continental control area, control zones, terminal control areas, airport radar service areas, and transition areas within which some or all aircraft may be subject to air traffic control.

   a. Control Zones

   Upward from the surface and terminate at the base of the continental control area. Normally a circular radius of 5 statute miles from the primary airport to include extensions where necessary for arrivals and departures.

b.   Control Areas

Airspace designated as VOR federal airways, colored federal airways, additional control areas, and control area extensions but does not include the continental control area.

3.   VOR Federal Airways

Formed from one navigational aid or intersection to another navigational aid. The lateral limits are 4 nautical miles each side of centerline. Vertical limits begin at 1,200 feet A.G.L. up to but not including 18,000 feet MSL. They are spoken as "Victor" plus the number in group form (i.e., V13 would be "Victor Thirteen").

4.   Alternate Airways

Alternate airways are identified by location with respect to the main airway. A north/south airway would have an alternate east or west. An east/west airway would have an alternate to the north or south.

5.   Control Area

The control area normally included in the airspace between the main VOR airway and the alternate.

c.   Continental Control Area (CCA)

Airspace of the 48 counterminous U.S. states. The base of the CCA begins at 14,500 feet MSL and has no upper limit. It does not include airspace less than 1,500 above ground level (AGL) or prohibited or restricted areas.

d.   Positive Control Area (PCA)

Airspace where positive control of aircraft is exercised. Flight is normally under IFR and applies to counterminous United States. The base of the PCA is 18,000 feet MSL extending up to and including flight level 600 (60,000 feet MSL).

6.   Jet Routes

Jet routes are direct courses between NAVAIDS and/or intersections. The vertical limits begin at 18,000 feet MSL up to FL450 inclusive. They are identified by the letter "J" plus the number in group form "Jay one hundred."

D.   Special Use Airspace

Airspace wherein activities must be confined because of their nature, or wherein limitations are imposed upon aircraft operations that are not part of those activities.

1.   Prohibited Area

Airspace of defined dimensions identified by an area on the surface of the earth within which the flight of aircraft is prohibited. It's identified by the letter "P" and a number spoken in group form; i.e., P57, spoken "Pee Fifty Seven."

2. Restricted Area

Airspace identified by an area on the surface of the earth within which the flight of aircraft, while not wholly prohibited, is subject to restrictions. This area may be extremely hazardous to aircraft. It's identified by the letter "R" and a number spoken in group form; i.e., R931A, spoken "Romeo Nine Thirty-One Alpha."

3. Warning Area

Airspace that may contain hazards to nonparticipating aircraft in international airspace. It is identified by the letter "W" and a number spoken in group form; i.e., "Whiskey One Fifty-One, W151."

4. Military Operations Area (MOA)

Airspace of defined vertical and lateral limits established for the purpose of separating certain military training activities from IFR traffic.

Aircraft Categories

1. Purpose

Facilitates application of ATC procedures by providing immediate recognition within a specific category. Grouping helps when studying performance characteristics and aircraft recognition.

2. Category I

Lightweight single engine, personal type, propeller driven aircraft.
Speed—100–160 knots
Altitude—15,000 and below
Climb/Descent Rate—1,000 feet per minute
Weight Class—small

3. Category II

Lightweight, twin engine, propeller driven aircraft 12,500 pounds or less.
Speed—160–250 knots
Altitude—FL240 and below
Climb/Descent Rate—2,000 fpm
Weight Class—small

4. Category III

All other aircraft such as higher performance, single engine, large twin engine, four engine, and turbo jet.
Speed—300–550 knots
Altitude—FL450 and below
Climb/Descent Rate—2,000/4,000 fpm
Weight class—as specified in the ATC handbook

Weight Classes

1. Purpose

To provide wake turbulence separation between arrivals and/or departures. Groupings are general in nature and based on manufacturers' published performance data and/or FAA certificated stopping distance.

2. Definitions

   a. Heavy—Aircraft capable of takeoff weight of 300,000 lbs. or more regardless of whether they're operating at this weight.

   b. Large—Aircraft of more than 12,500 lbs. maximum certificated takeoff weight up to 300,000 lbs.

   c. Small—Aircraft of 12,500 lbs. or less maximum certificated weight.

FAR TERMINOLOGY
END-OF-LESSON TEST

DIRECTIONS: *Items 1 through 16 are multiple-choice. Indicate your selection by circling the appropriate letter for each test item. Correct answers appear at the end of the chapter.*

1. Which statement about FARS is correct?
   (A) FARS give directions that promote the safety of flight.
   (B) FARS apply only to registered aircrafts in the United States.
   (C) FARS do not require pilots to comply with Air Traffic Clearances.

2. Match the definitions with the appropriate terms.

   _____ Aircraft

   _____ Air Traffic Clearance

   _____ Air Traffic Control

   _____ Aircarrier

   _____ Shall

   A. A service operated by appropriate authority to promote the safe, orderly, and expeditious flow of air traffic.
   B. A device used or intended to be used for flight in the air.
   C. A person who by lease or other arrangement engages in air transportation.
   D. An authorization by air traffic control, for the purpose of preventing collision between known aircrafts; for an aircraft to proceed under specified traffic conditions within controlled airspace.
   E. Means a procedure is mandatory.
   F. Control of all air traffic within designated airspace by air traffic control.
   G. Means a procedure is optional.
   H. A geographical location to which the position of an aircraft is reported.

3. The lower limit of a control zone is
   (A) 1,200 feet A.G.L.   (B) 1,220 feet M.S.L.
   (C) 1,500 feet A.G.L.   (D) the surface

4. VOR airways are based on a centerline extending from one
   (A) NAVAID to another NAVAID.
   (B) intersection to another intersection.
   (C) NAVAID or intersection to another NAVAID.
   (D) NAVAID to an intersection.

5. A control zone has a normal radius of
   (A) 5 SM.   (B) 5 NM.   (C) 8 SM.   (D) 8 NM.

6. The width of a federal airway is normally _____ each side of the airway centerline.
   (A) 4 SM   (B) 4 NM   (C) 8 SM   (D) 8 NM

7. In the conterminous United States, the airspace at and above 14,500 M.S.L. is designated as
   (A) control area.   (B) control zone.
   (C) continental control area.   (D) positive control area.

8. Which airspace areas are considered special use airspace?
   (A) Alert area   (B) PCA   (C) Prohibited area
   (D) Restricted area   (E) Warning area   (F) MOA

9. Which airspace may be extremely hazardous to aircraft?
   (A) Restricted area   (B) Prohibited area
   (C) Military operations area   (D) Alert area

10. The general speed range of Category I aircraft is
    (A) 90-120 knots.   (B) 100-160 knots.
    (C) 120-160 knots.   (D) 160-200 knots.

11. The normal climb/descent rate of a Category I aircraft is
    (A) 1,000 feet per minute or less.   (B) 1,000-2,000 feet per minute.
    (C) 2,000 feet per minute or less.   (D) 1,500-3,000 feet per minute.

12. The normal climb/descent rate of a Category II aircraft is
    (A) 1,000-2,000 feet per minute.   (B) 2,000-3,000 feet per minute.
    (C) 2,000-4,000 feet per minute.   (D) 3,000-4,000 feet per minute.

13. The general speed range of a Category II aircraft is
    (A) 90-120 knots.   (B) 120-160 knots.
    (C) 160-250 knots.   (D) more than 250 knots.

14. The normal descent rate for a Category III aircraft is
    (A) 1,000 feet per minute.   (B) 1,000-2,000 feet per minute.
    (C) 2,000 feet per minute.   (D) 2,000-4,000 feet per minute.

15. The purpose of weight classes small, large, and heavy is
    (A) to provide groupings of aircraft.
    (B) to provide stopping distances.
    (C) to provide aircraft flight capabilities.
    (D) to provide wake turbulence separation between arrivals and departures.

16. In order to be classified as a heavy, an aircraft must be capable of takeoff weight of more than _____ pounds.
    (A) 400,000   (B) 300,000   (C) 200,000   (D) 100,000

LESSON 2
AERO CENTER MAP STUDY

Of all the academic subjects to be presented in this course, the ZAE map study is one of the most important. It is both the foundation for many of your academic studies and a keystone to running lab problems. In the future each facility to which you are assigned will have a map that has to be mastered, prior to certification. For this phase, ZAE is your facility, and an in-depth knowledge of the ZAE map is an absolute requirement. A copy of the ZAE map is included at the end of this book. For instructions on how to use it, see page 37.

Objectives

Given an unlabeled map, without references, and in accordance with the Aero Center map, you will draw and label all:

1. NAVAIDs

2. Airways, jet routes, and radials

3. Alternate airways and radials

4. Mileages

5. Approach control boundaries and altitude limits

6. Charted holding patterns

7. VOR intersections

8. DME fixes

9. MEAs, MRAs, MOCAs, MCAs

10. Airports

11. Sector and adjacent facility boundaries

12. Uncontrolled airspace and restricted areas

Lesson Guide

A. Boundaries

Boundaries between D1, D2, and adjacent centers.

B. VORTACs

D1—OKC, SNL, PNC, END   ZKC—MKC, ICT, GCK
D2—TUL, MIO, MLC   ZAB—AMA, CDS
ZME—HOT, FSM, FYV, SGF   ZFW—ABI, DAL, PRX

C. Airways, Jet Routes, and Radials

J100—AMA 120—SNL 300; SNL 115—PRX 295
V1—GCK 165—END 345; END 165—OKC 345; OKC 150—DAL 330
V2—AMA 090—END 270; END 090—PNC 270; PNC 090—MIO 270
  MIO 090—FYV
V3—ABI 050—OKC 230; OKC 030—PNC 210; PNC 060—MKC 240
V4—ABI 050—OKC 230; OKC 065—TUL 245; TUL 050—SGF 230
  V4N—OKC 045—TUL 270
V5—DAL 360—SNL 180; SNL 360—PNC 180; PNC 360—TO ICT
V6—CDS 090—OKC 270; OKC 090—SNL 270; SNL 090—MLC 270
  MLC 090—TO HOT
V6N—CDS 075—OKC 285
V6S—OKC 105—MLC 255
V7—PRX 330—MLC 150; MLC 345—TUL 165; TUL 020—MIO 200
  MIO—030—MKC 210
V8—GCK 120—PNC 300; PNC 120—TUL 300; TUL 090—FSM 270
V9—DAL 040—MLC 220; MLC 020—MIO 150; MIO 325—TO ICT
V10—TUL 020—MIO 200; MIO 070—SGF 250
V11—PRX 330—MLC 150; MLC 300—PNC 180; PNC 360— TO ICT
V13—END 035—TO ICT

D. Intersections, DME Fixes, and Radials

D1 SECTOR—TRYON, SLICK, ASHER, DAVIS, KARNS, COYLE,
JONES, BOLEY, MOORE, MINCO, YUKON
ZKC—BLUFF, MAPLE
D2 SECTOR—DEPEW, PRYOR, AFTON, MAYES, ATOKA

E. R931A

The vertical limits of R931A are at and below 8,000 feet. It is operational continuously. Aerocenter and flight service station are controlling agencies.

F. Uncontrolled Airspace

Airspace at and below 14,500 feet north of Oklahoma City VORTAC. The southern boundary is a 40 NM arc north of Oklahoma City VORTAC. The east, west, and northern boundaries are 5 NM from the respective airways, and the northeast and northwest boundaries are 20 NM arcs from Ponca City VORTAC and Enid VORTAC.

G. NDBs and Airports

NDBs in D1 sector —   FAU/Fairview NDB, END 240030
                         F22/Perry NDB, PNC 240030

Airports in D1   —   OKC Oklahoma City Airport, OKC 180005
Sector   PWA, Wiley Post Airport, OKC 005020
                       6K4, Fairview Airport, 5NM SE FAU NDB Bearing 130
                       END, Enid Airport, END 250005
                       F22, Perry Airport, PNC 240030, collocated with F22
                           NDB
                       PNC, Ponca City Airport, PNC 030005

NDBs in D2 sector —   BVO/Bartlesville NDB, PNC 105055 or MIO 225025

Airports in D2   —   TUL, Tulsa Airport, TUL 105005
Sector   BVO, Bartlesville Airport, 5NM SE BVO NDB Bearing
                         170
                       MIO, Miami Airport, MIO 360005
                       MLC, McAlester Airport, MLC 180005

H.   MRA, MOCA, MCA, MEAs

MRA—Minimum Reception Altitude/Signal reception at Mayes 4,000 feet and above.

MOCA—Minimum Obstruction Clearance Altitude/28 feet at PNC, NE bound on V3 used within 22 NM of PNC VORTAC.

MCA—Minimum Crossing Altitude/6,000 feet at Maple intersection NE bound on V3.

MEA—Minimum En route Altitude/the MEA is the lowest altitude assignable to aircraft (see map for altitudes).

I.   OKC Apch Control Airspace

A 20 NM radium from Oklahoma City VORTAC with a 5 NM arc extension around PWA at and below 5,000 feet.

J.   TUL Apch Control Airspace

Airspace at and below 5,000 within lateral limits as detailed on the aero center map.

K.   APCH/Tower Frequencies

Oklahoma City Approach—119.1/259.1
Tulsa Approach   —119.2/259.2
PNC Tower   —118.1/258.1
MLC Tower   —118.2/258.2

L.   Airway and Route Mileages

Airway and route mileages are annotated on the aero center map.

M.   ARTCC Frequencies   ZAE   D1—124.0/334.0   D2—125.0/335.0

ZAB — 126.0/336.0
ZME — 128.0/338.0
ZKC — 127.0/337.0
ZFW — 129.0/339.0

AERO CENTER MAP STUDY
END-OF-LESSON TEST

DIRECTIONS:

Using an unlabeled version of the ZAE map at the end of this book

1. Draw and/or label the following items, as depicted on the Aero Center (ZAE) map

    A. Boundaries

        (1) ZAE

        (2) Adjacent centers

        (3) ZAE sectors

        (4) OKC and TUL approach controls, including

            (a) Vertical limits

        (5) Uncontrolled airspace area

        (6) Restricted area, including

            (a) Vertical limits

            (b) Hours of operation

            (c) Controlling authority

    B. VORTACs, including

        (1) Depicted VORTACs

        (2) Garden City

        (3) Indicator for VORTACs off map area

    C. NDBs

    D. Airport(s) location

        (1) In relation to their NAVAID

    E. Victor airways and jet route

        (1) Extend airways/route to first VORTAC outside ZAE area

        (2) If unable to do item (1), extend airways outside ZAE area, and identify next VORTAC along that airway, including

            (a) Identified intersections outside ZAE area

F. Intersections

    (1) Within ZAE area

    (2) First intersection outside ZAE area

    (3) DME fixes, including

        (a) Mileage

G. Radials from identified VORTACs, that make up

    (1) Airways and routes

    (2) Intersection(s)/DME fix(es)

H. Mileages between

    (1) Intersections

    (2) Intersections and VORTACs

    (3) VORTAC to VORTAC (total), including

        (a) Depicted and nondepicted (off map) VORTACs

I. MEAs for airways and routes

    (1) At least once for each airway/route segment, for each direction from a VORTAC

    (2) At least once in each ZAE sector

J. MCAs, MOCAs, MRAs

K. Holding patterns

ZAE MAP INSTRUCTIONS

At the end of this book you will find the two-page ZAE map to use with these exercises. Follow the instructions given to remove the map from the book.

You will need to make separate copies to use with the different exercises. Before beginning, take one copy and white out all numbers and letter codes. Make copies of this unlabeled map to use when called for in the exercises.

LESSON 3
NAVIGATION AIDS

The NAVAIDs presented in this lesson are used for en route navigation and instrument approaches. It is essential that you understand the capabilities and limitations of NAVAIDs in order to control aircraft and to provide assistance to pilots.

Objective

Without references, you will identify the functions of nondirectional radio beacons and VORTACs in accordance with the *Airman's Information Manual.*

Lesson Guide

A. Radio Beacons

    1. Directional-Marker Beacons

       Radio aid used to identify a particular location in space along an airway or on the approach to an instrument runway. The signal is transmitted vertically, and the pilot receives the signal when flying over the beacon. The VHF (very high frequency) is 75 megahertz (MHZ) with an elliptal or bone-shaped antenna pattern. It is identified by transmitting dots and/or dashes which activate a light in the aircraft to indicate passing the beacon.

    2. Nondirectional

       A nondirectional radio beacon (NDB) transmits nondirectional signals whereby the pilot of an aircraft properly equipped can determine his or her bearing and "home" on the station. The NDB is used in airborne radio direction finding and instrument approaches. Holding the signal is a low to medium frequency (L/MF) operating from 190 to 535 kilohertz (KHZ). The antenna pattern is a circular nondirectional pattern, which radiates in all directions. Its identification is continuous three letters in morse code with no exceptions, during voice transmission or when used as a compass locator. NDB are classified according to the usable distance of the signal.

Class	Distance
HH	75NM
H	50NM
MH	25NM
Compass Locator*	15NM

       The limitations of NDB may include erroneous bearing information caused by other stations, lightning, or precipitation static.

---

* NOTE: Compass locators are associated with the ILS (Instrument Landing System).

B.   VOR

1.   Definition

The VHF omnidirectional range is a ground-based electronic navigation aid transmitting very high frequency navigation signals, 360 degrees in azimuth, oriented from magnetic north.

2.   Uses

The VOR is the basis for navigation in the national airspace system, with voice transmission possible.

3.   Signal

The VHF signal operates between 108.0—117.95 MHZ. Its line-of-sight signals will not penetrate mountains, go through the curvature of the earth, or bounce off ionosphere to form skywaves, resulting in short-range transmission. The reception distance increases with altitude.

4.   Antenna Pattern

Radials are emitted from the station in all (OMNI) directions. Directional information is part of the signal, and the aircraft equipment provides the bearing. It transmits 160 usable magnetic radials measures outbound from the station.

5.   Identification

VOR's are identified by three letters in morse code. Some VOR's also include voice, which alternates with morse code. Morse code or voice identification are the only positive methods of identification; without identification the VOR is unreliable.

6.   Classification

VORs are classified according to their standard service volume, which defines the usable distance for signal reception. VOR's are classified as "H" (high), "L" (low), or "T" (terminal). SSV limitations do not apply to published routes or published procedures.

7.   Accuracy

The signal is accurate to plus or minus one degree within the standard service volume within line-of-sight.

C.   TACAN

1.   Definition

An ultra-high frequency electronic air navigation aid that provides suitably equipped aircraft a continuous indication of bearing and distance to the TACAN station.

2.   Uses

Used widely for navigation by the military in the national airspace system.

3.   Signal

The signals provide azimuth and distance-measuring equipment (DME). It operates between 960–1,215 MHZ and assigned channel numbers. It is line-of-sight, as is the VOR.

4.   Antenna Pattern

The TACAN transmits 360 usable magnetic radials in all directions measured outbound from the station.

5.   Identification

Three letter ID in morse code with no voice frequency assigned in 126 paired channels. When selected, the equipment automatically tunes azimuth frequency and DME frequency.

6.   Classification

H, L, T—same as VOR.

7.   Accuracy

Plus or minus one degree.

8.   DME

Distance Measuring Equipment/DME Equipment (airborne and ground) used to measure in nautical miles. The slant range distance of an aircraft from the DME navigational aid.

The aircraft's interrogator sends a signal to the ground-based transponder and receives a reply. The interrogator translates the reply to distance in slant range displayed in nautical miles.

D.   VORTAC

1.   Definition

A navigation providing VOR azimuth, TACAN azimuth, and TACAN distance measuring equipment (DME) at one sight.

2.   Uses

VOR aircraft equipped with DME can select the appropriate VOR frequency and receive both azimuth and distance information (DME from TACAN).

TACAN aircraft that select the appropriate channel will receive both azimuth and distance information.

3.   Signals

VOR and TACAN frequencies are paired.

4.   Antennas

Antennas are collocated with the TACAN placed on top of the VOR.

NAVIGATION AIDS
END-OF-LESSON TEST

DIRECTIONS: *For each of the following questions circle the letter of the answer you think is best. Correct answers appear at the end of the chapter.*

1. Which is the purpose of a marker beacon?
   (A) Provide directional information   (B) Identify a particular location
   (C) Airborne radio direction finding   (D) Transmit signals for homing

2. On what frequency do marker beacons operate?
   (A) 130 MHz   (B) 190 kHz   (C) 75 MHz   (D) 75 kHz

3. NDB is the term given to an L/MF aid used in
   (A) approaches, marking runway location, and holding.
   (B) holding, automatic direction finding, and locating weather.
   (C) automatic direction finding, approaches, and holding.
   (D) marking runway location, locating weather, and approaches.

4. Nondirectional radio beacons operate in the radio frequency range of
   (A) 190-535 kHz.   (B) 190-535 MHz.   (C) 135-590 kHz.   (D) 135-590 MHz.

5. How are all NDBs except compass locators identified?
   (A) Continuous dots and/or dashes
   (B) Three letters in Morse Code with light signal in aircraft
   (C) Three letters in Morse Code with voice identification possible
   (D) Three letters in Morse Code

6. What is the usable distance of a Class "HH" NDB in miles?
   (A) 15   (B) 25   (C) 50   (D) 75

7. What is the usable distance of a Class "H" NDB in miles?
   (A) 15   (B) 25   (C) 50   (D) 75

8. When an NDB is used in conjunction with the Instrument Landing System, it is called a/an
   (A) compass locator.   (B) marker beacon.   (C) outer marker.   (D) ADF.

9. Which NAVAID is the basis for navigation in the National Airspace System?
   (A) Marker Beacons   (B) VORs   (C) NDBs   (D) TACANs

10. VORs operate in the VHF frequency band from
    (A) 108.0 - 117.95 MHz.   (B) 112.0 - 118.50 MHz.
    (C) 118.0 - 135.95 MHz.   (D) 960.0 - 1215.0 MHz.

11. A VOR has how many usable radials?
    (A) 90   (B) 180   (C) 360   (D) Infinite

12. Due to "Line-of-Sight" principle, VOR
    (A) signals bounce off the ionosphere to form sky waves.
    (B) signals provide long-range transmission.
    (C) reception distance decreases with altitude.
    (D) reception distance increases with altitude.

13. VORs are identified by
    (A) continuous dots and/or dashes.
    (B) three letters in Morse Code with light signal in aircraft.
    (C) three letters in Morse Code with voice identification possible.
    (D) three letters in Morse Code without voice identification possible.

14. The VOR classes are
    (A) HH, H, MH, and Compass Locator.   (B) H, L, and Terminal.
    (C) H, MH, L, and Terminal.   (D) H, L, and Compass Locator.

15. TACANs operate in the _____ frequency band.
    (A) L/MF   (B) VHF   (C) UHF   (D) HF

16. The required equipment for DME is a/an _____ in the aircraft and a/an _____ on the ground.
    (A) interrogator, transponder   (B) transponder, interrogator
    (C) receiver, transmitter   (D) transmitter, receiver

17. Distance information from DME equipment is _____ distance in _____ miles.
    (A) horizontal, statute   (B) horizontal, nautical
    (C) slant range, statute   (D) slant range, nautical

18. TACANs are identified by
    (A) continuous dots and/or dashes.
    (B) three letters in Morse Code with light signal in aircraft.
    (C) three letters in Morse Code with voice identification possible.
    (D) three letters in Morse Code without voice identification possible.

19. A VORTAC facility provides
    (A) VHF distance and UHF distance/direction.
    (B) UHF distance and VHF distance/direction.
    (C) VHF direction and UHF distance/direction.
    (D) UHF direction and VHF distance/direction.

20. The VOR and TACAN antennas that comprise a VORTAC are
    (A) collocated.   (B) noncollocated.
    (C) within one mile of each other.   (D) within two miles of each other.

LESSON 4
RADIO AND INTERPHONE COMMUNICATION

Having been exposed to many new items in your new training, you need to know how to say and use them. This lesson contains the basics of radio and interphone communications. Remember, anyone can be heard—but a professional will be understood. How well you communicate will directly relate to your ability to control traffic.

Objectives

Given examples of radio and interphone activities and procedures, without references, and in accordance with 7110.65, you will:

1. Identify requirements for monitoring radio frequencies and interphone circuits.

2. Identify the conditions under which controllers relay operational messages to and from aircraft and operators.

3. Select, in order, the four message priorities.

4. Identify the words used for priority message interruptions.

5. Select the formats used for initial call-up to, and reply to call-up from, aircraft and facilities.

6. Identify standard phraseologies to be used in radio and interphone messages.

7. Identify methods used to abbreviate radio and interphone messages.

Lesson Guide

A.   Communication Language

It is imperative that radio and interphone procedures be standardized to ensure that both pilots and controllers understand all communications related to air traffic control.

B.   Radio Frequencies

Use radio frequencies for the special purposes intended.

C.   Monitoring

Monitor interphones and assigned frequencies continuously. Maintain adequate volumes to hear all calls.

D.   Authorized Transmissions

Transmit messages necessary for air traffic control and contributing to air safety.

E. Pilot Acknowledgement

Ensure acknowledgement from pilot for all issued clearances, instruction, and information. If the read back is not correct, or if it is incomplete, make corrections as appropriate.

F. Authorized Interruptions

A pilot may be authorized by ATC to interrupt communications guard. The pilot must request this, and his or her request should come if only one operative radio is available. The pilot should return to frequency after a mutually agreed time.

G. Authorized Relays

Operational information to aircraft or aircraft operators as necessary. These should not be handled on a regular basis. Relay authorized FAA messages. The FAA Administrator is called "Safe Air One," Deputy Administrator "Safe Air Two." Relay operational information to military aircraft.

H. Initial Call

1. ID of the aircraft being called

2. ID of the calling unit

3. Type of message to follow (if necessary)

4. The word "over" (if required)

I. Reply

1. ID of the aircraft initiating the call up

2. ID of the replying unit

3. Message

4. The word "over" (if required)

J. Communications Established

After communications are established use the same format for initial call up and reply, except after stating ID of calling or replying unit; in this instance, state message or acknowledge message received.

K. Clearance for Specific Aircraft

Always use aircraft ID when issuing clearance or instructions to aircraft.

L. Abbreviated Transmissions

General aviation and military call signs may be abbreviated. Use the ID prefix and last 3 digits of letters after communications have been established and the type of aircraft is known. Do not abbreviate call signs of air carriers, civil aircraft with FAA authorized call signs, or aircraft with similar sounding ID's.

— Omit facility ID after communication is established.
— Transmit ID and message simultaneously after initial call up if message is short and receipt is assured.
— Omit the word "over" if a reply is obvious.

M. Interphone Priority

First: Emergency messages
Second: Clearance and control instructions
Third: Movement and control messages
              a. Progress reports
              b. Departure or arrival reports
              c. Flight plans
Fourth: Movement messages on UFR aircraft

N. Priority Interruption

Use the words "emergency" or "control" for interrupting lower priority messages.

O. Interphone Message Format

Intra/Interfacility

1. Call format: State the ID of position called and ID of position calling.

2. Response format: State position ID and acknowledgement of call.

3. Caller states message.

4. Caller position responds and states operating initials.

5. Caller states operating initials.

P. Interphone Message Termination

Terminate interphone messages with your operating initials.

Q. Words and Phrases

As contained in the glossary, use the word "heavy." In inter/intra facility for heavy jet identification and in communications heavy jet aircraft.

R. Emphasis for Clarity

Emphasize for clarity similar sounding words, letters, digits, and call signs. Notify each pilot concerned if call signs are similar.

S. ICAO Phonetics

Use the ICAO phonetic alphabet to clarify individual letters as necessary.

T. Number Usage

The numeral "0" is spoken "zero" with separate digit requirements, spoken "OH" in group form, or remains silent. Numeral "9" is "niner."

ALTITUDES AND FLIGHT LEVELS

ALTITUDES
STATE THE SEPARATE DIGITS OF THE THOUSAND PLUS THE HUNDREDS.

Altitude	Written	Phraseology
6,000	60	"six thousand"
8,500	85	"eight thousand five hundred"
10,000	100	"one zero thousand"
14,000	140	"one four thousand"

FLIGHT LEVELS
STATE THE WORDS "FLIGHT LEVEL" FOLLOWED BY THE SEPARATE DIGITS OF THE FLIGHT LEVEL.

Altitude	Written	Phraseology
18,000	180	"flight level one eight zero"
21,000	210	"flight level two one zero"
37,000	370	"flight level three seven zero"

TIME

TIME
FOR GENERAL TIME, STATE THE 4 SEPARATE DIGITS BASED ON THE 24-HOUR CLOCK IN TERMS OF COORDINATED UNIVERSAL TIME (UTC).

12 hr	24 hr	Phraseology
2:25 AM	0225	"zero two two five"
2:25 PM	1425	"one four two five"
midnight	0000	"zero zero zero zero"

PILOT REQUEST LOCAL TIME
STATE THE 4 SEPARATE DIGITS OF UTC, THEN THE WORD "ZULU," FOLLOWED BY THE 4-DIGIT LOCAL TIME AND THE APPROPRIATE ZONE.

Example	Phraseology
1545(UTC)0945(CST)	"one five four five zulu, zero niner four five central"

TIME CHECK
STATE THE WORD "TIME" FOLLOWED BY THE 4 DIGITS OF THE HOUR AND MINUTES, AND THE NEAREST QUARTER MINUTE.

Time	Phraseology
1622:30	"time, one six two two and one half."
1643:10	"time, one six four three and one quarter"

ALTIMETER SETTING

ALTIMETER SETTING
STATE THE WORD "ALTIMETER" FOLLOWED BY THE 4 SEPARATE DIGITS.

Setting	Phraseology
29.92	"altimeter, two niner niner two"
30.04	"altimeter, three zero zero four"

HEADING

HEADING
STATE THE WORD "HEADING" FOLLOWED BY THE 3 DIGITS OF THE NUMBER OF DEGREES. OMIT THE WORD "DEGREES."

Heading	Phraseology
5°	"heading, zero zero five"
90°	"heading, zero niner zero"
165°	"heading, one six five"
360°	"heading, three six zero"

RUNWAYS

RUNWAYS
STATE THE WORD "RUNWAY" FOLLOWED BY THE SEPARATE DIGIT(S) OF THE RUNWAY.

Designation	Phraseology
7	"runway, seven"
21	"runway, two one"
36	"runway, three six"

FREQUENCIES

FREQUENCIES
STATE THE SEPARATE DIGITS OF THE FREQUENCY. INSERT THE WORD "POINT" WHERE THE DECIMAL OCCURS.

Frequency	Phraseology
118.2 MHz	"one one eight point two"
119.1 MHz	"one one niner point one"
124.0 MHz	"one two four point zero"
336.0 MHz	"three three six point zero"

Aero Center Frequency Usage
Military = UHF
Others = VHF

SPEEDS

AIRCRAFT SPEEDS
STATE THE SEPARATE DIGITS OF THE SPEED FOLLOWED BY THE WORD "KNOTS."

Speed	Phraseology
250	"two five zero knots"
160	"one six zero knots"
90	"niner zero knots"

MILES

MILES
STATE THE SEPARATE DIGITS OF THE MILEAGE FOLLOWED BY THE WORD "MILE(S)."

Phraseology

"two niner mile arc southwest of TULSA VORTAC"
"cross one seven miles east of ENID VORTAC"
"cross five miles east of MIAMI VORTAC"

FIELD ELEVATION
STATE THE WORDS "FIELD ELEVATION" FOLLOWED BY THE SEPARATE DIGIT(S) OF THE ELEVATION.

Elevation	Phraseology
8 feet	"field elevation eight"
916 feet	"field elevation niner one six"
2047 feet	"field elevation two zero four seven"

FACILITY IDENTIFICATION

ARTCC—ATCT
STATE THE FACILITY NAME FOLLOWED BY THE WORD "CENTER" OR "TOWER."

Facility	Phraseology
aero (ZAE)	"aero center"
memphis (ZME)	"memphis center"
ponca city (PNC)	"ponca city tower"
mcalester (MLC)	"mcalester tower"

A/C—FSS
A/C: STATE THE FACILITY NAME FOLLOWED BY THE WORD "APPROACH."
FSS: STATE THE STATION NAME FOLLOWED BY THE WORD "RADIO."

Facility	Phraseology
TUL A/C	"tulsa approach"
END FSS	"enid radio"

AIRCRAFT ID

Use the same ID in reply as the pilot used in initial call-up. Use the correct ID after communications have been established. Use full ID to aircraft with similar call signs.

CIVIL AIRCRAFT
STATE AIRCRAFT TYPE, MODEL, MANUFACTURER'S NAME, OR PREFIX "NOVEMBER," FOLLOWED BY REGISTRATION NUMBERS/LETTERS.

Civil Designator	Call Sign	Phraseology
BE10	N692MT	"(___*___) six niner two mike tango"
		* King Air or Beech or November

AIR CARRIER/CIVIL AIRCRAFT WITH FAA CALL SIGNS
STATE CALL SIGN FOLLOWED BY THE FLIGHT NUMBERS IN GROUP FORM.

Designator	Phraseology
UAL211	"United two eleven"
AAL1010	"American ten ten"
FDX66	"Express sixty-six"

AIR TAXI/COMMERCIAL OPERATORS WITHOUT FAA CALL SIGNS
STATE THE PREFIX "TANGO" ON INITIAL CONTACT, IF USED BY PILOT, FOLLOWED BY REGISTRATION NUMBERS.

Civil Designators	Call Sign	Phraseology
BE80	TN216K	"tango two one six kilo"
MO21	TN941G	"tango mooney niner four one golf"

State the prefix "Tango" on initial contact if used by the pilot. The prefix may be dropped after initial contact.

AMBULANCE
CIVILIAN AIRBORNE: STATE THE WORD "LIFEGUARD" FOLLOWED BY TYPE AND REGISTRATION NUMBER.
MILITARY MEDICAL AIR EVACUATION: STATE SERVICE NAME (IF DESIGNATED) FOLLOWED BY THE WORDS "AIR EVAC" AND LAST 5 DIGITS OF SERIAL NUMBER.

Call Sign	Phraseology
LN21R	"lifeguard beech two one romeo"
E16522	"air evac one six five two two"

U.S. MILITARY
STATE THE SERVICE NAME, OR SPECIAL MILITARY OPERATION, FOLLOWED BY THE LAST 5 DIGITS OF THE SERIAL NUMBER.

Call sign	Phraseology
R92141	"army niner two one four one"
A16226	"air force one six two two six"
VM42617	"marine four two six one seven"
G12158	"guard one two one five eight"

PRESIDENTIAL AIRCRAFT

Type	President	Vice President
military	"(service) one"	"(service) two"
civil	"executive one"	"executive two"
family—any	"executive one foxtrot"	"executive two foxtrot"

President

On military aircraft state the service name and word "One." On civil aircraft, "Executive One."

President's Family

On civil aircraft, "Executive One Foxtrot."

Vice President

On military aircraft state service name and word "Two." On civilian aircraft use "Executive Two."

Vice President's Family

Use "Executive Two Foxtrot."

SPECIAL FLIGHTS

For semiautomatic flight inspection, state the code name "SAFI" followed by separate digits of grid number.

For flight inspection aircraft, state the call sign "Flight Check," followed by separate digits of registration number.

AIRCRAFT TYPES

MILITARY
STATE THE MILITARY DESIGNATOR WITH NUMBERS IN GROUP FORM.

Type	Phraseology
F15	"F fifteen"
B1	"B one"
B52	"B fifty-two"
C130	"C one thirty"

AIR CARRIER
STATE THE MANUFACTURER'S NAME OR MODEL, AND/OR COMPANY NAME FOLLOWED BY THE NUMBERS IN GROUP FORM.

Type	Phraseology
B737	"Boeing seven thirty-seven"
L1011	"(__*__) ten eleven"
	* Lockheed or Heavy Delta

GENERAL AVIATION AND AIR TAXI
STATE MANUFACTURER'S NAME, MODEL, OR DESIGNATOR.

Type	Phraseology
BE33	"(__*__) thirty-three"
	* Bonanza, Beech, or B-E
PAZT	"(__*__)"
	* P-A-Z-T, or Aztec

RADIO AND INTERPHONE COMMUNICATION END-OF-LESSON TEST

DIRECTIONS: *For items 1 through 10, indicate your selection by circling the appropriate letter for each test item. For items 11 through 20, write the phraseology required immediately below each item. Correct answers appear at the end of the chapter.*

1. The interphone and assigned radio frequencies should be monitored
   (A) continuously.   (B) during heavy traffic periods.
   (C) at controller's discretion.   (D) when ordered by supervisor.

2. What messages are you NOT authorized to transmit?
   (A) Weather advisories to aircraft operators
   (B) Official FAA messages
   (C) Request for aircraft servicing
   (D) Operational information to military aircraft

3. Operational information may be relayed to an aircraft or to aircraft operators
   (A) as necessary.   (B) on a regular basis.
   (C) at controller's discretion.   (D) of military aircraft only.

4. The radio message format for initial call-up to an aircraft, in the order of usage, is identification of
   (A) aircraft being called, message, and word "OVER."
   (B) aircraft being called, identification of calling unit, type of message if necessary, and word "OVER," if required.
   (C) aircraft being called, identification of calling unit, and message.
   (D) aircraft being called, identification of calling unit, and word "OVER."

5. The radio message format for replying to a call-up from an aircraft, in the order of usage, is identification of
   (A) aircraft initiating call-up, identification of replying unit, message, and word "OVER", if required.
   (B) aircraft initiating call-up message, and word "OVER."
   (C) replying unit, identification of aircraft initiating call-up, and message.
   (D) replying unit, message, and word "OVER."

6. When may the word "OVER" be omitted?
   (A) At controller's discretion
   (B) When message obviously requires reply
   (C) Always
   (D) Never

7. When may you omit facility identification in a radio message?
   (A) After communications have been established
   (B) When the message has high priority
   (C) When communicating with FAA aircraft
   (D) When relaying information to military aircraft

8. Which two types of aircraft identifications MAY NOT be abbreviated?
   (A) Air carrier and military
   (B) Air carrier and FAA airraft
   (C) Civil aircraft with FAA authorized call sign and military
   (D) Air carrier and civil aircraft with FAA authorized call sign.

9. The four interphone priorities in their order of precedence are
   (A) emergency messages, movement and control messages, clearance and control instructions, movement messages on VFR aircraft
   (B) emergency messages, clearance and control instructions, movement and control messages, movement messages on VFR aircraft
   (C) clearance and control instructions, emergency messages, movement and control instructions, movement messages on VFR aircraft
   (D) emergency messages, clearance and control instructions, movement messages on VFR aircraft, movement and control messages

10. What words are used to interrupt lower priority messages?
   (A) BREAK THE LINE   (B) PRIORITY MESSAGE
   (C) BREAK, BREAK   (D) EMERGENCY OR CONTROL

11. How is altitude 15,700 feet spoken?

12. How is flight level 310 spoken?

13. What is the phraseology to issue a time of 2:45 PM?

14. How is a heading of 090 spoken?

15. What is the phraseology to call the approach control at Tulsa?

16. What is the phraseology to call the ARTCC at Memphis?

17. What phraseology should you use to identify Aztec N111MH?

18. What phraseology should you use for a semiautomatic flight inspection aircraft, flight (grid) number 532?

19. What phraseology should you use for the presidential aircraft if the president is riding in an army transport, serial number 15763?

20. What word do air taxi and commercial operators NOT having authorized FAA call signs use to prefix their civil aircraft identification?

LESSON 5
PROPOSED FLIGHT PLANS AND FIX POSTINGS

So far in Block 1 you have studied the map and radio/interphone procedures. We are now going to venture on to strip usage. The relationship of the previous lessons to the strips will become evident as you proceed. Proper strip usage and strip marketing are essential to knowing what your traffic is and how you are going to separate it. As you will see, separation is the ultimate goal of air traffic control.

Objectives

1. Given flight plan proposals, you will enter all proposal items in the designated spaces on the flight progress strips without references, and in accordance with 7110.65.

2. Using proposed routes of flight, you will determine the number of fix positions required for each proposal without references, and in accordance with the Aero Center map.

3. Using the fix postings determined for each proposal, you will enter all en route data in the designated spaces on the flight progress strips without references, and in accordance with 7110.65.

Lesson Guide

Proposed Flight Plans

A. Fix Postings

A geographical location within a sector, where information is recorded and displayed on flight progress strips for the purpose of determining separation of active and proposed traffic.

B. Spaces

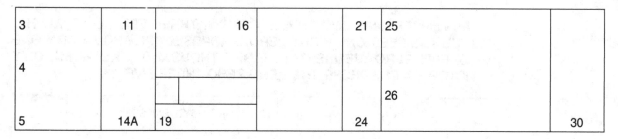

1. Space 3—Aircraft Identification—Appropriate prefix followed by a combination of letters and/or numbers. Maximum allowable characters, seven.

2. Space 4—Number of aircraft, heavy aircraft indicator, type of aircraft, and equipment suffix.

3.   Space 5—Filed true airspeed.

4.   Space 19—Departure point and proposed departure time.

5.   Space 24—Requested altitude—Two or three digits representing altitudes in hundreds of feet.

6.   Space 25—Point of origin, route of flight, destination, and estimated time enroute (ETE), or estimated time of arrival (ETA).

7.   Space 26—Pertinent remarks—Use plain language or approved words or phrases contained in 7110.65, App. A.

8.   Space 16—Departure arrow.

9.   Space 21—Next fix (next compulsory reporting point—can only be a three-letter identifier).

10.   Space 30—Coordination indicator (if required).

11.   Space 11—Previous fix—May be a three-letter identifier or a five-letter identifier.

12.   Space 14A—Plus time (from previous fix to posted fix).

SPEED TO MILES-PER-MINUTE CONVERSION CHART

KNOTS	MPM
0–85	1
90–145	2
150–205	3
210–265	4
270–325	5
330–385	6
390–445	7
450–505	8

Flight Plans And Fix Posting

EXAMPLES:

1.   "NOVEMBER ONE TWO THREE, CESSNA THREE TEN SLANT ALPHA, TRUE AIRSPEED ONE EIGHT ZERO, PROPOSED OKLAHOMA CITY ONE SIX FIVE ZERO, REQUESTING EIGHT THOUSAND, OKLAHOMA CITY VICTOR SIX CHILDRESS, ETE ZERO ZERO THREE FIVE."

N123			↑		CDS	OKC V6 CDS/0035	
C310/A							
T180		OKC P1650			80		ZAB

2. "AHAB FIVE SIX HEAVY A HEAVY B FIFTY-TWO SLANT ALPHA, TRUE AIR-
SPEED FOUR FOUR ZERO, PROPOSED OKLAHOMA CITY ONE SIX THREE
ZERO, REQUESTING FLIGHT LEVEL TWO FIVE ZERO, OKLAHOMA CITY
VICTOR SIX SHAWNEE JAY ONE HUNDRED PARIS."

AHAB56		↑		SNL	OKC V6 SNL J100 PRX
H/B52/A					
T440		OKC P1630		250	

AHAB56	OKC			PRX	OKC V6 SNL J100 PRX
H/B52/A					
T440	+7	SNL			

AHAB56	SNL			PRX	OKC V6 SNL J100 PRX
H/B52/A					
T440	+9	MLC220035			ZFW

3. "UNITED FIFTY, BOEING SEVEN TWENTY-SEVEN SLANT ALPHA, TRUE
AIRSPEED FOUR FIVE ZERO, PROPOSED OKLAHOMA CITY ONE SIX
THREE ZERO, REQUESTING ONE SEVEN THOUSAND, OKLAHOMA CITY
VICTOR FOUR NORTH TULSA VICTOR EIGHT FORT SMITH."

UAL50		↑		TUL	OKC V4N TUL V8 FSM
B727/A					
T450		OKC P1630		170	

UAL 50	OKC			TUL	OCK V4N TUL V8 FSM
B727/A					
T450	+9	TRYON			

UAL50	TRYON			FSM	OKC V4N TUL V8 FSM	
B727/A						
T450	+8	TUL				ZME

4. "AIR FORCE ONE TWO SIX EIGHT SEVEN, C-ONE THIRTY SLANT ALPHA, TRUE AIRSPEED THREE TWO ZERO, PROPOSED OKLAHOMA CITY ONE SEVEN THREE FIVE, REQUESTING ONE TWO THOUSAND, OKLAHOMA CITY VICTOR ONE GARDEN CITY VICTOR EIGHT DENVER."

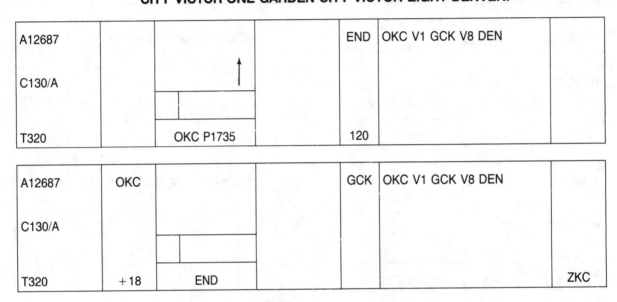

A12687				END	OKC V1 GCK V8 DEN	
C130/A						
T320		OKC P1735		120		

A12687	OKC			GCK	OKC V1 GCK V8 DEN	
C130/A						
T320	+18	END				ZKC

5. "NOVEMBER FOUR FIVE SIX, CESSNA THREE TEN SLANT UNIFORM, TRUE AIRSPEED ONE EIGHT ZERO, PROPOSED TULSA ONE SIX THREE ZERO, REQUESTING ONE ZERO THOUSAND, TULSA VICTOR FOUR ABILENE, ETE ZERO ONE ONE FIVE."

N456				OKC	TUL V4 ABI/0115	
C310/U						
T180		TUL P1630		100		

N456	TUL			OKC	TUL V4 ABI	
C310/U						
T180	+22	SLICK				

N456	SLICK			ABI	TUL V4 ABI	
C310/U						
T180	+19	OKC				ZFW

6. "NOVEMBER TWO SEVEN THREE X-RAY, CESSNA THREE TWENTY SLANT ALPHA, TRUE AIRSPEED ONE NINER ZERO, PROPOSED TULSA ONE SIX THREE ZERO, REQUESTING EIGHT THOUSAND, TULSA VICTOR FOUR DEPEW VICTOR ELEVEN MCALESTER VICTOR SIX HOT SPRINGS, ETE ZERO ONE TWO FIVE IFR TRAINING FLIGHT."

N273X				MLC	TUL V4 DEPEW V11 MLC V6 HOT/0125	
C320/A						
T190		TUL P1630		80	IFR TRAINING FLT	

N273X	TUL			HOT	TUL V4 DEPEW V11 MLC V6 HOT/0125	
C320/A						
T190	+34	MLC			IFR TRAINING FLIGHT	ZME

PROPOSED FLIGHT PLANS AND FIX POSTINGS END-OF-LESSON TEST

DIRECTIONS: *Read the flight plan above the strips, then review and follow required fix postings and en route data that should be inserted.*

1. "AERO CENTER, ENID RADIO WITH A PROPOSAL."

    "AERO CENTER, GO AHEAD."

    "NOVEMBER TWO THREE EIGHT, A CESSNA ONE FIFTY SLANT UNIFORM, TRUE AIRSPEED NINER FIVE, PROPOSED ENID ONE SIX THREE ZERO, REQUESTING SEVEN THOUSAND, ENID VICTOR TWO PONCA CITY VICTOR THREE KANSAS CITY, ESTIMATED TIME ENROUTE ZERO ONE FOUR THREE."

N238				PNC	END V2 PNC V3 MKC/	
			↑		0143	
C150/U						
T95		END P1630		70		

N238	END			MKC	END V2 PNC V3 MKC	
C150/U						
T95	+38	PNC				ZKC

2. "AERO CENTER, TINKER OPERATIONS WITH A PROPOSAL."

    "AERO CENTER GO AHEAD."

    "AIR FORCE ONE TWO FOUR EIGHT SEVEN, AN F-FOUR SLANT BRAVO, TRUE AIR SPEED FOUR FIVE ZERO PROPOSED OKLAHOMA CITY ONE SIX THREE ZERO, REQUESTING ONE SEVEN THOUSAND, OKLAHOMA CITY VICTOR SIX HOT SPRINGS. MS DX."

A12487				SNL	OKC V6 HOT	
			↑			
F4/B						
T450		OKC P1630				

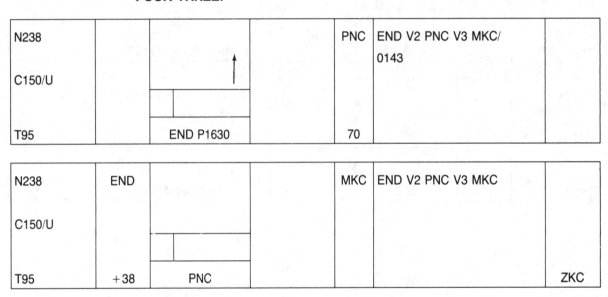

A12467	OKC			MLC	OKC V6 HOT	
F4/B						
T450	+6	SNL				

A12487	SNL			HOT		
F4/B						
T450	+9	MLC				ZME

3. "AERO CENTER, AMERICAN OPERATIONS WITH A PROPOSAL."

   "AERO CENTER GO AHEAD."

   "AMERICAN FIFTY, A BOEING SEVEN TWENTY-SEVEN SLANT ALFA, TRUE AIRSPEED FOUR EIGHT ZERO, PROPOSED OKLAHOMA CITY ONE FOUR FIVE ZERO, REQUESTING ONE SEVEN THOUSAND, OKLAHOMA CITY VICTOR FOUR SPRINGFIELD. MS DX."

AAL50				TUL	OKC V4 SGF	
B727/A		↑				
T420		OKC P1450		170		

AAL50	OKC			TUL	OKC V4 SGF	
B727/A						
T420	+7	SLICK				

AAL50	SLICK			SGF	OKC V4 SGF	
B727/A						
T420	+9	TUL				

AAL50	TUL			SGF	OKC V4 SGF	
B727/A						
T480	+7	AFTON				ZME

4. "AERO CENTER, TULSA APPROACH CONTROL WITH A PROPOSAL."

"AERO CENTER GO AHEAD."

"NOVEMBER TWO THREE FOUR, A CESSNA THREE TEN SLANT ALFA, TRUE AIRSPEED ONE EIGHT ZERO, PROPOSED TULSA ONE FOUR FIVE FIVE, REQUESTING EIGHT THOUSAND, TULSA VICTOR FOUR NORTH TRYON VICTOR FIVE PONCA CITY VICTOR TWO AMARILLO, ESTIMATED TIME EN ROUTE ZERO ONE TWO ZERO. DX CO."

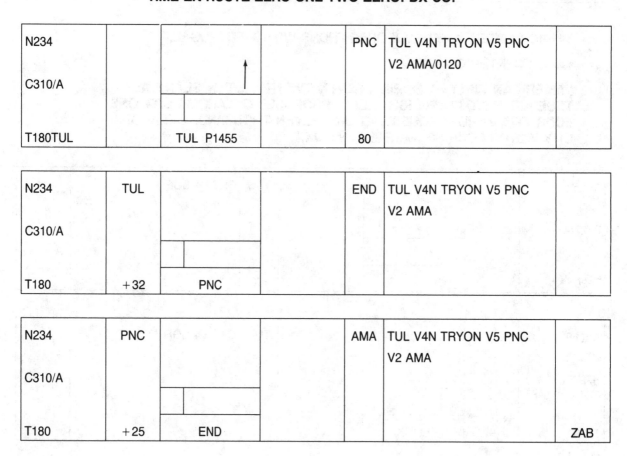

N234				PNC	TUL V4N TRYON V5 PNC	
C310/A		↑			V2 AMA/0120	
T180TUL		TUL P1455		80		

N234	TUL			END	TUL V4N TRYON V5 PNC	
C310/A					V2 AMA	
T180	+32	PNC				

N234	PNC			AMA	TUL V4N TRYON V5 PNC	
C310/A					V2 AMA	
T180	+25	END				ZAB

5. "AERO CENTER, MCALESTER TOWER WITH A PROPOSAL."

"AERO CENTER GO AHEAD."

"NOVEMBER FOUR FIVE SIX, A CESSNA ONE SEVENTY-TWO SLANT UNIFORM, TRUE AIRSPEED ONE ZERO FIVE, PROPOSED MCALESTER ONE SIX ZERO ZERO, REQUESTING SIX THOUSAND, MCALESTER VICTOR SIX CHILDRESS, ESTIMATED TIME EN ROUTE ZERO ONE FIVE THREE. DX MS."

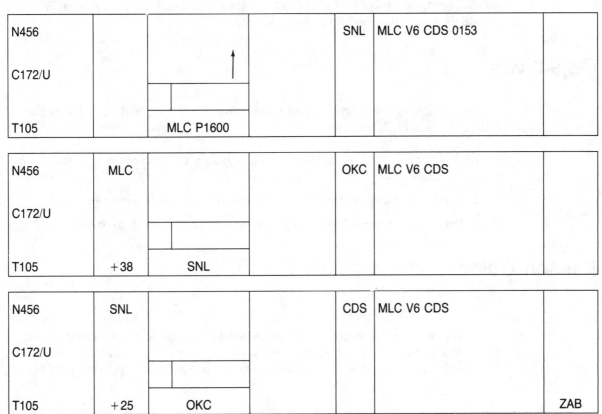

LESSON 6
ESTIMATING EN ROUTE FLIGHT PLANS

The previous lesson introduced you to the correct positioning of information on flight strips, required strips for various routes of flight in Aero Center, and the process of computing "plus times." This lesson reviews what you previously learned and introduces you to the use of additional spaces.

Objectives

Given flight progress strips, en route and arrival flight data, without references, and in accordance with 7110.65, you will:

1. Enter times/estimates in the designated spaces for en route and arrival aircraft in Aero Center.

2. Determine estimates for en route and arrival aircraft in Aero Center.

3. Determine fix postings for en route and arrival aircraft in Aero Center.

Lesson Guide

A. Receiving Estimates

You may receive estimates of flights from other areas of specialization within your center on aircraft landing or overflying your sector. You may also receive estimates from adjacent centers on flights landing in or overflying your sector.

B. New Spaces

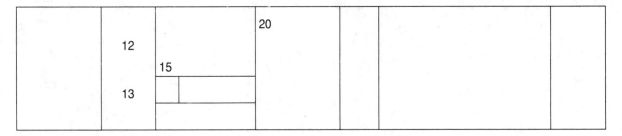

1. Space 12

Center estimated time over previous fix.

2. Space 13

Center revised estimated time over previous fix.

3. Space 15

Center estimated time over fix.

4. Space 20

Altitude information.

C.   Differences between proposed and en route strips

Space 15—dual purpose space.
   Enroute strip—center—estimated time over posted fix.
   Proposal strip—used for clearance information.
Space 20—en route altitude.
Space 24—proposed requested altitude.

D.   Determine center estimated time over posted fix
Compute plus time (space 14A)—
   Estimated en route time between previous fix and posted to be posted in
   space 14A.
Compute posted fix time (space 15)—
   "Plus time" added to center estimated time over previous fix (space 12) will
   result in the estimate time for space 15.

COMPUTING POSTED FIX ESTIMATE

SPACE 12 + SPACE 14A = SPACE 15
OR
TIME ESTIMATED OVER THE PREVIOUS FIX
ADDED TO THE PLUS TIME RESULTS IN THE
CENTER ESTIMATE FOR THE POSTED FIX.

DETERMINING CENTER-ESTIMATED TIME

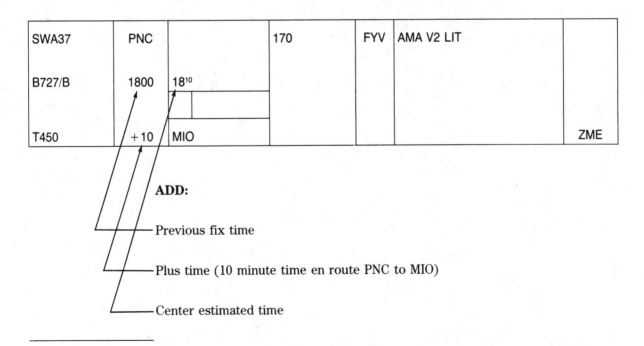

ADD:

——— Previous fix time

——— Plus time (10 minute time en route PNC to MIO)

——— Center estimated time

NOTE: Ponca City To Miami Is 75 Miles. SWA 37 Speed Is 450 (8 Miles Per Minute). It Will Take
Approximately 10 Minutes For SWA 37 To Travel 80 Miles (Space 14A).

E.   Determine required fix postings

AERO CENTER FIX POSTINGS

V1	OKC END
V2	END PNC MIO
V3	OKC PNC
V4	OKC SLICK TUL AFTON
V5	SNL PNC
V6	OKC SNL MLC
V7	MLC TUL MIO
V8	PNC TUL
V9	MLC MAYES MIO
V10	TUL MIO
V11	MLC DEPEW PNC
V13	END
V4N	OKC TRYON TUL
V6N	OKC
V6S	OKC ASHER MLC

ESTIMATING EN ROUTE FLIGHT PLANS
PRACTICE EXERCISE

Directions:

3	11		20	21	25			
	12	15	16					
4	13							
5	14A	19		24	26			30

1. Using the above strip, list the required items in the designated space.

3. _____	15. _____
4. _____	16. _____
_____	19. _____
_____	20. _____
5. _____	21. _____
11. _____	24. _____
12. _____	25. _____
13. _____	26. _____
14A. _____	30. _____

2. On the following strips compute and record the plus times and posted fix estimates.

N17C	AMA		90	AMA V2 MIO V7 PRX	
	1600				
C310/B					
180		END			

N17C	END		90	AMA V2 MIO V7 PRX	
C310/B					
180		PNC			

N17C	PNC		90		AMA V2 MIO V7 PRX	
C310/B						
180		MIO				

N17C	MIO		90		AMA MIO V7 PRX	
C310/B						
180		TUL				

N17C	TUL		90		AMA MIO V7 PRX	
C310/B						
180		MLC				ZFW

ESTIMATING EN ROUTE FLIGHT PLANS
END-OF-LESSON TEST

DIRECTIONS: *List the required fix posting identifiers under each of the routes of flight given below. Correct answers appear at the end of the chapter.*

1. DEN V1 OKC

_____

_____

_____

_____

2. AMA V2 PNC V8 TUL V7 PRX

_____

_____

_____

3. STL V4 ABI

_____

_____

_____

_____

4. ABI V4 OKC V4N TUL

_____

_____

_____

_____

DIRECTIONS: *On items 5 and 6, process the flight strips from the flight plans given. All available strips may not be needed.*

5. **"EASTER ONE NINETY SEVEN, BOEING SEVEN TWENTY-SEVEN SLANT ALPHA, TRUE AIRSPEED FOUR TWO ZERO, ESTIMATED CHILDRESS AT ONE SEVEN ZERO FOUR, AT ONE FIVE THOUSAND, LOS ANGELES VICTOR SIX HOT SPRINGS."**

EAL197

6. "AIR FORCE ONE EIGHT EIGHT ONE SEVEN, C-ONE THIRTY SLANT BRAVO, TRUE AIRSPEED TWO NINER ZERO, ESTIMATED FORT SMITH AT ONE TWO ZERO SEVEN, AT ONE TWO THOUSAND, MEMPHIS VICTOR EIGHT PONCA CITY VICTOR TWO ENID VICTOR ONE OKLAHOMA CITY."

A18817

LESSON 7
PROCESSING DEPARTURE FLIGHT PLANS

This lesson is a continuation of the study of spaces concerning flight progress strips. You will cover five new spaces involving departure strips and figuring estimates for en route fix postings.

Objectives

Given flight progress strips and proposal flight data, without references, and in accordance with 7110.65, you will:

1. Prepare a proposal strip and en route fix postings.

2. Determine fix times/estimates for each proposal and en route strip, accurate within three minutes.

3. Enter data in designated spaces on all proposal and en route strips in Aero Center.

Lesson Guide

				22 23		28
		18				
	14					

A.   Space 18

Departure time (actual or assumed) or actual time over fix for en route aircraft.

Departure Strip

Assumed Departure Time — time clearance requested, recorded on left side of space in red in four digits. Actual Departure Time — recorded on right side of space in black in four digits.

En route/Arrival Strip

Actual time over fix (two digits in black).
Cancellation time (four digits in black).
Arrival time at nonapproach control airport (four digits, in black).

B.   Space 14

Actual time over previous fix or actual time entered on first fix posting after departure (ZAE procedures normally use assumed departure time).

C. Space 22

Pilot's estimated time over next fix. Given when pilot arrives over the posted fix.

D. Space 23

Shows direction of flight, used on departures, arrivals, and en route. Use is optional. Direction arrow is in red.

E. Space 28

Miscellaneous Control Data
    D = Cleared to depart from the fix;
    A = Cleared to airport.

F. ETA

Estimated time of arrival, space 25. The ETE added to the assumed departure time in space 18 will give you the ETA.

PROCESSING DEPARTURE FLIGHT PLANS
PRACTICE EXERCISE

DIRECTIONS:

Step 1: On the following pages process the proposed flight plans, read by the instructor, on the strips provided.

Step 2: When step 1 is completed, the instructor will read the appropriate clearances from which you will:

1. Copy the clearances.
2. Process the strips from the plus times.
3. Convert the ETE to ETA.

All available strips may not be needed.

1. **Time: 0910**

   Step 1 Process the proposed flight plan on the first strip.

   SWA521, DC9/A T400 END P0910 150 END VI OKC V6 MLC VII PRX

   Step 2 Read the following clearance, process the necessary strips, and convert ETE to ETA.

   "SWA 521 CLEARED FROM ENID AIRPORT TO PARIS AIRPORT VIA VI OKC V6 MLC VII, CLIMB AND MAINTAIN 15,000."

SWA521			↑ 150	OKC	END V1 OKC V6 MLC V11 PRX	
DC9/A				↘		D-A
		0910/				
T400		END P0910		150		

SWA 521	END	23	↑ 150	SNL	END V1 OKC V6 MLC V11 PRX	
DC9/A	09			↘		
	0910					
T400	+13	OKC				

SWA521	OKC			↑150	MLC	END OKC V6 MLC V11	
	0923		31			PRX	
DC9/A		09					
						→	
T400	+8		SNL				

SWA521	SNL			↑150	PRX	END OKC V6 MLC V11	
	0931		42			PRX	
DC9/A		09					
						↘	
T400	+11		MLC				ZFW

2.   **Time: 1455**

   Step 1   Process the proposed flight plan on the first strip.
   N88KM PA31/B T180 OKC P1455 110 OKC V4 SGF ETE 0108

   Step 2   Read the following clearance, process the necessary strips, and convert ETE to ETA.

   "N88KM CLEARED TO SGF AIRPORT VIA V4, CLIMB AND MAINTAIN 11,000."

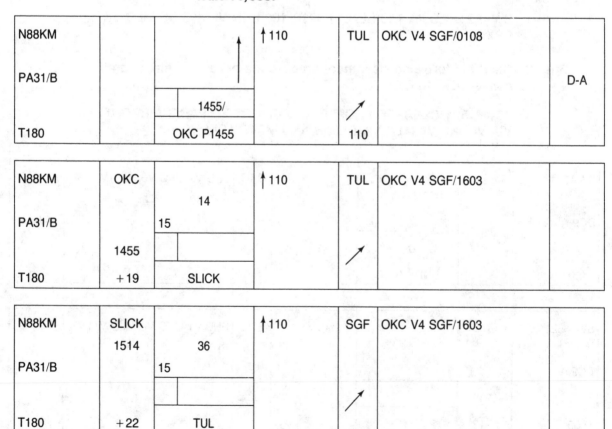

N88KM			↑	↑110	TUL	OKC V4 SGF/0108	
PA31/B							D-A
			1455/			↗	
T180			OKC P1455			110	

N88KM	OKC			↑110	TUL	OKC V4 SGF/1603	
			14				
PA31/B		15					
	1455					↗	
T180	+19		SLICK				

N88KM	SLICK			↑110	SGF	OKC V4 SGF/1603	
	1514		36				
PA31/B		15					
						↗	
T180	+22		TUL				

N88KM	TUL			↑ 110	SGF	OKC V4 SGF/1603	
	1536		55				
PA31/B		15					
					↗		
T180	+19		AFTON				ZME

3. **Time: 2122**

   Step 1 **Process the proposed flight plan on the first strip.**
   VV71378 P31P T300 PRX P2125 140 PRX V7 MKC

   Step 2 **Read the following clearance, process the necessary strips, and convert ETE to ETA.**
   "APPROVAL REQUEST: VVT1378 ASSUMED PARIS DEPARTURE 2125, CLIMBING TO 14,000."

VV71378	PRX			↑ 140	TUL	PRX V7 MKC	
	P2125		37				
P3/P		21					
					↖		
T300	+11		MCL				

VV71378	MLC			↑ 140	MIO	PRX V7 MKC	
	2137		48				
P3/P		21					
					↙		
T300	+11		TUL				

VV7138	MLC			↑ 140	MKC	PRX V7 MKC	
	2148		56				
P3/P		21					
					↗		
T300	+8		MIO				ZKC

PROCESSING DEPARTURE FLIGHT PLANS
END-OF-LESSON TEST

DIRECTIONS: *Process the following flight plans on the strips provided.*

1. TIME: 0530

   TWA514 DC9/A T480 SGF E0533 160 IND V10 TUL V4 ELP

2. TIME: 0638

N683B PA24/A T150 MLC P0640 80 MLC V9 ICT/0115

NOTE: After the proper flight plans have been posted, the assumed departure time for N683B is 0638. Process this time.

3. TIME: 1258

TWA 333 B727/A T450 OKC P1301 170 OKC V6S MLC

NOTE: After the proper flight plans have been posted, the assumed departure time for TWA 333 is 1258. Process this time.

4.   **TIME: 0010**
     COA26 B727/A T450 TUL P0008 150 TUL V4 SGF

FLIGHT PLAN PROCESSING PRACTICE EXERCISES

PURPOSE

These exercises are designed as a review of flight plan processing and the Aero Center map.

DIRECTIONS:
Practice Exercise 1: *Process the proposed flight plans.*
Practice Exercise 2: *Process the en route flight plans.*
Practice Exercise 3: *Read the clearances, then process the flight plans.*

PRACTICE EXERCISE 1
PROPOSED FLIGHT PLANS AND FIX POSTINGS

1. SWA 123 B727/A T440 OKC P2220 170 OKC V4N V5 PNC V3 MKC

2. N6245C C310/A T180 OKC P2245 100 OKC V1 END V2 AMA V430 ABQ/
    0250

3.   A76241 F104/A T480 OKC P2350 170 OKC V6 MLC V7 PRX SHV MGM MXF

4.   VV76PH P3/B T280 TUL P1140 140 TUL V8 PNC V2 AMA

5.   N269T PAZT/A T160 MLC P1420 80 MLC V7 MIO/0034

6.   R61589 U11/A T160 END P2210 90 END V2 PNC V8 TUL V7 MLC V6 HOT

7.   N21AC C310/A T180 PNC P1136 70 PNC V8 TUL/0025

8.   N99224 C150/X T100 END P2113 50 END V2 PNC/0045

9.   DAL313 DC9/A T430 OKC P1816 150 OKC V4 TUL

10.   A96143 C130/B T290 TUL P0016 170 TUL V8 LIT LRF

PRACTICE EXERCISE 2
ESTIMATING EN ROUTE FLIGHT PLANS

1. **N12345 L188/B T360 AMA E1700 170 ABQ V2 PNC/1725**

2. **USA868 DC9/A T440 FSM E1410 160 MEM V8 DEN**

3. **A44411 C135/B T475 CDS E2215 170 PHX V6 LRF**

4.   N622G BE65/X T170 SGF E0705 80 STL V10 V2 AMA/0844

5.   N47G C310/X T180 PRX E1615 80 HOU V11 PNC/1720

6.   AAL212 B727/A T450 MAPLE E1530 120 MKC V3 PNC V5 DAL

7.   VV32115 P3/B T360 BLUFF E2105 100 ICT V13 VI OKC

8. DAL613 DC9/A T450 ABI E1235 150 ELP ABI V4 OKC V4N TUL V4 SGF

9. N26254 BE65/U T180 BLUFF E1020 90 DEN V8 TUL/1108

10.   A96213 C130/B T290 FSM E2259 120 STL V8 TUL V7 MLC V6 OKC

PRACTICE EXERCISE 3
PROCESSING DEPARTURE FLIGHT PLANS

1. **TIME: 0625**

   "DAL810 CLEARED TO DENVER AIRPORT VIA VICTOR ONE VICTOR EIGHT, CLIMB AND MAINTAIN ONE SIX THOUSAND."

DAL810				OKC V1 V8 DEN	
DC9/A					
T430		OKC P0628	160		

2. **TIME: 2104**

   "AIR FORCE TWO SIX ONE FOUR FIVE CLEARED TO DENVER AIRPORT VIA VICTOR SEVEN TULSA VICTOR EIGHT, CLIMB AND MAINTAIN ONE TWO THOUSAND."

A26145				MLC V7 TUL V8 DEN	
C130/A					
T290		MLC P2104	120		

3.   TIME: 1632

"N8421C CLEARED FROM MIAMI AIRPORT TO LOS ANGELES AIRPORT VIA VICTOR TWO, CLIMB AND MAINTAIN ONE ZERO THOUSAND."

N8421C				MIO V2 LAX/0305	
C310/A					
T200		MIO P1630	100		

4.   TIME: 0630

"EAL694 CLEARED TO DALLAS AIRPORT VIA VICTOR FIVE, CLIMB AND MAINTAIN ONE SIX THOUSAND."

EAL694				PCN V5 DAL	
B727/A					
T400		PNC P0630	160		

5. TIME: 1417

"APPROVAL REQUEST: AAL12 ASSUMED CHILDRESS DEPARTURE AT 1420 CLIMBING TO ONE SEVEN THOUSAND."

AAL12 B727/A T450	CDS P1420				CDS V6 OKC V3 PNC V5 ICT	

6. TIME: 1431

"APPROVAL REQUEST: AAL22 DEPARTED HOT SPRINGS AT 1430 AT ONE FOUR THOUSAND."

AAL22 L188/A T280	HOT P1430			140	HOT V6 MLC V7 TUL V8 DEN	

7. TIME: 1432

"APPROVAL REQUEST: EAL421 ASSUMED SGF DEPARTURE AT 1435 CLIMBING TO ONE TWO THOUSAND."

EAL421	SGF			SGF V10 MIO V2 SLC	
CV58/A					
T270			120		

8. TIME: 1437

"APPROVAL REQUEST: USA160 ASSUMED DAL DEPARTURE AT 1440 AT ONE ZERO THOUSAND."

USA160	DAL			DAL V1 GCK	
	P1435				
L188/A					
T280			100		

9. TIME: 1444

"APPROVAL REQUEST: C3418 ASSUMED GCK DEPARTURE AT 1445 CLIMBING TO ONE SEVEN THOUSAND."

| C3418

CV34/A

T230 | GCK
P1444 | | | 170 | GCK V1 OKC V6 MLC
V11 PRX | |

10. TIME: 1655

"AAL65 CLEARED TO SHV AIRPORT VIA VICTOR SEVEN, CLIMB AND MAINTAIN ONE FIVE THOUSAND."

AAL65 B707/A T420		TUL P1654		TUL V7 SHV 170	

LESSON 8
RECORDING CLEARANCE AND CONTROL INFORMATION

You have practiced copying and processing basic flight plan information. You must be able to mark, correct, and update flight progress strips in a clear and concise manner. Correct strip marketing is THE method of communicating to other controllers what you are planning to do or have done with aircraft under your control. Your strip marketing will be scrutinized during the rest of your career as an air traffic controller. You should make every effort to master this means of communication in order to form a solid foundation for the lessons to follow.

Objectives

Given flight progess strips, sample clearances, and control information, without references, and in accordance with 7110.65, you will:

1. Record clearance and control information using approved symbols and abbreviations.

2. Enter all data in the designated spaces on the strips.

Lesson Guide

A. Flight Progress Strip Marking

   1. Recording Information

       Enter in designated spaces, without delay, estimated times and position reports, and all other IFR flight data using approved symbols and abbreviations.

   2. Making Corrections

       Do not erase or overwrite data. Draw a horizontal line through data to be corrected or updated. Do not draw a horizontal line through an altitude until the aircraft has reported leaving the altitude. Use an X to delete climb/descend and maintain arrow, at or above/below symbol, cruise symbol, unwanted altitude information. Write new data adjacent to old.

   3. Preplanning

       Accomplish preplanning in red pencil. Allow room in the space for the information to be rewritten in black without overwriting. When clearance is issued, preplanned data is rewritten in black in the appropriate space.

   4. Manually Prepared Strips

       Use machine generated format for manually prepared strips.

B. Control Symbols and Abbreviations

D = CLEARED TO DEPART FROM THE FIX (DEPARTURE STRIPS—SPACE 28)

A, (FIX) = DESTINATION AIRPORT, CLEARANCE LIMIT (SPACE 28)

T → = DEPART (DIRECTION, IF SPECIFIED) (SPACE 15)

TR/TL = TURN RIGHT/TURN LEFT (SPACE 15)

/ = UNTIL (ANY SPACE)

⇌ = JOIN OR INTERCEPT (SPACE 15, 20, 25)

_ = RESTRICTION BAR (SPACE 20)

↑,↓ = CLIMB/DESCEND AND MAINTAIN (SPACE 20)

× = CROSS (SPACE 20)

↕,↥ = AT OR BELOW/ABOVE (SPACE 20)

∨< = VOID IF NOT OFF BY (SPACE 15)

C (TIME/FIX/ALT) = CONTACT (TIME/FIX/ALTITUDE) (SPACE 26)

CTL = CONTROL (SPACE 26)

CC = COMMUNICATIONS AND CONTROL (SPACE 26)

>,< = BEFORE/AFTER (ANY SPACE)

(MILES)⌒ (DIRECTION) = DME ARC (SPACE 25)

(   ) = ALTERNATE INSTRUCTIONS (ANY SPACE)

HFR = HOLD FOR RELEASE (SPACE 15)

RLS = RELEASE (SPACE 15)

SYD = RELEASED YOUR DISCRETION (SPACE 15)

→ = CRUISE (SPACE 20)

↘ = DIRECTION OF FLIGHT (IN RED, SPACE 23)

√ = REPORTED LEVEL (SPACE 20)

㊿ = OTHER THAN ASSIGNED ALTITUDE REPORTED, CIRCLE ALTITUDE IN BLACK (SPACE 20)

(ALT) = INAPPROPRIATE ALTITUDE/FLIGHT LEVEL FOR DIRECTION OF FLIGHT (UNDERLINE ALTITUDE IN RED, SPACE 20)

RR = REPORT REACHING (SPACE 20)

RL = REPORT LEAVING (SPACE 20)

RP = REPORT PASSING (SPACE 26)

RX = REPORT CROSSING (SPACE 26)

E = EMERGENCY (SPACE 26)

W = WARNING, TO ALERT YOURSELF ACTION MUST BE TAKEN (SPACE 20, 24)

¢ (TIME) = PILOT CANCELLED IFR (SPACE 18)

F = CLEARED TO POSTED FIX (SPACE 28)

F (FIX) = CLEARED TO OTHER THAN POSTED FIX

RECORDING CLEARANCE AND CONTROL INFORMATION EXAMPLE

DIRECTIONS: *Using approved symbology and abbreviations, record the following clearances and control information on the flight progress strips.*

1. TIME: 1155   RUNWAY: 21

DAL150		T→PNC	↑130	TUL	PNC V8 TUL	
DC9/A						D-A
		1155/			LU30	
T460		PNC P1200		130		

Controller clearance:

"DELTA ONE FIFTY CLEARED TO TULSA AIRPORT VIA DIRECT PONCA CITY VORTAC VICTOR EIGHT CLIMB AND MAINTAIN ONE THREE THOUSAND, CONTACT AERO CENTER ONE TWO FOUR POINT ZERO LEAVING THREE THOUSAND."

2. TIME: 1156

EAL120		T→SW TL 130/⇌VI	↑150 ↓60 ×KARNS@ 60	OKC	END V1 OKC	
B727/A						D-
		1156/			LU30	KARNS
T480		PNC P1200		150		

Controller clearance:

"EASTERN ONE TWENTY CLEARED FROM ENID AIRPORT TO KARNS INTERSECTION, DEPART SOUTHWEST, TURN LEFT, HEADING ONE THREE ZERO UNTIL JOINING VICTOR ONE, VICTOR ONE, CLIMB AND MAINTAIN ONE FIVE THOUSAND, CROSS KARNS AT AND MAINTAIN SIX THOUSAND. CONTACT AERO CENTER ONE TWO FOUR POINT ZERO LEAVING THREE THOUSAND."

3. TIME: 1155   RUNWAY: 21

N265Q		T→RY21 PNC	↑100 ↓60	OKC	PNC V3 OKC/0035	
			×17SW ↕60			
BE65/B		V<1210	×COYLE			D-
		1155/	@60		LV30	COYLE
T175		PNC P1200		100		

Controller clearance:

"QUEEN AIR TWO SIX FIVE QUEBEC CLEARED TO COYLE INTERSECTION, DEPART RUNWAY TWO ONE DIRECT PONCA CITY VORTAC, VICTOR THREE, CROSS ONE SEVEN MILES SOUTHWEST OF PONCA CITY VORTAC AT OR BELOW SIX THOUSAND. CLIMB AND MAINTAIN ONE ZERO THOUSAND, CROSS COYLE AT AND MAINTAIN SIX THOUSAND. CLEARANCE VOID IF NOT OFF BY ONE TWO ONE ZERO. CONTACT AERO CENTER ONE TWO FOUR POINT ZERO LEAVING THREE THOUSAND."

4. TIME: 1156

DAL10			↑170	SNL	OKC V6 HOT	
			×BOLEY ↕70			
DC9/A			×5WSNL ↕			D-A
		1156/	110×5ESNL			
T460		OKC P1200	↕160	170		

Controller clearance

"DELTA TEN CLEARED TO HOT SPRINGS AIRPORT VIA VICTOR SIX CROSS BOLEY AT OR BELOW SEVEN THOUSAND CROSS FIVE MILES WEST OF SHAWNEE VORTAC AT OR ABOVE ONE THOUSAND, CROSS FIVE MILES EAST OF SHAWNEE VORTAC AT OR BELOW SIX THOUSAND, CLIMB AND MAINTAIN ONE SEVEN THOUSAND."

RECORDING CLEARANCE AND CONTROL INFORMATION PRACTICE EXERCISE 1

DIRECTIONS: *Using approval symbology and abbreviations, record the following clearances and control information on the flight progress strips.*

1. TIME: 1558   RUNWAY: 3

N234				PNC V8 TUL V7	
				MLC/0045	
C310/A					
T180		PNC P1600		90	

"CESSNA TWO THREE FOUR CLEARED TO MCALESTER AIRPORT VIA DEPART NORTHEAST. TURN RIGHT HEADING ONE SIX ZERO UNTIL JOINING VICTOR EIGHT, VICTOR EIGHT TULSA VICTOR SEVEN, MAINTAIN NINER THOUSAND CONTACT AERO CENTER ONE TWO FOUR POINT ZERO LEAVING THREE THOUSAND."

2. TIME: 1555 Pilot will accept northeast departure.

N456				OKC	END V1 DFW/0135	
C310/A						
T180		END P1600		90		

"TWIN CESSNA FOUR FIVE SIX CLEARED FROM ENID AIRPORT TO OKLAHOMA CITY VORTAC. DEPART NORTHEAST DIRECT ENID VORTAC VICTOR ONE, CROSS TWO ZERO MILES NORTHWEST OF OKLAHOMA CITY VORTAC AT OR ABOVE SIX THOUSAND, MAINTAIN NINER THOUSAND, CONTACT AERO CENTER ONE TWO FOUR POINT ZERO LEAVING THREE THOUSAND."

3. TIME: 1620

N234	HOT			120		SNL	SHV V6 OKC/1720	
	1550		30					
C310/A		16						
T180		MLC						

"TWIN CESSNA TWO THREE FOUR MAINTAIN ONE TWO THOUSAND UNTIL FOUR SEVEN MILES EAST OF MCALESTER VORTAC, CROSS EIGHT MILES WEST OF MCALESTER VORTAC AT OR ABOVE ONE ZERO THOUSAND, DESCEND AND MAINTAIN SIX THOUSAND."

4. TIME: 1620

N156	TUL			100			ICT V7 MLC/1648	
	1618		32					
PAZT/A		16						
T180		MLC						

"AZTEC ONE FIVE SIX CLEARED TO MCALESTER VORTAC, DESCEND AND MAINTAIN SIX THOUSAND, HOLD NORTH ON THREE SIX ZERO RADIAL, EXCEPT FURTHER CLEARANCE ONE SIX FOUR TWO."

5. TIME: 1625

N16S	MKC			120		TUL	MKC V7 TUL V4	
	1605		30				OKC/1728	
BE35/A		16						
T180		MIO						

"BONANZA ONE SIX SIERRA MAINTAIN ONE TWO THOUSAND UNTIL THREE FIVE MILES NORTHEAST MIAMI VORTAC, CROSS SIX MILES SOUTHWEST OF MIAMI VORTAC AT OR ABOVE ONE ZERO THOUSAND, DESCEND AND MAINTAIN EIGHT THOUSAND, REPORT LEAVING NINER THOUSAND, REPORT PASSING ONE SEVEN MILES SOUTHWEST OF MIAMI VORTAC."

6. TIME: 1625

DAL10	HOT			160		BHM V6 MLC	
	1608		30				
B727/A		16					
T450		MLC					

Indicate DL10 coordinated with McAlester tower.

"DELTA TEN MAINTAIN ONE SIX THOUSAND UNTIL FOUR SEVEN MILES EAST OF MCALESTER VORTAC, CROSS SIX MILES EAST OF MCALESTER VORTAC AT OR BELOW SEVEN THOUSAND, CLEARED FOR APPROACH CONTACT MCALESTER TOWER ONE ONE EIGHT POINT TWO PROCEDURE TURN."

7. TIME: 1712

N234					PNC	TUL V8 DEN	
C310/A							
T180		TUL P1717			100		

"TWIN CESSNA TWO THREE FOUR CLEARED TO DENVER AIRPORT VIA REVISED ROUTE VICTOR FOUR NORTH TWO NINER MILE ARC NORTH-WEST TULSA VORTAC UNTIL JOINING VICTOR EIGHT, VICTOR EIGHT, CROSS ONE SEVEN MILES WEST TULSA VORTAC AT OR BELOW FIVE THOUSAND, CROSS TULSA VORTAC TWO EIGHT FIVE RADIAL AT OR ABOVE NINER THOUSAND MAINTAIN ONE ZERO THOUSAND."

8.

N234	OKC			90	MKC	OKC V3 MKC/1745	
			30				
C310/A		16					
	1603						
T180	+27	PNC					ZKC

Mark the strip as if you had passed the estimate to Kansas City Center.

RECORDING CLEARANCE AND CONTROL INFORMATION END-OF-LESSON TEST

DIRECTIONS: *Using approved symbols and abbreviations, record the following clearances and control information in the designated spaces on the flight progress strips. Correct answers appear at the end of the chapter.*

1.

N234	MIO		80	END	FYV V2 AMA/1750	
	1605	30				
C310/A		16				
T180		PNC				

Pilot initial report:

"AERO CENTER, TWIN CESSNA TWO THREE FOUR ESTIMATING PONCA CITY ONE SIX THREE TWO, EIGHT THOUSAND, ENID NEXT."

2.

N456	MIO		100	END	FYV V2 AMA/1750	
	1605	30				
PAZT/A		16				
T180		PNC				

Pilot initial report:

"AERO CENTER, AZTEC FOUR FIVE SIX ESTIMATING PONCA CITY ONE SIX THREE THREE, EIGHT THOUSAND, ENID NEXT."

3. TIME:1625   RUNWAY: 3

N678				MKC	PNC V3 MKC/0100	
M021/A						
T180		PNC P1630		110		ZKC

Controller clearance:

"MOONEY SIX SEVEN EIGHT CLEARED TO KANSAS CITY AIRPORT, DEPART NORTHEAST TURN RIGHT HEADING ZERO NINER ZERO UNTIL JOINING VICTOR THREE, VICTOR THREE, CLIMB AND MAINTAIN ONE ONE THOUSAND, CONTACT AERO CENTER ONE TWO FOUR POINT ZERO LEAVING THREE THOUSAND, RELEASE MOONEY SIX SEVEN EIGHT ONE MINUTE AFTER BARRON FOUR FIVE THREE DEPARTS."

4. TIME: 1628

N521	SNL		110	CDS V6 MLC/1700	
	1623	48			
BE35/A		16			
T180		MLC			

Controller clearance:

"BONANZA FIVE TWO ONE AERO CENTER, CLEARED TO MCALESTER VORTAC, MAINTAIN ONE ONE THOUSAND UNTIL ONE EIGHT MILES EAST OF SHAWNEE VORTAC, CROSS EIGHT MILES WEST OF MCALESTER VORTAC AT OR BELOW SEVEN THOUSAND, CROSS MCALESTER VORTAC AT AND MAINTAIN SIX THOUSAND, REPORT LEAVING EIGHT THOUSAND. HOLD NORTH ON THE THREE SIX ZERO RADIAL, EXPECT FURTHER CLEARANCE, ONE SIX FIVE EIGHT."

5. TIME: 1615

N147	MIO			80		FYV V2 PNC/1640	
	1605		30				
C310/A		16					
T180		PNC					

Controller clearance:

"TWIN CESSNA ONE FOUR SEVEN, AERO CENTER, CLEARED TO PONCA CITY VORTAC, HOLD SOUTHWEST ON TWO ONE ZERO RADIAL, EXPECT FURTHER CLEARANCE ONE SIX FOUR ZERO."

6. TIME: 1640   RUNWAY: 21

N231				END	PNC V2 AMA/0051	
PAZT/A						
T180		PNC P1640		80		

Controller clearance:

"AZTEC TWO THREE ONE CLEARED TO AMARILLO AIRPORT, DEPART SOUTHWEST DIRECT PONCA CITY VORTAC, VICTOR EIGHT, THREE ZERO MILE ARC NORTHWEST OF PONCA CITY VORTAC UNTIL JOINING VICTOR TWO, VICTOR TWO CROSS NINER MILES NORTHWEST OF PONCA CITY VORTAC AT OR BELOW SIX THOUSAND, CROSS PONCA CITY TWO EIGHT FIVE RADIAL AT AND MAINTAIN EIGHT THOUSAND, CONTACT AERO CENTER ONE TWO FOUR POINT ZERO LEAVING THREE THOUSAND."

7.   TIME: 1643

N268	MIO 1617	50	100	MIO V9 MLC/1655	
PA31/A	16				
T180	MLC				

Controller clearance:

"NAVAJO TWO SIX EIGHT, CLEARED FOR APPROACH, REPORT PASSING FOUR FOUR MILES NORTHEAST MCALESTER VORTAC, CONTACT MCALESTER TOWER ONE ONE EIGHT POINT TWO PROCEDURE TURN."

8.   TIME: 1600

AAL29	AFTON 1606	18	160	SGF V4 OKC	
B727/A	16				
T420	TUL				

Controller clearance:

"AMERICAN TWENTY-NINE, CLEARED TO TULSA ZERO FIVE ZERO RADIAL TWO ZERO MILE FIX, HOLD NORTHEAST ON VICTOR FOUR, ONE ZERO MILE LEG, EXCEPT FURTHER CLEARANCE ONE SIX TWO EIGHT."

9.   TIME: 1615

AAL16	FSM 1612	27	150	MEM V8 TUL	
B707/A	16				
T420	TUL				

Indicate AA16 is at wrong altitude for direction of flight and has declared an emergency because of a fuel leak.

10.

UAL50	HOT		160	SNL	NYP V6 LAX	
	1620	42				
DC8/A		16				
T420		MLC				

Indicate UA50:

1. is in confliction at 160.

2. estimating MLC 1642, 160.

3. progressed MLC 1642, 160.

4. estimating SNL 1649.

5. requesting BOMB SQUAD AT LAX.

6. is declaring emergency.

7. was instructed to contact Aero Center 124.0 18 miles east of SNL.

Indicate all information has been coordinated.

11.   TIME: 1620

UAL52	SNL		160	CDS	HOT V6 CDS	
	1629	40				
B727/A		16				
T420		OKC				

Controller clearance:

"UNITED FIFTY-TWO, MAINTAIN ONE SIX THOUSAND UNTIL ONE EIGHT MILES EAST OF SHAWNEE VORTAC, DESCEND TO REACH ONE FOUR THOUSAND AT OR BEFORE ONE SIX THREE ZERO, DESCEND AND MAINTAIN ONE TWO THOUSAND."

LESSONS 1–8 ANSWERS

FAR TERMINOLOGY
END-OF-LESSON TEST

1. **A**
2. **B, D, A, C, E**
3. **D**
4. **C**
5. **A**
6. **B**
7. **C**
8. **C, D, E, F**

9. **A**
10. **B**
11. **A**
12. **A**
13. **C**
14. **D**
15. **D**
16. **B**

NAVIGATION AIDS
END-OF-LESSON TEST

1. **B**
2. **C**
3. **C**
4. **A**
5. **C**

6. **D**
7. **C**
8. **A**
9. **B**
10. **A**

11. **C**
12. **D**
13. **C**
14. **B**
15. **C**

16. **A**
17. **D**
18. **D**
19. **C**
20. **A**

RADIO AND INTERPHONE COMMUNICATIONS
END-OF-LESSON TEST

1. **A**
2. **C**
3. **C**
4. **B**
5. **A**
6. **B**
7. **A**
8. **D**
9. **B**
10. **D**
11. **"ONE FIVE THOUSAND SEVEN HUNDRED"**

12. **"FLIGHT LEVEL THREE ONE ZERO"**
13. **"ONE FOUR FOUR FIVE"**
14. **"ZERO NINE ZERO"**
15. **"TULSA APPROACH"**
16. **"MEMPHIS CENTER"**
17. **"NOVEMBER ONE ONE ONE MIKE HOTEL"**
18. **"SAFI FIVE THREE TWO"**
19. **"ARMY ONE"**
20. **TANGO**

PROPOSED FLIGHT PLANS AND FIX POSTINGS
END-OF-LESSON TEST

1.

N238				PNC	END V2 PNC V3
C150/U		↑			MKC/0143
T95		END P1630		70	

N238	END			MKC	END V2 PNC V3
C150/U					MKC/0143
T95	+38	PNC			ZKC

2.

A12487				SNL	OKC V6 HOT
F4/B		↑			
T450		OKC P1630		170	

A12487	OKC			MLC	OKC V6 HOT
F4/B					
T450	+6	SNL			

A12487	SNL			HOT	OKC V6 HOT
F4/B					
T450	+9	MLC			ZME

3.

AAL50			↑		TUL	OKC V4 SGF	
B727/A							
T480		OKC P1450			170		

AAL50	OKC				TUL	OKC V4 SGF	
B727/A							
T480	+7	SLICK					

AAL50	SLICK				SGF	OKC V4 SGF	
B727/A							
T480	+9	TUL					

AAL50	TUL				SGF	OKC V4 SGF	
B727/A							
T480	+7	AFTON					ZME

4.

N234			↑		PNC	TUL V4N TRYON	
C310/A						V5 PNC V2	
T180		TUL P1455			80	AMA/0120	

| N234 C310/A T180 | TUL +32 | PNC | | END | TUL V4N TRYON V5 PNC V2 AMA/ 0120 | |

| N234 C310/A T180 | PNC +25 | END | | AMA | TUL V4N TRYON V5 PNC V2 AMA/ 0120 | ZAB |

5.

| N456 C172/U T105 | | MLC P1600 | | SNL 60 | MLC V6 CDS/0153 | |

| N456 C172/U T105 | MLC +38 | SNL | | OKC | MLC V6 CDS/0153 | |

| N456 C172/U T105 | SNL +25 | OKC | | CDS | MLC V6 CDS/0153 | ZAB |

ESTIMATING EN ROUTE FLIGHT PLANS
EXAMPLE 1

Directions:

3	11			20	21	25		
	12	15	16					
4	13							
5	14A	19			24	26		30

1. Using the above strip, list the required items in the designated space.

3.	AIRCRAFT I.D.	15.	ETA OVER POSTED FIX
4.	NUMBER OF AIRCRAFT	16.	ARR./DEPT. ARROW
	HEAVY INDICATION, TYPE	19.	POSTED FIX/PROPOSAL TIME
	OF AIRCRAFT, EQUIPMENT SUFFIX	20.	ALT. INFORMATION
5.	TRUE AIR SPEED	21.	NEXT FIX
11.	PREVIOUS FIX	24.	PILOT'S REQUESTED ALT.
12.	ETA OVER PREVIOUS FIX	25.	DEPT. POINT, ROUTE, DESTINATION, ETA AT DESTINATION
13.	REVISED ETA OVER PREVIOUS FIX	26.	PERTINENT REMARKS
14A.	PLUS TIME	30.	COORDINATION INDICATOR

2. On the following strips compute and record the plus times and posted fix estimates.

N17C	AMA		24	90	PNC	AMA V2 MIO V7 PRX	
	1600	16					
C310/B							
180	+24	END					

N17C	END		49	90		MIO	AMA V2 MIO V7 PRX	
	1624	16						
C310/B								
180	+25	PNC						

N17C	PNC		14	90		TUL	AMA V2 MIO V7 PRX	
	1649	17						
C310/B								
180	+25	MIO						

N17C	MIO		27	90		MLC	AMA MIO V7 PRX	
	1714	17						
C310/B								
180	+13	TUL						

N17C	TUL		45	90		PRX	AMA MIO V7 PRX	
	1727	17						
C310/B								
180	+18	MLC						ZFW

ESTIMATING EN ROUTE FLIGHT PLANS
END-OF-LESSON TEST

1. DEN V1 OKC

	END
	OKC

3. STL V4 ABI

	AFTON
	TUL
	SLICK
	OKC

2. AMA V2 PNC V8 TUL V7 PRX

	END
	PNC
	TUL
	MLC

4. ABI V4 OKC V4N TUL

	OKC
	TRYON
	TUL

5.

EAL197 B727/A T420	CDS 1704		150		LAX V6 HOT	

EAL197 B727/A T420	CDS 1704 +15	1719 OKC	150	SNL	LAX V6 HOT	

EAL197 B727/A T420	OKC 1717 +8	1727 SNL	150	MLC	LAX V6 HOT	

EAL197 B727/A T420	SNL 1724 +11	1735 MLC	150	HOT	LAX V6 HOT	ZME

6.

A18817 C130/B T290	FSM 1207		120		MEM V8 PNC V2 END V1 OKC	

A18817 C130/B T290	FSM 1207 +20	27 12 TUL	120	PNC	MEM V8 PNC V2 END V1 CKC	

A18817 C130/B T290	TUL 1227 +14	41 12 PNC	120	END	MEM V8 PNC V2 END V1 OKC	

A18817 C130/B T290	PNC 1241 +15	56 12 End	120	OKC	MEM V8 PNC V2 END V1 OKC	

A18817	END		120		MEM V8 PNC V2	
	1256	14			END V1 OKC	
C130/B		13 ↓				
T290	+18	OKC				

PROCESSING DEPARTURE FLIGHT PLANS
END-OF-LESSON TEST

1. TIME: 0530

TWA514 DC9/A T480 SGF E0533 160 IND V10 TUL V4 ELP

TWA514	SGF		160	TUL	IND V10 TUL V4 ELP	
	E0533	40				
DC9/A		05				
T480	+7	MIO				

TWA514	MIO		160	OKC	IND V10 TUL V4 ELP	
		45				
DC9/A		05				
T480	+5	TUL				

TWA514	TUL		160		IND V10 TUL V4 ELP	
		54				
DC9/A		05				
T480	+9	SLICK				

TWA514	SLICK		160	ABI	IND V10 TUL V4 ELP	
		01				
DC9/A		06				
T480	+7	OKC				ZFW

2. TIME: 0638

N683B PA24/A T150 MLC P0640 80 MLC V9ICT/0115

N683B		↑		MIO	MLC V9 ICT/0115	
PA24/A						
T150		MLC P0640		80		

N683B	MLC			MIO	MLC V9 ICT	
PA24/A						
T150	+18	MAYES				

N683B	MAYES			ICT	MLC V9 ICT	
PA24/A						
T150	+13	MIO				ZKC

3. TIME: 1258

TWA333 B727/A T450 OKC P1301 170 OKC V6S MLC

TWA333		↑		MLC	OKC V6S MLC	
B727/A						
T450		OKC P1301		170		

TWA333	OKC			MLC	OKC V6S MLC	
B727/A						
T450	+7	ASHER				

TWA333	ASHER				OKC V6S MLC	
B727/A		↓				
T450	+11	MLC				

4. **TIME: 0010**

   COA26 B727/A T450 TUL P0008 150 TUL V4 SGF

COA26				SGF	TUL V4 SGF	
B727/A						
T450		TUL P0008		150		

COA26				SGF	TUL V4 SGF	
B727/A						
T450	+7	AFTON				ZME

PRACTICE EXERCISE 1
PROPOSED FLIGHT PLANS AND FIX POSTINGS

1.   SWA 123 B727/A T440 OKC P2220 170 OKC V4N V5 PNC V3 MKC

SWA123				PNC	OKC V4N TRYON V5 PNC V3 MKC	
B727/A		↑				
T440		OKC P2220		170		

SWA123	OKC			MKC	OKC V4N TRYON V5 PNC V3 MKC	
B727/A						
T440	+15	PNC				ZKC

2.   N6245C C310/A T180 OKC P2245 100 OKC V1 END V2 AMA V430 ABQ/ 0250

N6245C				END	OKC V1 END V2 AMA V430 ABQ /0250	
C310/A		↑				
T180		OKC P2245		100		

N6245C	OKC			AMA	OKC V1 END V2 AMA V430 ABQ	
C310/A						
T180	+30	END				ZAB

3. **A76241 F104/A T480 OKC P2350 170 OKC V6 MLC V7 PRX SHV MGM MXF**

A76241 F104/A T480		↑ OKC P2350		SNL 170	OKC V6 MLC V7 PRX SHV MGM MXF	

A76241 F104/A T480	OKC +7	SNL		MLC	OKC V6 MLC V7 PRX SHV MGM MXF	

A76241 F104/A T480	SNL +10	MLC		PRX	OKC V6 MLC V7 PRX SHV MGM MXF	ZFW

4. **VV76PH P3/B T280 TUL P1140 140 TUL V8 PNC V2 AMA**

VV76PH P3/B T280		↑ TUL P1140		PNC 140	TUL V8 PNC V2 AMA	

VV76PH P3/B T280	TUL +14	PNC		END	TUL V8 PNC V2 AMA	

VV76PH	PNC			AMA	TUL V8 PNC V2 AMA	
P3/B						
T280	+15	END				ZAB

5.   N269T PAZT/A T160 MLC P1420 80 MLC V7 MIO/0034

N269T		↑		TUL	MLC V7 M10 /0034	
PAZT/A						
T160		MLC P1420		80		

N269T	MLC			M10	MLC V7 M10	
PAZT/A						
T160	+18	TUL				

N269T	TUL	↓			MLC V7 M10	
PAZT/A						
T160	+13	M10				

6.   R61589 U11/A T160 END P2210 90 END V2 PNC V8 TUL V7 MLC V6 HOT

R61589		↑		PNC	END V2 PNC V8 TUL V7 MLC V6 HOT	
U11/A						
T160		END P2210		90		

R61589	END			TUL	END V2 PNC V8	
U11/A					TUL V7 MLC V6	
					HOT	
T160	+25	PNC				

R61589	PNC			MLC	END V2 PNC V8	
U11/A					TUL V7 MLC V6	
					HOT	
T160	+24	TUL				

R61589	TUL			HOT	END V2 PNC V8	
U11/A					TUL V7 MLC V6	
					HOT	
T160	+18	MLC				ZME

7. N21AC C310/A T180 PNC P1136 70 PNC V8 TUL/0025

N21AC		↑		TUL	PNC V8 TUL	
C310/A					/0025	
T180		PNC P1136		70		

N21AC	PNC	↓			PNC V8 TUL	
C310/A						
T180	+24	TUL				

8.   N99224 C150/X T100 END P2113 50 END V2 PNC/0045

N99224		↑	PNC	END V2 PNC /0045
C150/X				
T100		END P2113	50	

N99224	END	↓		END V2 PNC
C150/X				
T100	+38	PNC		

9.   DAL313 DC9/A T430 OKC P1816 150 OKC V4 TUL

DAL313		↑	TUL	OKC V4 TUL
DC9/A				
T430		OKC P1816	150	

DAL313	OKC		TUL	OKC V4 TUL
DC9/A				
T430	+8	SLICK		

DAL313	SLICK	↓		OKC V4 TUL
DC9/A				
T430	+10	TUL		

10.   A96143 C130/B T290 TUL P0016 170 TUL V8 LIT LRF

A96143 C130/B T290		↑ TUL P0016		FSM 170	TUL V8 LIT LRF ZME

PRACTICE EXERCISE 2
ESTIMATING EN ROUTE FLIGHT PLANS

1.　N12345 L188/B T360 AMA E1700 170 ABQ V2 PNC/1725

	AMA		170	PNC	ABQ V2 PNC
N12345		12			/1725
	1700	17			
L188/B					
T360	+12	END			

	END		170	PNC	ABQ V2 PNC
N12345		25 ↓			/1725
	1712	17			
L188/B					
T360	+13	PNC			

2.　USA868 DC9/A T440 FSM E1410 160 MEM V8 DEN

	FSM		160	PNC	MEM V8 DEN
USA868		25			
	1410	14			
DC9/A					
T440	+15	TUL			

	TUL		160	GCK	MEM V8 DEN	
USA868		35				
	1425	14				
DC9/A						
T440	+10	PNC				ZKC

3.　A44411 C135/B T475 CDS E2215 170 PHX V6 LRF

	CDS		170	SNL	PHX V6 LRF
A44411		28			
	2215	22			
C135/B					
T475	+13	OKC			

	OKC		170	MLC	PHX V6 LRF	
A44411		35				
	2228	22				
C135/B						
T475	+7	SNL				

	SNL		170	HOT	PHX V6 LRF	
A44411		45				
	2235	22				
C135/B						
T475	+10	MLC				ZME

4. N622G BE65/X T170 SGF E0705 80 STL V10 V2 AMA/0844

	SGF		80	PNC	STL V10 V2 AMA	
N622G		22			/0844	
	0705	07				
BE65/X						
T170	+17	MIO				

	MIO		80	END	STL V10 V2 AMA	
N622G		47			/0844	
	0722	07				
BE65/X						
T170	+25	PNC				

	PNC		80	AMA	STL V10 V2 AMA	
N622G		12			/0844	
	0747	08				
BE65/X						
T170	+25	END				ZAB

5. N47G C310/X T180 PRX E1615 80 HOU V11 PNC/1720

	PRX		80	PNC	HOU V11 PNC	
N47G	1615	35			/1720	
		16				
C310/X						
T180	+20	MLC				

N47G	MLC 1635	56		80	PNC	HOU V11 PNC /1720	
		16					
C310/X							
T180	+21	DEPEW					

N47G	DEPEW 1656	18 ↓		80		HOU V11 PNC /1720	
		17					
C310/X							
T180	+22	PNC					

6. AAL212 B727/A T450 MAPLE E1530 120 MKC V3 PNC V5 DAL

AAL212	MAPLE	38		120	SNL	MKC V3 PNC V5 DAL	
	1530	15					
B727/A							
T450	+8	PNC					

AAL212	PNC	49		120	DAL	MKC V3 PNC V5 DAL	
	1538	15					
B727/A							
T450	+11	SNL					ZFW

7. VV32115 P3/B T360 BLUFF E2105 100 ICT V13 VI OKC

VV32115	BLUFF	12		100	OKC	ICT V13 V1 OKC	
	2105	21					
P3/B							
T360	+7	END					

VV32115	END	27 ↓		100		ICT V13 V1 OKC	
	2112	21					
P3/B							
T360	+15	OKC					

8. DAL613 DC9/A T450 ABI E1235 150 ELP ABI V4 OKC V4N TUL V4 SGF

	ABI		150	TUL	ELP ABI V4 OKC	
DAL613	1235	48			V4N TUL V4 SGF	
DC9/A		12				
T450	+13	OKC				

	OKC		150	TUL	ELP OKC V4N	
DAL613	1248	57			TUL V4 SGF	
DC9/A		12				
T450	+9	TRYON				

	TRYON		150	SGF	ELP OKC V4N	
DAL613	1235	05			V4N TUL V4 SGF	
DC9/A		13				
T450	+8	TUL				

	TUL		150	SGF	ELP TUL V4 SGF	
DAL613	1305	12				
DC9/A		13				
T450	+7	AFTON				ZME

9. N26254 BE65/U T180 BLUFF E1020 90 DEN V8 TUL/1108

	BLUFF		90	TUL	DEN V8 TUL	
N26254	1020	41			/1108	
BE65/U		10				
T180	+21	PNC				

	PNC		90		DEN V8 TUL	
N26254	1041	05 ↓			/1108	
BE65/U		11				
T180	+24	TUL				

10. A96213 C130/B T290 FSM E2259 120 STL V8 TUL V7 MLC V6 OKC

				120	MLC	STL V8 TUL V7	
A96213	FSM	19				MLC V6 OKC	
	2259	23					
C130/B							
T290	+20	TUL					

				120	SNL	STL V8 TUL V7	
A96213	TUL	30				MLC V6 OKC	
	2319	23					
C130/B							
T290	+11	MLC					

				120	OKC	STL V8 TUL V7	
A96213	MLC	45				MLC V6 OKC	
	2330	23					
C130/B							
T290	+15	SNL					

				120		STL V8 TUL V7	
A96213	SNL	55	↓			MLC V6 OKC	
	2345	23					
C130/B							
T290	+10	OKC					

PRACTICE EXERCISE 3
PROCESSING DEPARTURE FLIGHT PLANS

1. TIME: 0625

"DAL810 CLEARED TO DENVER AIRPORT VIA VICTOR ONE VICTOR EIGHT, CLIMB AND MAINTAIN ONE SIX THOUSAND."

DAL810 DC9/A T430		↑ 0625/0625 OKC P0628	↑ 160	END 160	OKC V1 GCK V8 DEN	D-A

DAL810 DC9/A T430	OKC 0625 +13	38 06 END	↑ 160	GCK	OKC V1 V8 DEN	ZKC

2. TIME: 2104

"AIR FORCE TWO SIX ONE FOUR FIVE CLEARED TO DENVER AIRPORT VIA VICTOR SEVEN TULSA VICTOR EIGHT, CLIMB AND MAINTAIN ONE TWO THOUSAND."

A26145 C130/A T290		↑ 2104/ MLC P2104	↑ 120	TUL 120	MLC V7 TUL V8 DEN	D-A

A26145 C130/A T290	MLC 2104 +11	15 21 TUL	↑ 120	PNC	MLC V7 TUL V8 DEN	

A26145	TUL	29	↑120	GCK	MLC V7 TUL V8 DEN	
	2115	21				
C130/A						
T290	+14	PNC				ZKC

3. TIME: 1632

"N8421C CLEARED FROM MIAMI AIRPORT TO LOS ANGELES AIRPORT VIA VICTOR TWO, CLIMB AND MAINTAIN ONE ZERO THOUSAND."

N8421C		↑	↑100	PNC	MIO V2 LAX	
					/0305	D-A
C310/A						
		1632/				
T200		MIO P1630		100		

N8421C	MIO	57	↑100	END	MIO V2 LAX/1937	
	16					
C310/A						
	1632					
T200	+25	PNC				

N8421C	PNC	22	↑100	AMA	MIO V2 LAX/1937	
	17					
C310/A						
	1657					
T200	+25	END				ZAB

4. TIME: 0630

"EAL694 CLEARED TO DALLAS AIRPORT VIA VICTOR FIVE, CLIMB AND MAINTAIN ONE SIX THOUSAND."

EAL694		↑	↑160	SNL	PNC V5 DAL	
						D-A
B727/A						
		0630/				
T400		PNC P0630		160		

EAL694	PNC	43	↑160	DAL	PNC V5 DAL	
		06				
B727/A						
	0630					
T400	+13	SNL				ZFW

5. TIME: 1417

"APPROVAL REQUEST: AAL12 ASSUMED CHILDRESS DEPARTURE AT 1420 CLIMBING TO ONE SEVEN THOUSAND."

AAL12	CDS	33	↑170	PNC	CDS V6 OKC V3	
	P1420	14			PNC V5 ICT	
B727/A	1420					
T450	+13	OKC		170		

AAL12	OKC	46	↑170	ICT	CDS V6 OKC V3 PNC	
	1433	14			V5 ICT	
B727/A						
T450	+13	PNC				ZKC

6. TIME: 1431

"APPROVAL REQUEST: AAL22 DEPARTED HOT SPRINGS AT 1430 AT ONE FOUR THOUSAND."

AAL22	HOT	00	140	TUL	HOT V6 MLC V7	
	P1430	15			TUL V8 DEN	
L188/A						
	1430					
T280	+30	MLC		140		

AAL22	MLC	11	140	PNC	HOT V6 MLC V7 TUL	
		15			V8 DEN	
L188/A						
	1500					
T280	+11	TUL				

AAL22	TUL	25	140	GCK	HOT V6 MLC V7 TUL	
		15			V8 DEN	
L188/A						
	1511					
T280	+14	PNC				ZKC

7.   TIME: 1432

"APPROVAL REQUEST: EAL421 ASSUMED SGF DEPARTURE AT 1435 CLIMBING TO ONE TWO THOUSAND."

EAL421	SGF	46	↑120	PNC	SGF V10 MIO V2	
	P1435	14			SLC	
CV58/A						
	1435					
T270	+12	MIO		120		

EAL421	MIO	01	↑120	END	SGF V10 MIO V2	
		15			SLC	
CV58/A						
	1446					
T270	+15	PNC				

EAL421	PNC	16	↑120	AMA	SGF V10 MIO V2	
		15			SLC	
CV58/A						
	1501					
T270	+15	END				ZAB

8.   TIME: 1437

"APPROVAL REQUEST: USA160 ASSUMED DAL DEPARTURE AT 1440 AT ONE ZERO THOUSAND."

USA160	DAL	00	100	END	DAL V1 GCK	
	P1435	15				
L188/A						
	1440					
T280	+20	OKC		100		

USA160	OKC	18		100	GCK	DAL V1 GCK	
		15					
L188/A							
	1500						
T280	+18	END					ZKC

9. TIME: 1444

"APPROVAL REQUEST: C3418 ASSUMED GCK DEPARTURE AT 1445 CLIMBING TO ONE SEVEN THOUSAND."

C3418	GCK	59	↑170	OKC	GCK V1 OKC V6	
	P1444	14			MLC V11 PRX	
CV34/A						
	1445					
T230	+14	END		170		

C3418	END	22	↑170	SNL	GCK V1 OKC V6	
		15			MLC V11 PRX	
CV34/A						
	1459					
T230	+23	OKC				

C3418	OKC	35	↑170	MLC	GCK OKC V6 MLC	
		15			V11 PRX	
CV34/A						
	1522					
T230	+13	SNL				

C3418	SNL	54	↑170	PRX	GCK OKC V6 MLC	
		15			V11 PRX	
CV34/A						
	1535					
T230	+19	MLC				ZFW

10.   TIME: 1655

"AAL65 CLEARED TO SHV AIRPORT VIA VICTOR SEVEN, CLIMB AND MAINTAIN ONE FIVE THOUSAND."

AAL65		↑	↑ 150	MLC	TUL V7 SHV	D-A
B707/A		1655/				
T420		TUL P1654		170		

AAL65	TUL	03	↑ 150	PRX	TUL V7 SHV	
B707/A	17					
	1655					
T420	+8	MLC				ZFW

RECORDING CLEARANCE AND CONTROL INFORMATION
EXAMPLE 1

DIRECTIONS: *Using approval symbology and abbreviations, record the following clearances and control information on the flight progress strips.*

1. TIME: 1558   RUNWAY: 3

N234		T→ NE TR	↑ 90		PNC V8 TUL V7	
		160/-V8			MLC/0045	
C310/A						D-A
					LV30	
T180		PNC P1600	90			

"CESSNA TWO THREE FOUR CLEARED TO MCALESTER AIRPORT VIA DEPART NORTHEAST. TURN RIGHT HEADING ONE SIX ZERO UNTIL JOINING VICTOR EIGHT, VICTOR EIGHT TULSA VICTOR SEVEN, MAINTAIN NINER THOUSAND CONTACT AERO CENTER ONE TWO FOUR POINT ZERO LEAVING THREE THOUSAND."

2. TIME: 1555 Pilot will accept northeast departure.

N456		T→ NE END	↑ 90	OKC	END V1 DFW/0135	
			X20NWOKC			D-OKC
C310/A			↕ 60			
					LV30	
T180		END P1600	90			

"TWIN CESSNA FOUR FIVE SIX CLEARED FROM ENID AIRPORT TO OKLAHOMA CITY VORTAC. DEPART NORTHEAST DIRECT ENID VORTAC VICTOR ONE, CROSS TWO ZERO MILES NORTHWEST OF OKLAHOMA CITY VORTAC AT OR ABOVE SIX THOUSAND, MAINTAIN NINER THOUSAND, CONTACT AERO CENTER ONE TWO FOUR POINT ZERO LEAVING THREE THOUSAND."

3. TIME: 1620

N234	HOT			120 ↓ 60	SNL	SHV V6 OKC/1720	
	1550		30	120/47E			
C310/A		16					
				X8W ↕ 100			
T180		MLC					

"TWIN CESSNA TWO THREE FOUR MAINTAIN ONE TWO THOUSAND
UNTIL FOUR SEVEN MILES EAST OF MCALESTER VORTAC, CROSS
EIGHT MILES WEST OF MCALESTER VORTAC AT OR ABOVE ONE
ZERO THOUSAND, DESCEND AND MAINTAIN SIX THOUSAND."

4. TIME: 1620

N156	TUL			100 ↓ 60		ICT V7 MLC/1648	
	1618		32				N
PAZT/A		16					H360
							1642
T180		MLC					

"AZTEC ONE FIVE SIX CLEARED TO MCALESTER VORTAC, DESCEND
AND MAINTAIN SIX THOUSAND, HOLD NORTH ON THREE SIX ZERO
RADIAL, EXCEPT FURTHER CLEARANCE ONE SIX FOUR TWO."

5. TIME: 1625

N16S	MKC			120 ↓ 80	TUL	MKC V7 TUL V4	
	1605		30	120/35NE		OKC/1728	
BE35/A		16		X6 SW ↕ 100			
				RL90		RP17SW/	
T180		MIO					

"BONANZA ONE SIX SIERRA MAINTAIN ONE TWO THOUSAND UNTIL
THREE FIVE MILES NORTHEAST MIAMI VORTAC, CROSS SIX MILES
SOUTHWEST OF MIAMI VORTAC AT OR ABOVE ONE ZERO THOUSAND,
DESCEND AND MAINTAIN EIGHT THOUSAND, REPORT LEAVING NINER
THOUSAND, REPORT PASSING ONE SEVEN MILES SOUTHWEST OF
MIAMI VORTAC."

6.   TIME: 1625

DAL10	HOT			160		BHM V6 MLC		APCH
	1608		㉚	160/47E				APCH
B727/A		16		X6E ↕ 70				1625
							PT	
T450		MLC						

Indicate DL10 coordinated with McAlester tower.

"DELTA TEN MAINTAIN ONE SIX THOUSAND UNTIL FOUR SEVEN MILES EAST OF MCALESTER VORTAC, CROSS SIX MILES EAST OF MCALESTER VORTAC AT OR BELOW SEVEN THOUSAND, CLEARED FOR APPROACH CONTACT MCALESTER TOWER ONE ONE EIGHT POINT TWO PROCEDURE TURN."

7.   TIME: 1712

N234			↑ 100	PNC	TUL V4N V8 DEN	
			X17W ↕ 50		29NW/-V8	
C310/A			X285R ↕ 90			D-A
T180		TUL P1717		100		

"TWIN CESSNA TWO THREE FOUR CLEARED TO DENVER AIRPORT VIA REVISED ROUTE VICTOR FOUR NORTH TWO NINER MILE ARC NORTH-WEST TULSA VORTAC UNTIL JOINING VICTOR EIGHT, VICTOR EIGHT, CROSS ONE SEVEN MILES WEST TULSA VORTAC AT OR BELOW FIVE THOUSAND, CROSS TULSA VORTAC TWO EIGHT FIVE RADIAL AT OR ABOVE NINER THOUSAND MAINTAIN ONE ZERO THOUSAND."

8.

N234	OKC			⑨⓪	MKC	OKC V3 MKC ⟨1745⟩	
			㉚				
C310/A		16					
	1603						
T180	+ 27	PNC					ZKC

Mark the strip as if you had passed the estimate to Kansas City Center.

RECORDING CLEARANCE AND CONTROL INFORMATION
END-OF-LESSON TEST

1.

| N234

C310/A

T180 | MIO
1605

PNC | 30
16

32 | 80✓ | END

← | FYV V2 AMA/1750 | |

Pilot initial report:

"AERO CENTER, TWIN CESSNA TWO THREE FOUR ESTIMATING PONCA CITY ONE SIX THREE TWO, EIGHT THOUSAND, ENID NEXT."

2.

| N456

PAZT/A

T180 | MIO
1605

PNC | 30
16
33 | 100 80✓ | END

← | FYV V2 AMA/1750 | |

Pilot initial report:

"AERO CENTER, AZTEC FOUR FIVE SIX ESTIMATING PONCA CITY ONE SIX THREE THREE, EIGHT THOUSAND, ENID NEXT."

3.   TIME: 1625   RUNWAY: 3

| N678

M021/A

T180 | | T→ TR
090/⇒V3
RLS1<N453
1625/
PNC P1630 | ↑110

110 | MKC

↗ | PNC V3 MKC/0100

LV30 | D-A

ZKC |

Controller Clearance:

"MOONEY SIX SEVEN EIGHT CLEARED TO KANSAS CITY AIRPORT, DEPART NORTHEAST TURN RIGHT HEADING ZERO NINER ZERO UNTIL JOINING VICTOR THREE, VICTOR THREE, MAINTAIN ONE ONE THOUSAND, CONTACT AERO CENTER ONE TWO FOUR POINT ZERO LEAVING THREE THOUSAND, RELEASE MOONEY SIX SEVEN EIGHT ONE MINUTE AFTER BARRON FOUR FIVE THREE DEPARTS."

4. TIME: 1628

N521	SNL			110 ↓ 60	CDS V6 MLC/1700		N
	1623			110/18E SNL			360
BE35/A		16⁴⁸		× 8W ↕ 70			
			48	× @60	→		1658
T180		MLC		RL80			

Controller clearance:

"BONANZA FIVE TWO ONE AERO CENTER, CLEARED TO MCALESTER VORTAC, MAINTAIN ONE ONE THOUSAND UNTIL ONE EIGHT MILES EAST OF SHAWNEE VORTAC, CROSS EIGHT MILES WEST OF MCALESTER VORTAC AT OR BELOW SEVEN THOUSAND, CROSS MCALESTER VORTAC AT AND MAINTAIN SIX THOUSAND, REPORT LEAVING EIGHT THOUSAND. HOLD NORTH ON THE THREE SIX ZERO RADIAL, EXPECT FURTHER CLEARANCE, ONE SIX FIVE EIGHT."

5. TIME: 1615

N147	MIO			80	FYV V2 PNC/1640		SW
	1605		30	↓			210
C310/A		16					
		32			←		1640
T180		PNC					

Controller clearance:

"TWIN CESSNA ONE FOUR SEVEN, AERO CENTER, CLEARED. TO PONCA CITY VORTAC, HOLD SOUTHWEST ON TWO ONE ZERO RADIAL, EXPECT FURTHER CLEARANCE ONE SIX FOUR ZERO."

6.   TIME: 1640   RUNWAY: 21

N231		T→SW-PNC	↑80	END	PNC V2 AMA/0051	D-A
			×9W ↕60		V8 30 NW/⇒V2	
PAZT/A			×285R@80			
		1640/		←	LV30	
T180		PNC P1640		80		

Controller clearance:

"AZTEC TWO THREE ONE CLEARED TO AMARILLO AIRPORT, DEPART SOUTHWEST DIRECT PONCA CITY VORTAC, VICTOR EIGHT, THREE ZERO MILE ARC NORTHWEST OF PONCA CITY VORTAC UNTIL JOINING VICTOR TWO, VICTOR TWO CROSS NINER MILES NORTHWEST OF PONCA CITY VORTAC AT OR BELOW SIX THOUSAND, CROSS PONCA CITY TWO EIGHT FIVE RADIAL AT AND MAINTAIN EIGHT THOUSAND, CONTACT AERO CENTER ONE TWO FOUR POINT ZERO LEAVING THREE THOUSAND."

7.   TIME: 1643

N268	MIO		100	MIO V9 MLC/1655	APCH
	1617	㊿ ↓			APCH
PA31/A	16				1643
				RP 44NE/	
T180	MLC			PT	

Controller clearance:

"NAVAJO TWO SIX EIGHT, CLEARED FOR APPROACH, REPORT PASSING FOUR FOUR MILES NORTHEAST MCALESTER VORTAC, CONTACT MCALESTER TOWER ONE ONE EIGHT POINT TWO PROCEDURE TURN."

8. TIME: 1600

AAL29	AFTON		160√	OKC	SGF V4 OKC	
	1606	18				120 NE
B727/A	16					110 V4
	17			↙		1628
T420	TUL					

Controller clearance:

"AMERICAN TWENTY-NINE, CLEARED TO TULSA ZERO FIVE ZERO RADIAL TWO ZERO MILE FIX, HOLD NORTHEAST ON VICTOR FOUR, ONE ZERO MILE LEG, EXCEPT FURTHER CLEARANCE ONE SIX TWO EIGHT."

9. TIME: 1615

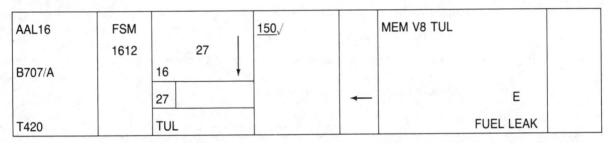

AAL16	FSM		150√		MEM V8 TUL	
	1612	27				
B707/A	16	↓				
	27			←	E	
T420	TUL				FUEL LEAK	

Indicate AA16 is at wrong altitude for direction of flight and has declared an emergency because of a fuel leak.

10.

UAL50	HOT			160W	SNL	NYP V6 LAX	
	1620		42		1649		
DC8/A		16					
		42	42		←	18ESNL	
T420		MLC				RQST BOMB SPO LAX E	

Indicate UA50:

    1. is in confliction at 160.

    2. estimating MLC 1642, 160.

    3. progressed MLC 1642, 160.

    4. estimating SNL 1649.

    5. requesting BOMB SQUAD AT LAX.

    6. is declaring emergency.

    7. was instructed to contact Aero Center 124.0 18 miles east of SNL.

Indicate all information has been coordinated.

11.   TIME: 1620

UAL52	SNL			160 ↓ 120	CDS	HOT V6 CDS	
	1629		40	16018E SNL			
B727/A		16		↓ 140>1630			
					←		
T420		OKC					ZAB

Controller clearance:

"UNITED FIFTY-TWO, MAINTAIN ONE SIX THOUSAND UNTIL ONE EIGHT MILES EAST OF SHAWNEE VORTAC, DESCEND TO REACH ONE FOUR THOUSAND AT OR BEFORE ONE SIX THREE ZERO, DESCEND AND MAINTAIN ONE TWO THOUSAND."

CHAPTER II

Lessons 9–12

FORWARDING FLIGHT PLAN AND CONTROL INFORMATION
FLIGHT PLAN AND CONTROL INFORMATION REVISION
GENERAL CONTROL
BOARD MANAGEMENT

LESSON 9
FORWARDING FLIGHT PLAN AND CONTROL INFORMATION

Previous lessons covered copying proposal and estimated flight plans, including processing and appropriate flight progress strips. This lesson will cover other pertinent information concerning flight progress data.

Mastering this phase of your training will add to the time-saving tools necessary to become a professional air traffic control specialist.

OBJECTIVE

Given sample flight progress strips, without references, and in accordance with 7110.65 and Aero Center procedures, you will be able to identify:

1. Flight data to be passed to en route facilities.

2. Sequence to pass flight data.

3. To whom flight data is passed.

4. Flight data to be passed to arrival facilities.

5. Time parameter for passing flight data between sectors/facilities.

6. Where to obtain missing flight data.

LESSON GUIDE

A. Standard Flight Plan

The flight plan form is completed by the pilot and is filed at a flight service station, operations office, or air field with an FAA facility. The flight service station or operations office forwards the flight plan to the assistant controller. The assistant controller disseminates the strips and forwards the information to adjacent centers/sectors.

B. Sequence and Data to be Forwarded for Departures in a Manual Mode

Space 3 — Aircraft identification.
Space 4 — Number of aircraft, type, equipment suffix.
Space 5 — Filed true airspeed.
Space 19 — Fix identifier.
Space 24 — Requested altitude.
Space 25 — Point of origin, route of flight, destination airport, ETE.
Space 26 — Pertinent remarks.

C. Sequence and Data to be Forwarded for Departures in a Suspense Mode

Space 3 — Aircraft identification.
Space 19 — Fix identifier.
Space 18 — Assumed or actual departure time.

Space 20 — Assigned altitude — pertinent restrictions
Space 26 — Pertinent remarks.
Space 28 — Forward clearance limit if other than destination airport.

D. Time Parameters for Departure Flight Plans

Forward departure flight plans within 3 minutes after finishing the clearance. When issuing multiple clearances, within 3 minutes after finishing the last clearance. Giving initials in Aero Center constitutes finishing the clearance.

E. Sequence and Data to be Forwarded for En Route Flights

Space 3 — Aircraft identification.
Space 4 — Number of Aircraft, type, equipment suffix.
Space 5 — Filed true airspeed.
Space 19 — Last fix posting in sector.
Space 15 — Center Estimate for fix shown in space 19.
Space 20 — Altitude assignment.
Space 24 — Altitude requested by pilot.
Space 25 — Route of flight information.
Space 26 — Pertinent remarks.
Space 28 — Control Information, clearance limit if other than destination airport.

F. Time Parameters for Forwarding En Route Data

Forward flight plan information at least 15 minutes before the aircraft is estimated to enter the receiving facility's area or before the center estimate for the last posted fix in the sector/center, whichever is the latest time.

G. Sequence and Data to be Forwarded to Approach Control for Tower En Route Flights

Space 3 — Aircraft identification.
Space 4 — Number, type, equipment suffix.
Space 5 — True air speed.
Space 19 — OKC or TUL VORTAC.
Space 15 — Center estimate for OKC or TUL VORTAC.
Space 20 — Assigned altitude, 5,000 ft. or below.
Space 25 — Route of flight.
Space 26 — Pertinent remarks affecting safety.
Space 29 — Transfer of control point (time, place, altitude).

H. Time Parameters for Data to be Forwarded for Tower En Route Flights

At least 10 minutes before center estimate of VORTAC serving that facility, OKC VORTAC or TUL VORTAC. May be reduced by letter of agreement and may be increased because of manual data processing or nonradar operations.

I. Sequence and Data to be Forwarded to Approach Control for Arrival Flights

Space 3 — Aircraft identification.
Space 4 — Number, type, equipment suffix.
Space 19 — Clearance limit.
Space 15 — Center estimate for clearance limit.
Space 20 — Center assigned altitude.
Space 25 — Forward destination airport if other than primary airport.
Space 26 — Forward remarks and pertinent information.
Space 29 — Forward transfer of control point.

J. Time Parameters for Forwarding Data to Approach Control for Arrival Flights

Prior to transfer of control point.

K. Sequence and Data to be Forwarded to VFR Towers for Arrival Flights

Space 3 — Aircraft identification.
Space 4 — Number, type.
Space 19 — Fix from which approach will be made.
Space 15 — Center estimate for NAVAID serving approach fix for destination airport.
Space 26 — Forward any information that will affect safety of flight.
Space 28 — Control Information — Type of approach, ZAE phraseology "for approach."

L. Time Parameters for Forwarding Data to VFR Towers for Arrival Flights

Arrival information must be forwarded to VFR towers before approach clearance is issued to the arrival flight, and soon enough to permit adjustment of the traffic flow.

M. Sequence and Data to be Forwarded to FSS for Arrival Flights

Space 3 — Aircraft identification.
Space 4 — Number, type.
Space 19 — Fix showing navigational aid from which approach will be made.
Space 15 — Center estimate for NAVAID serving the approach.
Space 26 — Remarks that might affect safety of flight.
Space 28 — Control information — phraseology "for approach."

N. Time Parameters for Forwarding Data to FSS for Arrival Flights

Forward flight information prior to center estimate for approach fix. If the flight is in hold, pass the information before issuing approach clearance. Forward information soon enough to provide airport advisory service.

O. Sources to Obtain Data for Missing Information on Flight Plans.

Obtain missing information from previous sector/center, organization where flight plan was filed, or the pilot.

FORWARDING FLIGHT PLAN AND CONTROL INFORMATION END-OF-LESSON TEST

DIRECTIONS: *Items 1, 2, 5, 7, 8, 11, 12, and 13 are multiple-choice. Indicate your selection by circling the appropriate letter for each item. Items 3, 4, 6, 9, 10, 14, 16, 17, and 18 are completion statements. Fill in the blank(s) with the appropriate words or phrases. Item 15 is a matching test item. Write information given in the correct spaces. Correct answers appear at the end of the chapter.*

1. What is the correct sequence for information to be forwarded on a proposed departure in a manual mode?
   (A) Spaces 3, 4, 5, 19, 24, 25, 26   (B) Spaces 3, 4, 14A, 19, 20, 25, 26
   (C) Spaces 3, 4, 5, 25, 19, 24, 26   (D) Spaces 3, 4, 5, 24, 25, 26, 28

2. What is the correct sequence for information to be forwarded on a departure in a suspense mode?
   (A) Spaces 19, 18, 20, 25, 26, 28   (B) Spaces 4, 19, 18, 20, 25, 26, 28
   (C) Spaces 3, 4, 5, 19, 15, 20, 24, 25, 26, 28   (D) Spaces 3, 19, 18, 20, 25, 26, 28

3. MLC tower requests two clearances at the same time, AAL10 and UAL15. Controller finishes clearance on AAL10 at time 1013 and starts clearance on UAL15. Controller completes clearance on UAL15 at time 1017. By what time must these flights be coordinated with ZFW center? _____

4.

N716				MKC	PNC V3 MKC/1645	
CV54/A						
T300		PNC P1604		90		ZKC

   What is the latest time that data on N716 must be forwarded to Kansas City Center to meet the time requirements for passing flight plan data?

5. The correct sequence to forward en route information in a suspense mode is
   (A) spaces 3, 4, 5, 6, 24, 25, 26, 28   (B) spaces 3, 19, 15, 20, 25, 26, 28
   (C) spaces 19, 18, 20, 25, 26, 28   (D) spaces 34, 19, 20, 25, 26, 29

6.

AAL61	OKC			MKC	OKC V3 MKC	
B707/A						
T450	PNC					ZKC

What time is the latest time that data on AAL61 must be passed to ZKC Center to meet the time requirements for passing flight data?

_____

7.

N38TV	TUL		90	ICT	TUL V10 V9 ICT	
CV48/D		11 13				
T280	MIO					ZKC

N38TV must be passed to Kansas City by
(A) 1105.   (B) 1108.   (C) 1113.   (D) 1115.

8. What spaces are used to forward arrival data to approach control?
   (A) Spaces 3, 5, 19, 18, 15, 20, 29, 28, 26, 25
   (B) Spaces 3, 4, 5, 19, 15, 20, 24, 25, 26, 28, 29
   (C) Spaces 3, 4, 5, 18, 24, 25, 26, 28, 29
   (D) Spaces 3, 4, 19, 15, 20, 25, 26, 28, 29

9. The letters TCP stand for _____.

10. When should arrival information be forwarded on arrivals to approach control facilities? _____

11. What is the correct sequence for information to be forwarded to a flight service station and VFR tower?
   (A) Space 4, 3, 15, 20, 19, 25, 26, 28   (B) Space 3, 15, 19, 28, 26, 4
   (C) Space 3, 4, 19, 15, 26, 28   (D) Space 3, 19, 4, 26, 15, 28

12. Arrival data for inbound aircraft must be forwarded to VFR towers before the
   (A) aircraft is cleared for approach.   (B) flight enters control zone.
   (C) center estimate for approach fix.   (D) aircraft enters holding.

13. In Aero Center, arrival information for inbound aircraft must be forwarded to FSSs before the
    (A) aircraft makes procedure turn.
    (B) flight leaves adjacent sector/center airspace.
    (C) center estimate for approach fix.
    (D) aircraft enters FSS area of jurisdiction.

14.

A90012				GCK	END V1 DEN	
T29/B						
T200		END P1900		60		ZKC

N450T	PNC 0317	42	60	FYV V2 END/0345	
M404/D	03				
T200	END				

N56WP	BLUF 1110	31	70	DEN V8 PNC/1135	
BE90/D	11				
T190	PNC				

UAL562	SLICK 1127	40	170	ABI V4 TUL	
L188/A	11				
T300	TUL				

Using the above flight progress strips, determine which facility should be passed information. On the lines below, write the aircraft identification adjacent to the facility receiving the information.

Aircraft Identification	Receiving Facility
_____	_____
_____	_____
_____	_____
_____	_____

15.

On the above strip enter the following flight data in the appropriate spaces:

= 90		= 1856 (MIO departure time)
= MIO P1859		= UAL716
= MIO V2 FYV		= T420
= B727/A		= 90

16. TIME: 1003

A68542				PNC	OKC V3 MKC	
C124/B						
T230		OKC P1000		90		

A68542	OKC			MKC	OKC V3 MKC	
C124/B						
T230		PNC				

Does the PNC strip contain all the information required to be passed?

YES ‒‒‒‒
NO ‒‒‒‒

If no, what information is missing?

‒‒

‒‒

‒‒

17.

N3002W	OKC			90	MKC	ABI V3 MKC	
	0218		53				
PA23/D		02					
T160		PNC					ZKC

What information is missing that should be passed?

_____

_____

_____

18.

COA86	ABI			170	PNC	ELP V3 PNC V2 MIO	
	1123		36				
B737/A		11					
T480	1123	OKC					

COA86	OKC			170	MIO	ELP V3 PNC V2 MIO	
			49				
B737/A		11					
T480		PNC					

COA86	PNC			170		PNC V2 MIO	
	1149						
B737							
T480		MIO					

Fill in the missing data on the above strips.

LESSON 10
FLIGHT PLAN AND CONTROL INFORMATION REVISION

You have received instructions on how to copy flight plans, recognize and correct errors and omissions, forward required information in the correct sequence, in a timely manner, and indicate the information has been forwarded. Since posted information is in a constant state of change, it is of the utmost importance that this information be amended and forwarded. The next logical step is to study the procedure used to record and forward revisions.

Objectives

Given sample flight progress strips, without references, and in accordance with 7110.65, you will:

1. Record revisions, using standard strip marking.

2. Forward revisions to appropriate facility, using standard strip marking.

3. Indicate when revised information has been forwarded by using standard strip marking.

Lesson Guide

A.   Revisions of Flight Plans and Control Information

　　1.   Updating Within Your Sector

　　　　a.   Guidelines — update revisions on all strips within your sector. Maintain only necessary and current data, and do not erase or overwrite any information. Line through information to be revised. Use an "X" to delete unwanted altitude information, climb or descend arrow, or at or above/below symbols. Write correct information adjacent to original information.

　　2.   Forward To Adjacent Sector or Facility

　　　　a.   Format — Use standard phraseology to forward revised information.

　　　　b.   Aircraft Identification — "... revised aircraft identification (revised identification)."

　　　　c.   Aircraft Type — "... revised aircraft type (type aircraft)."

　　　　d.   Equipment Suffix — "... revised equipment suffix (revised equipment suffix)."

　　　　e.   Airspeed — "... revised true airspeed (speed) knots."

　　　　f.   Time — Revise and coordinate aircraft time changes if center estimate of last posted fix in transferring facility's area is different by more than 3 minutes. Also coordinate time if the position report over last reporting point in transferring facility's area differs more than 3 minutes from estimate given.

Phraseology: "AT (first fix inside receiving controller's airspace) (aircraft ID), REVISED ESTIMATE (last fix your airspace) (time)."

Example: "AT CHILDRESS, NOVEMBER ONE TWO THREE, REVISED ESTIMATE OKLAHOMA CITY ONE ONE FOUR FIVE."

Coordination must be timely, prior to one of the following, whichever is later: (1) center estimate for last fix posting in sector, (2) 15 minutes before center estimate for center/sector boundary.

g. Altitude — "AT (first fix inside receiving controller's airspace) (aircraft identification) REVISED ALTITUDE."

h. Route and/or Destination — "AT (first fix inside receiving controller's airspace) REVISED ROUTE (route)."

i. Pilot's ETA at Destination — coordinate general aviation aircraft revisions if different by more than 3 minutes.

3. Airborne Military Aircraft

a. Forward to FSS — IFR flight plans and changes to IFR flight plans concerning destination, pilot ETA at destination, and fuel exhaustion time.

FLIGHT PLAN AND CONTROL INFORMATION REVISION EXAMPLE 1

DIRECTIONS: *Revise the strips where necessary, and answer each question in the space provided.*

1. TIME: 1502

TWA431	PNC			150		MLC	END V8 TUL V7 PRX	
	1508 ~~1508~~		~~14~~ 19					
DC9/A	08	15						
T450		TUL						

TWA431	TUL			150		PRX	END V7 PRX	
	15~~14~~		~~21~~ 26					
DC9/A	19	15						
T450		MLC						ZFW

D-1 forwards you a revised Ponca City estimate of one five zero eight on TWA Four Thirty-One. To what sector or facility should you forward the revision after revising your strips?

<u>FORT WORTH CENTER</u>

2. TIME: 1056

AAL211	OKC		50	170√		MLC	CDS V6 HOT	
	1040					1106		
B727/A	1043	10						
		53	54					
T310		SNL						

What action needs to be taken on the above strip? You are working the aircraft in Sector D-1.

<u>FORWARD SNL PROGRESS AND MLC ESTIMATE TO D2 SECTOR</u>

3.   TIME: 1718

N34T	SNL			~~70~~ 50	HOT	OKC V6 HOT	
	1720		39				
C310/A		17					
T190		MLC					ZME

D-1 forwards you a revised altitude of five thousand on Twin Cessna Three Four Tango. To what sector or facility should you forward the revision after revising your strip?

MEMPHIS CENTER

4.   TIME: 1158

EAL410	MIO			160	END	MIO V2 AMA	
	1204		15				
B~~737~~/A		12					
727							
T520		PNC					

EAL410	PNC			160	AMA	MIO V2 AMA	
			24				
B~~737~~/A		12					
727	1204						
T520		END					ZAB

D-2 forwards you a revised aircraft type on Eastern Four Ten to a Boeing Seven Twenty-Seven slant alfa. After revising your strip, to what sector or facility should you forward the revision?

ALBUQUERQUE CENTER

5.   TIME: 1610

WAL311	ABI			130	TUL	HOU V4 OKC ~~V4N~~ TUL V4N	
	1615		27				
B727/A		16					
T510		OKC					

WAL311	OKC	34	130		TUL	HOU V4 OKC ~~V4N~~ TUL	
	1627					V4N	
B727/A		16					
T510		~~SLICK~~ TRYON					

Fort Worth Center forwards you a revised route on Western Three Eleven on V4 Oklahoma City, V4N Tulsa. After revising your strip, to what sector or facility should you forward the revision?

D2 _____

FLIGHT PLAN AND CONTROL INFORMATION REVISION EXAMPLE 2

DIRECTIONS:
A. *Revise each strip according to information given.*
B. *On the lines provided, write the phraseology necessary to forward the revised information.*
C. *Indicate on each strip information forwarded.*

1. TIME: 1515

TWA431	TUL	21(26)	150√		PRX	END TUL V7 PRX	
	151~~5~~						
DC9/A	19	15					
		26					
T450		MLC					ZFW

PILOT REPORT:

"AERO CENTER TWA FOUR THIRTY-ONE PROGRESSED TULSA VORTAC ONE FIVE ONE NINER, ONE FIVE THOUSAND, ESTIMATING MCALESTER VORTAC ONE FIVE TWO SIX PARIS NEXT."

"FORT WORTH CENTER, AERO CENTER, ACTIVE AT PARIS, T-W-A FOUR THIRTY-ONE REVISED McALESTER VORTAC ESTIMATE ONE FIVE TWO SIX." _____

2. TIME: 2110

DAL616	SNL 2121		30	170	HOT	OKC V6 HOT	
~~DC9/A~~ B727/B		21					
T480		MLC					ZME

PREVIOUS SECTOR REVISION:

"D2, D1, AT MCALESTER, DELTA SIX SIXTEEN REVISED TYPE AIRCRAFT AND EQUIPMENT BOEING SEVEN TWENTY-SEVEN SLANT BRAVO."

"MEMPHIS CENTER, AERO CENTER, ACTIVE AT HOT SPRINGS DELTA SIX SIXTEEN REVISED TYPE AIRCRAFT AND EQUIPMENT SUFFIX BOEING SEVEN TWENTY-SEVEN SLANT BRAVO."

3. TIME: 2302

N34T	HOT 2236		26	~~30~~ (60)	DAL	HOT V6 MLC V9 DAL 0008	
BE90/A		23					
T190		MLC					ZFW

PREVIOUS CENTER REVISION:

"AT MCALESTER KING AIR THREE FOUR TANGO, REVISED ALTITUDE SIX THOUSAND."

"FORT WORTH CENTER AERO CENTER, ACTIVE AT DALLAS KING AIR THREE FOUR TANGO REVISED ALTITUDE SIX THOUSAND."

4.   TIME: 1047

AAL211	PNC			170√	DAL	ICT V5 DAL	
	1031		42		(1057)		
B727/A		10					
		46	(46)				
T490		SNL					ZFW

PILOT REPORT:

"AERO CENTER, AMERICAN TWO ELEVEN PROGRESSED SHAWNEE VORTAC ONE ZERO FOUR SIX, ONE SEVEN THOUSAND, ESTIMATING DALLAS ONE ZERO FIVE SEVEN, LANDING DALLAS."

"FORT WORTH CENTER AERO CENTER, ACTIVE AT DALLAS AMERICAN TWO ELEVEN PROGRESSED SHAWNEE VORTAC ONE ZERO FOUR SIX ONE SEVEN THOUSAND, ESTIMATED DALLAS VORTAC ONE ZERO FIVE SEVEN."

5.   TIME: 1615

WAL311	DAL			160	CDS	HOU V1 OKC V6 ABQ	
	1622		34			V6N CDS	
B727/A		16					
T500		OKC					ZAB

PREVIOUS CENTER REVISION:

"AT OKLAHOMA CITY WESTERN THREE ELEVEN REVISED ROUTE OKLA-HOMA CITY VORTAC VICTOR SIX NORTH CHILDRESS VICTOR 6 ALBU-QUERQUE."

"ALBUQUERQUE CENTER AERO CENTER, ACTIVE AT CHILDRESS WESTER THREE ELEVEN REVISED ROUTE VICTOR SIX NORTH CHIL-DRESS VICTOR SIX."

FLIGHT PLAN AND CONTROL INFORMATION REVISION END-OF-LESSON TEST

DIRECTIONS: *Items 1 through 11 are completion statements. Fill in the blank(s) with the appropriate words, phrases, or strip markings. Correct answers appear at the end of the chapter.*

Use the following strips to answer items 1 and 2.

UAL430	PRX 1715	17	23	140	TUL	MSY V7 MKC	
DC8/A							
T450		MLC					

UAL430	MLC 1723	17	30	140	MIO	MSY V7 MKC	
DC8/A							
T450		TUL					

UAL430	TUL 1730	17	35	140	MKC	MSY V7 MKC	
DC8/A							
T450		MIO					ZKC

1. Revise the above strips in accordance with the following data:

   A. Aircraft type and suffix changed to DC9/B.
   B. Altitude changed to 160.
   C. Paris time changes to 1721.

2. Write the phraseology for forwarding the revised aircraft type, equipment suffix, time, and altitude.

   _____

   _____

Use the following strip to answer items 3, 4, 5, and 6.

N401P	PNC 15~~10~~ 19	~~25~~ 34 15	✗ ↑ 90	FYV	END V2 FYV	
C310/A						
T190		MIO				ZME

3. To what facility or sector should you forward the revision?

_____

4. Write the phraseology for forwarding the revised time.

_____

_____

_____

5. Write the phraseology for forwarding the revised altitude.

_____

_____

_____

6. Mark the strip to indicate that the revised information has been forwarded properly. Delete any unwanted information.

Use the following strip to answer items 7 and 8.

A13597	SNL 1758	09 18	170	HOT	AMA V6 HOT LRF	
T39/B						
T420		MLC				ZME

7. A revised pilot ETA for LRF of 1850 will be forwarded to

_____

8. Mark the strip to indicate the revised information has been forwarded.

Use the following strips to answer items 9, 10, and 11.

USA278	MIO 1435	50 14	140	END	FYV V2 AMA	
CV58/A						
T280		PNC				

USA278	PNC 1450			140	AMA	FYV V2 AMA	
			05				
CV58/A		15					
T280		END					ZAB

9. Revise the strips in accordance with the following data:

    A.   MIO time revised to 1430.

    B.   Altitude revised to 120.

10. Write the phraseology for forwarding the revised time and altitude.

_____

_____

_____

11. Mark the strips to indicate all revised information has been forwarded.

LESSON 11
GENERAL CONTROL

It's time to tie it all together. You have completed the instruction that contained the rules and procedures used in air traffic control. By this point in your training, you should be ready to make rapid decisions applying all of the rules and procedures that have been presented. Your effectiveness as a controller will be judged by your ability to make sound decisions.

Objectives

Given air traffic situations, without references, and in accordance with 7110.65, you will:

1. Determine duty priority, procedural preference, and operational priority.

2. Select the procedure for control and radio communications transfer.

3. Select control procedures for a formation flight.

4. Approve/disapprove pilot's request as circumstances permit.

5. Identify standard phraseology requiring expeditious compliance of a clearance.

6. Determine appropriate action as a result of nonreceipt of position report.

7. Apply the term "heavy" in verbal communications.

Lesson Guide

A. Duty Priority

Give first priority to separating aircraft and issuing safety alerts.

B. Procedural Preference

Use automated over nonautomated procedures when permitted by workload, communications, and equipment capabilities.

C. Operational Priority

First come, first served with several exceptions. Exceptions: Aircraft in distress, air evacuation flights, SAR, flight check/SAFI, Presidential/Vice Presidential flights, nightwatch, flynet, garden plot, SAMP, IFR over FW/SVFR aircraft.

D. Coordinate Use of Airspace

Transfer control only after completing coordination.

E. Transfer Control Responsibility

At a time, fix/location, or altitude. Ensure you eliminate potential conflictions in your sector/area. Inform the receiving facility of altitude restrictions within your area/sector or altitude restrictions within the TCP.

F. Assume Control

Assume control after the aircraft enters your area unless specifically coordinated with the transferring sector/facility. When the aircraft is in the transferring facility's area you may coordinate for control, issue clearances through the transferring facility, or issue clearances with restrictions until the aircraft is in your area.

G. Transfer Radio Communications

Transfer radio communication before the aircraft enters receiving area/sector unless coordinated. Specify facility name or location name and terminal function. Specify frequency to use and when to contact next facility at time, fix, or altitude.

H. Formation Flights

Control formation flights as a single aircraft issuing control instructions to the formation leader when individual control requested; issue advisories that will assist in attaining separation. Once separation is established, issue individual control instructions.

I. Pilot's Request

Approve or disapprove a pilot's request as circumstances permit.

Phraseology:

"APPROVED AS REQUESTED."
"(requested operation) APPROVED."
"UNABLE (requested operation)."

J. Use of the word "Immediately"

Use the word "immediately" only when expeditious compliance is required to avoid an imminent situation. Include reason, time permitting.

K. No Position Report

Take action to obtain a position report no later than 5 minutes after fix estimate, if it affects separation.

L. Duplicate Position Reports

Do not require aircraft to report same position to more than one facility.

M. Heavy

Use the word "heavy" to identify heavy jet aircraft in all inter/intra facility communications.

GENERAL CONTROL
EXAMPLE 1

TIME: 0800   **SNL**

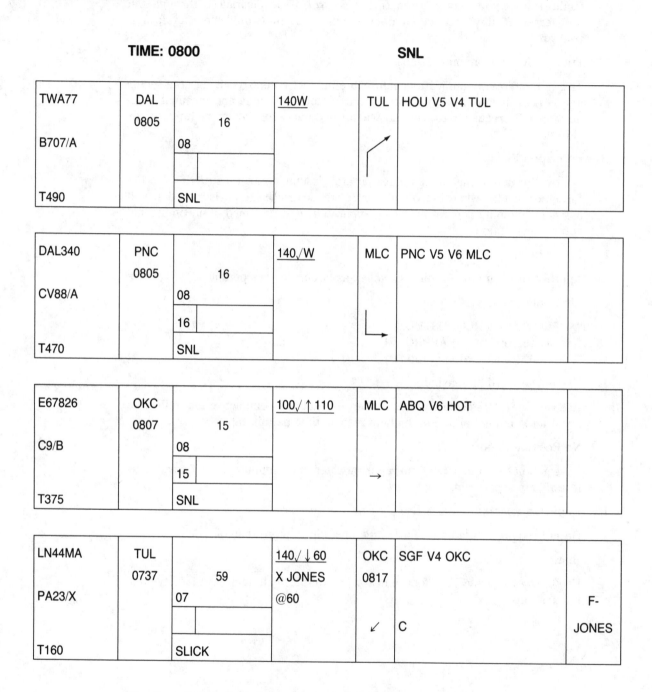

Use the above strips to answer questions 1, 2, and 3.

1. Which aircraft must be separated? Explain your answer.

DAL 340 AND TWA 77 RED W ON BOTH STRIPS INDICATES "WARNING," SHOWING AIRCRAFT ARE NOT SEPARATED.

2. Between E67826 and LN44MA, which aircraft has operational priority? Explain your answer.

   LN44MA, E67826, A MILITARY AIR EVACUATION FLIGHT, MUST REQUEST PRIORITY HANDLING WHILE LN44MA, A CIVILIAN AMBULANCE, DOES NOT.

3. List the priority of duties in the order of importance:
   A.   Coordinate altitude change on E67826.
   B.   Issue clearance to provide separation between DL340 and TW77.
   C.   Transfer radio communications on LN-44MA, which is approaching its clearance limit of Jones intersection.

   B, C, A

GENERAL CONTROL EXAMPLE 2

1. TIME: 1215

N306F	SNL 1206	25 (18) 12	⑥⓪√	OKC 1225	MLC V6 OKC	F
BE65/D						
						25E
T160		~~OKC~~-BOLEY				OKC

A. Write the phraseology to have N306F contact Oklahoma City Approach Control 30 miles from Oklahoma City VORTAC.

"QUEEN AIR ZERO SIX FOXTROT, CONTACT OKLAHOMA CITY APPROACH ONE ONE NINER POINT ONE THREE ZERO MILES EAST OF OKLAHOMA CITY VORTAC."

2. TIME: 1622

AAL14	CDS 1608	21 16	170√	DAL 1632	LAX V6 OKC V1 HOU	
B727/A						
		20 21				
T480		OKC			C	ZFW

A. Write the phraseology to have AAL14 contact Fort Worth Center at 1627.

"AMERICAN FOURTEEN, CONTACT FORT WORTH CENTER ONE TWO NINER POINT ZERO AT ONE SIX TWO SEVEN."

B. Write the phraseology to have AAL14 contact Fort Worth Center 46 miles from OKC VORTAC.

"AMERICAN FOURTEEN, CONTACT FORT WORTH CENTER ONE TWO NINER POINT ZERO FOUR SIX MILES SOUTHEAST OKLAHOMA CITY VORTAC."

3. TIME: 2130

VV29981	PNC		120√		FYV V2 END	
	2117	(32)	X 17E ↕ 50			
P3/N		21				APCH
		32				2130
T300		END			C	

A. **Write the phraseology to have VV29981 contact Enid FSS 255.4 at five thousand.**

"NAVY NINER EIGHT ONE, CONTACT ENID RADIO AT FIVE THOUSAND." (USE OF FREQUENCY IS OPTIONAL AT FSS)

B. **Write the phraseology to have VV29981 contact Enid FSS when starting procedure turn.**

"NAVY NINER EIGHT ONE, CONTACT ENID RADIO PROCEDURE TURN."

GENERAL CONTROL
END-OF-LESSON TEST

DIRECTIONS: *Items 1 through 12 are multiple-choice. Indicate your selection by circling the appropriate letter for each test item. Correct answers appear at the end of the chapter.*

1. What is the first priority of an air traffic controller?
   (A) Additional services
   (B) Separation of aircraft
   (C) Use of automated procedures over nonautomated
   (D) Issuing traffic information to IFR aircraft

2. Military air evacuation flights are given priority when
   (A) carrying patients.   (B) requested by pilot.
   (C) on a routine flight.   (D) deemed necessary by controller.

3. Which flight would receive priority?
   (A) SAFI mission
   (B) Air Force air evac aircraft
   (C) Air Force aircraft carrying a two star general
   (D) None of the above

4. Transfer control responsibility of an aircraft
   (A) at a time or fix only.
   (B) after aircraft enters the receiving facility's area.
   (C) after eliminating all potential conflictions.
   (D) only after transferring communications.

5. You have issued an altitude restriction to an aircraft that you will transfer to Tulsa approach. When coordinating transfer of control, you should
   (A) have aircraft inform Tulsa of the altitude restriction.
   (B) take no action in reference to the altitude restriction.
   (C) have aircraft change altitude at a time, fix, or specified position.
   (D) inform Tulsa of an altitude restriction within your area.

6. Assuming control of an aircraft, unless otherwise specified, can only be done after pilot
   (A) requests climb or descent.   (B) reports in your area.
   (C) reports last fix outside your area.   (D) reports on your frequency.

7. The phraseology used to transfer radio communications to another facility is
   (A) "UNITED SIX CONTACT OKLAHOMA CITY APPROACH THREE ZERO MILES WEST OF OKLAHOMA CITY ONE ONE NINER POINT ONE NOW."
   (B) "UNITED SIX CONTACT OKLAHOMA CITY APPROACH ONE ONE NINER POINT ONE THREE ZERO MILES WEST OF OKLAHOMA CITY VORTAC."

(C) "UNITED SIX CONTACT OKLAHOMA CITY APPROACH ONE ONE NINER ONE THREE ZERO MILES WEST OF OKLAHOMA CITY VORTAC."

(D) "UNITED SIX CONTACT OKLAHOMA CITY APPROACH ONE ONE NINER ONE APPROACHING THE THREE ZERO MILE FIX WEST OF OKLAHOMA CITY AIRPORT."

8. A formation flight shall be controlled
   (A) from the center of the formation.   (B) as separate aircraft.
   (C) as a single aircraft.   (D) on the position of the lead and trailing aircraft.

9. A pilot's request shall be approved or disapproved
   (A) upon approval by your supervisor.   (B) as circumstances permit.
   (C) when traffic is light to moderate.   (D) only if an emergency exists.

10. When is the word "immediately" used in a clearance?
    (A) When you need an aircraft to expedite descent
    (B) At no time should "immediately" be used.
    (C) Any time the controller is busy and wants an aircraft moved
    (D) Whenever expeditious compliance is required to avoid an imminent situation

11. Action should be taken to obtain a position report that affects separation no later than _____ minutes after the aircraft was estimated to pass the fix.
    (A) 3   (B) 5   (C) 7   (D) 10

12. When should the word "heavy" be used in reference to heavy jet identification?
    (A) Only in communications with heavy jet aircraft
    (B) In all inter/intrafacility communications and in communicating with jet aircraft
    (C) Only in interfacility communications
    (D) Only in intrafacility communications

LESSON 12
BOARD MANAGEMENT

When you are working the manual control position, you must be able to visualize traffic situations in your sector. This is often referred to as "Having the Big Picture." The "Big Picture" is actually many small pictures of what is occurring at each fix or on the airway. You must be able to rapidly scan from one small picture to the next, visualizing the traffic at each. This is a skill developed by experience and knowledge of the area. You may get the "Big Picture" early in your training, while for others it may take longer. If you get it early, great; but if you don't, do not become discouraged, frustrated, or upset. You must continue to study the map and the procedures that have been covered to develop this skill.

Objectives

Given an air traffic situation and flight progress strips, without references, and in accordance with 7110.65, you will be able to:

1. Identify the action to take prior to sequencing flight progress strips.

2. Compute approximate location of aircraft in flight, using the "quick estimate" procedure.

3. Detect and correct time errors on strips, using the "quick estimate" procedure.

4. Sequence, in order, flight progress strips.

Lesson Guide

A. Actions Prior to Sequencing Strips

Ensure accuracy and completeness of information.

B. Compute Location of Aircraft

Using quick estimating:

1. Aircraft Position—Fix time (FT) ETA/time over nearest fix less clock time (CT) multiplied by mile per minute (MPM) equal distance (DME).

$$(FT\text{-}CT) \times MPM = DME$$

2. Fix estimate—Distance to Fix (D) divided by miles per minute (MPM) plus previous fix time (PFT) equals fix estimate (ETA).

$$\frac{D}{MPM} + PFT = Fix\ ETA$$

C. Detect and Correct Time Errors

Use the quick estimating method to detect and correct time errors.

D. Sequencing Strips

Sequence strips under proper bay header. Post in chronological order of arrival time over a particular fix. If they have the same times, lower altitude is placed below higher altitude. Sequence arrivals, departures, and overflights together appear in ascending chronological order.

E. Scanning Strips

Scan strips for proper sequence, conflicting traffic, non-DME aircraft (T-V-X), wrong altitude for direction of flight (WAFDOF), altitude below MEA, and strips that need to be coordinated.

F. Preplanning

Authorized strip markings before problem begins:

1. Direction arrows

2. WAFDOF

3. Red "W"

4. Altitude check

5. Altimeter check

6. Outer fixes at OKC

7. Nonposted intersections

8. Next fix/intersection

9. Arrival/Departure

G. Deadwood

Remove strips when no longer required for control purposes.

BOARD MANAGEMENT
EXAMPLE 1

DIRECTIONS: *Inspect the strips provided for the Oklahoma City (OKC) and (END) fix postings. Using the "quick estimating" method previously taught, find the time errors. Correct as necessary.*

Check routes and strip markings on all flights through D1 for accuracy. Correct and revise as necessary.

OKC

A12389	END		110	SNL	COS V1 OKC V6 HOT	
	0810	~~36~~ 28				
C130/A		08				
T310		OKC				

EL7727	TUL		160		FSM V4 OKC	
	0805	~~28~~				
B727/A		08 20 ↓				
T410		~~OKC~~ JONES				

N12M	PNC		140		MKC V3 OKC	
	0801	11 ↓				
L118/B		08				
T300		~~OKC~~ COYLE				

UAL220	CDS		170	SNL	TUS MLC	
	0756	~~10~~				
DC9/A		08				
T420		OKC				

END

AAL210 DC9/A T310	OKC 0814 08 END	~~37~~ 27 ↓	160		DAL V1 END	

A21587 C130/A T310	AMA 0756 08 END	~~20~~ 10	150	PNC	TUS V2 MIO	

NWA2 B767/A T480	AMA 0804 08 END	15	170	ICT	AMA V2 END ~~V1~~ ICT V13	

N282T L188/B T300	ICT 0730 ~~06~~ 07 END	~~16~~ 56	140	OKC	TOP V13 END V1 OKC/ 0835	

BOARD MANAGEMENT
END-OF-LESSON TEST

DIRECTIONS: *Items 1 through 7 are multiple-choice. Indicate your selection by circling the appropriate letter to the left of each test item. Correct answers appear at the end of the chapter.*

1. Prior to sequencing flight progress strips, you should
   (A) check the accuracy and completeness of data and correct number of strips.
   (B) check remarks and destination.
   (C) compute position of aircraft.
   (D) check point of departure and clearance limit.

2. In Aero Center, strips shall be posted under the appropriate bay header
   (A) according to ascending altitude.
   (B) according to descending altitude.
   (C) in ascending chronological order.
   (D) in descending chronological order.

3. Select the correct order of sequence for the following flight progress strips.

A11918	MIO		120	MLC	MKC V7 PRX	
	1920	26				
T39/B		19				
T420	TUL					

N110	SLICK		110		ABI V4 TUL	
	1914	27				
CV58/A		19				
T300	TUL					

N134D	SLICK		70	FSM	CDS V4 TUL V8 FSM	
	1907	29				
PAZT/B		19				
T150	TUL					ZME

(A) N110, A11918, N134D   (B) N134D, N110, A11918
(C) A11918, N110, N134D   (D) N110, N134D, A11918

4. After placing strips under the appropriate bay header, the controller should scan the board for
   (A) required number of strips, type of equipment, remarks, and ETA.
   (B) proper sequence, conflictions, TUX, WAFDOF, MEA, and coordination.
   (C) point of departure, pilot's ETA, and remarks.
   (D) deadwood in each bay.

5. Strips should be removed from the board when
   (A) tower advises landing assured.
   (B) FSS advises aircraft in sight.
   (C) no longer required for control purposes.
   (D) pilot reports runway in sight.

Refer to the strip below and use the "quick estimating" procedure to answer questions 6 and 7.

N405B	FSM			80		OKC	LIT V8 TUL V4 OKC	
	1840		14					
C310/B		19						
T180		TUL						

6. What is the time error on N405B?
   (A) 5-minute error at TUL   (B) 10-minute error at TUL
   (C) 15-minute error at TUL   (D) No time error

7. What is the approximate position of N405B? (Present time is 1900.)
   (A) 10 miles west of FSM   (B) 19 miles west of FSM
   (C) 42 miles east of TUL   (D) 54 miles east of TUL

LESSONS 9–12 ANSWERS

FORWARDING FLIGHT PLAN AND CONTROL INFORMATION
END OF LESSON TEST

1. **A**
2. **D**
3. **1020**
4. **1608**
5. **B**
6. **1214**
7. **C**

8. **D**
9. **TRANSFER OF CONTROL POINT**
10. **PRIOR TO TCP**
11. **C**
12. **A**
13. **C**

14. | **AIRCRAFT IDENTIFICATION** | **RECEIVING FACILITY** |
|---|---|
| A 90012 | KANSAS CITY CENTER |
| N 450T | ENID RADIO |
| N 56WP | PONCA CITY TOWER |
| UAL 562 | TULSA APPROACH |

15.

UAL716			↑ 90		M10 V2 FYV	
B727/A		1856/1856				
F420		MIO P1859		90		

On the above strip enter the following flight data in the appropriate spaces.

- 90
- MIO P1859
- MIO V2 FYV
- B727/A

- 1856 (MIO departure time)
- UAL716
- T420
- 90

17.

N3002W	OKC		90	MKC	ABI V3 MKC	
	0218	53				
PA23/D	02					
T160	PNC					ZKC

What information is missing that should be passed?

ETA for MKC
_____
_____
_____

18.

COA86	ABI		170	PNC	ELP V3 PNC V2 MIO	
	1123	36				
B737/A	11					
T480	1123	OKC				

COA86	OKC		170	MIO	ELP V3 PNC V2 MIO	
	1136	49 /				
B737/A	11					
T480	PNC					

COA86	PNC		170		PNC V2 MIO	
	1149	59				
B737	11					
T480	MIO					

Fill in the missing data on the above strips.

FLIGHT PLAN AND CONTROL INFORMATION REVISION
END OF LESSON TEST

DIRECTIONS: *Items 1 through 11 are completion statements. Fill in the blank(s) with the appropriate words, phrases, or strip markings.*

Use the following strips to answer items 1 and 2.

UAL430	PRX		⊠	160	TUL	MSY V7 MKC	
	~~1715~~	2̶3̶					
~~DC8/A~~ DC9/B	1721	17 29					
T450		MLC					

UAL430	MLC		⊠	160	MIO	MSY V7 MKC	
	~~1723~~	3̶0̶					
~~DC8/A~~ DC9/B	1729	17 36					
T450		TUL					

UAL430	TUL		⊠	160	MKC	MSY V7 MKC	
	~~1730~~	3̶5̶					
~~DC8/A~~ DC9/B	1736	17 41					
T450		MIO				ZKC

1. Revise the above strips in accordance with the following data:
   (A) Aircraft type and suffix changed to DC9/B.
   (B) Altitude changed to 160.
   (C) Paris time changes to 1721.

2. Write the phraseology for forwarding the revised aircraft type, equipment suffix, time, and altitude.

"KANSAS CITY CENTER, AERO CENTER ACTIVE AT KANSAS CITY, UAL 430 REVISED TYPE AND SUFFIX DC9/B, REVISED ESTIMATE MIO VORTAC 1741, REVISED ALTITUDE 160. O.Z."

N401P	PNC			⭕↑90	FYV	END V2 FYV	
	1519		㉞				
C310/A		15					
T190		MIO					

3. To what facility or sector should you forward the revision?

ZME

4. Write the phraseology for forwarding the revised time.

"MEMPHIS CENTER AERO CENTER ACTIVE AT FAYETTEVILLE. N401P REVISED ESTIMATE MID VORTAC 1534 DEVISED MIO VORTAC ESTIMATE."

5. Write the phraseology for forwarding the revised altitude.

"MEMPHIS CENTER AERO CENTER ACTIVE AT FYV. N401P REVISED ALTITUDE CLIMBING TO NINER THOUSAND."

6. Mark the strip to indicate that the revised information has been forwarded properly. Delete any unwanted information.

A13597	SNL		170	HOT	AMA V6 HOT LRF	
	1758	09				⭕/1850
T39/B		18				
T420		MLC				ZME

7. A revised pilot ETA for LRF of 1850 will be forwarded to

MIAMI RADIO

8. Mark the strip to indicate the revised information has been forwarded.

USA278	MIO		~~140~~ 120	END	FYV V2 AMA	
	~~1435~~	~~50~~				
CV58/A	1430	14 45				
T280		PNC				

USA278	PNC			~~140~~ (120)	AMA	FYV V2 AMA	
	~~1450~~		05				
VC58/A	1445	~~15~~	00				
T280		END					ZAB

9. Revise the strips in accordance with the following data:
   - A. MIO time revised to 1430.
   - B. Altitude revised to 120.

10. Write the phraseology for forwarding the revised time and altitude.

   "ALBURQUERQUE CENTER AERO CENTER ACTIVE AT AMARILLO USAIR TWO SEVENTY EIGHT. REVISED ESTIMATE ENID VORTAC 1500, REVISED ALTITUDE 170.

11. Mark the strips to indicate all revised information has been forwarded.

GENERAL CONTROL
END-OF-LESSON TEST

1. **B**	4. **C**	7. **B**	10. **D**
2. **B**	5. **D**	8. **C**	11. **B**
3. **A**	6. **B**	9. **B**	12. **B**

BOARD MANAGEMENT
END-OF-LESSON TEST

1. **A**	3. **B**	5. **C**	7. **C**
2. **C**	4. **B**	6. **D**	

CHAPTER III

Lessons 13–16

LETTERS OF AGREEMENT
VERTICAL SEPARATION
LATERAL SEPARATION
LONGITUDINAL SEPARATION

LESSON 13
LETTERS OF AGREEMENT

You have received training on many rules in 7110.65. During this training you learned that an orderly and smooth flow of traffic depends largely upon the consistent application of those rules. This lesson concerns letters of agreement that are used to reduce coordination between facilities. Letters of agreement between Aero Center and tower facilities delegate airspace, and contain procedures for departures and arrivals, altitude assignments, and transfer of control responsibility. Letters of agreement with adjacent facilities establish interfacility nonradar coordination procedures.

A thorough knowledge of all letters of agreement that affect your sector of operation is essential for a safe, orderly, and expeditious flow of traffic.

Objectives

Without references, and in accordance with Aero Center Letters of Agreement, you will be able to identify and apply:

1. Clearance limits, altitude assignments, and transfer of control points for arrivals to airports within Oklahoma City and Tulsa Towers' airspace.

2. Procedures for Aero Center when issuing departure clearances to aircraft departing an airport within Oklahoma City and Tulsa Towers' airspace.

3. Use of Bolde One departure and Tulsa One arrival.

4. Frequencies assigned to arrival aircraft and to aircraft transiting Oklahoma City and Tulsa Towers' airspace.

5. Nonradar coordination procedures with adjacent centers.

Lesson Guide

A. Aero Center and Oklahoma City Letter of Agreement

1. Purpose

A letter of agreement delegates airspace and establishes coordination procedures.

2. Delegation of Responsibility

Outlines authority and responsibility for control of IFR arrivals, departures, and en route.

3. General

The receiving facility shall not alter assigned route while aircraft is within the transferring facility's area. Communications transfer shall be accomplished prior to aircraft's entering receiving facility's airspace. The tower shall advise center of NAVAID status. The tower controls overflights 5,000

MSL and below in terminal area. Procedures may be modified on individual basis with prior coordination. Situations not covered shall be coordinated on individual basis.

4.   Arrivals

Primary clearance limit is the outer fixes. The secondary clearance limit is the Oklamoma City VORTAC. Assigned altitude will be to cross the clearance limit at 6,000 or lowest available center altitude. Center will protect holding pattern airspace until the aircraft is tower control. Transfer of control is prior to aircraft's reaching clearance limit, normally 25 NM from Oklahoma City VORTAC. Center shall protect all altitudes below the aircraft's altitude from transfer of control point (TCP) to the clearance limit. Center shall transfer communications prior to the TCP. The TCP is normally 30 NM from OKC VORTAC.

5.   Departures

Issue IFR departure clearances to all IFR aircraft departing tower's airspace; aircraft on ground unless otherwise coordinated. Issue expect departure clearance (EDC) times if unable to issue departure clearance. Center separates departures from arrivals until arrival under tower control. Center specifies type for aircraft cleared same route; tower separates aircraft cleared different routes. Tower shall not clear aircraft above 5,000 until on center assigned route. All restrictions shall be complied with prior to communications transfer.

6.   Frequencies

Center shall assign to all aircraft entering tower's airspace 119.1 or 259.1. Tower shall assign to all aircraft entering center's airspace 124.0 or 334.0.

B.   Aero Center and Tulsa Letter of Agreement

1.   Purpose

Delegates airspace and establishes coordination procedures.

2.   Delegation of Responsibility

Outlines authority and responsibility for control of IFR arrivals, departures, and en route. The receiving facility shall not alter the assigned route while the aircraft is within transferring facility's area. Communications transfer shall be accomplished prior to aircraft's entering receiving facility's airspace. Tower will advise of NAVAID status. Tower controls overflights 5,000 MSL and below in terminal area. Procedures may be modified on an individual basis. Stiuations not covered shall be coordinated on an individual basis.

3.   Arrivals

Clearance limit is the Tulsa VORTAC, descending to the lowest usable center altitude. Holding pattern airspace will be protected until approach advises tower control. Transfer of control shall be effected at or before the TCP. The TCP is approach boundary with the exception of aircraft inbound on V4, the TCP is prior. Non-DME aircraft are coordinated on an individual basis. Altitudes at and below the aircraft's altitude are released to approach from the TCP to the clearance limit. Center shall forward to approach control, prior to transferring communications to tower, all restrictions inside the TCP. Transfer of communications shall occur at or prior to TCP. Center may assign the Tulsa one arrival when requested by the pilot or may be assigned at controller's discretion. Altitude restrictions may be issued.

4. Departures

Issue IFR departure clearances to all IFR aircraft departing tower's airspace. Aircraft are assumed on the ground unless coordinated otherwise. Issue expect departure clearance (EDC) times if unable to issue departure clearance. Center separates departures from arrivals until arrival is under tower control. Center specifies type separation for aircraft cleared same route; tower separates aircraft cleared different routes. Tower shall not clear above 5,000 until on center assigned route. The BOLDE ONE departure may be assigned at controller's discretion for Tulsa departures.

5. Frequencies

Center shall assign to all aircraft entering tower's airspace 119.2 or 259.2. Tower shall assign to all aircraft entering center's airspace 125.0 or 335.0.

C. Intercenter Letter of Agreement

1. Purpose

Establishes coordination and procedures between centers.

2. Nonradar Coordination Procedures

Proposed departures requiring approval must be forwarded prior to departure of the aircraft. If the departure point is less than 15 minutes' flying time from transferring facility's boundary, coordinate with the receiving facility before departure. Forward the assumed departure time within 3 minutes after giving initials for departure clearance; revise if the actual departure time differs by more than 3 minutes. Altitude assignments for aircraft going into the receiving center's airspace normally will be the correct altitude for direction of flight. WAFDOF altitudes may be used only after coordination and approval by the adjacent center. Estimates on en route aircraft shall be forwarded to the receiving centers at least 15 minutes prior to the aircraft's entering the receiving center area or prior to the last fix posting in your area, whichever is later. Each ARTCC shall advise the other of any NAVAID malfunction or frequency outages.

LETTERS OF AGREEMENT
EXERCISE 1

1.

N234	CDS			110		LAX V6 OKC	
	1617	50	↓				
C310/A		16					
T180		OKC					

In accordance with the Letter of Agreement, N234 would normally be cleared to __YUKON__ (clearance limit) at a minimum altitude of __6,000__ (altitude).

2.

N456			↑ 90	SNL	OKC V6 MLC	
C310/A						D-A
		1556/				
T180		OKC P1600		90		

N678			↑ 130	SNL	OKC V6S MLC	
			× 46 SE			
C310/A			↕ 90			
		1558/				
T180		OKC P1600		130		

In accordance with the Letter of Agreement, who is responsible for separation of N456 and N678 until they are established on diverging routes?

__OKLAHOMA CITY APPROACH CONTROL__

3.

N123	SLICK			60	OKC	TUL V4 OKC	
	1631	50 (45)	↓		1650		
C320/A		16					F
						C	25 NE
T190		~~OKC~~ JONES					OKC

DAL810			↑		PNC	OKC V4N TRYON ICT	
B727/A							
			1625/				
T420		OKC P1630			170		

The estimate on N123 has been passed to approach control. The time is now 1625, and DAL810 requests clearance. Who is responsible for separation of N123 and DL810 until they are laterally separated?

AERO CENTER

LETTERS OF AGREEMENT EXERCISE 2

1.

N268	SLICK			30	FSM	OKC V4 TUL V8 FSM	
	1622	00					
C172/A		17					
T105		TUL					ZME

This aircraft must be coordinated with Tulsa Approach Control because approach control is delegated __5,000__ (altitude) feet and below within their airspace.

2.

N987		↑	↑90	SGF	TUL V4 SGF	
C310/A		TUL P1600				D-A
		1555/				
T180				90		

DAL340		↑	↑170	SGF	TUL V4 SGF V92 MSP	
B727/A						D-A
		1550/				
T450		TUL P1555		170		

In accordance with the TUL Letter of Agreement, who determines the type of separation to be applied between DL340 and N987?

__AERO CENTER__

3.

N127	PNC		100	FYV	END V2 FYV	
	1625	50				
C310/A		16				
T180		MIO				ZME

N127 is at the wrong altitude for direction of flight. In accordance with the Intercenter Letter of Agreement, this is acceptable if __APPROVAL__ has been obtained from the receiving center.

4.

DAL846		T→N MLC	↑	↑	PRX	MLC V7 ATL		D-A
B727/A								
						C		
T490		MLC P1600			170			ZFW

In accordance with the Intercenter Letter of Agreement, Aero Center must coordinate this departure with Fort Worth Center because the aircraft is less than __15__ (minutes) flying time from the boundary.

5.

AAL42			↑	↑ 170	FSM	TUL V8 LGA		D-A
B727/A								
		1558/						
T420		TUL P1600			170			ZME

Tulsa Departure Control may clear AAL42 via the Tulsa 165 radial and a 15-mile arc SE of Tulsa VORTAC to intercept V8, but they must restrict the aircraft to remain at or below __5,000__ (altitude) feet until established on V8.

LETTERS OF AGREEMENT
END-OF-LESSON TEST

DIRECTIONS: *Items 1 through 12 are multiple-choice. Indicate your selection by circling the appropriate letter by each item. Correct answers appear at the end of the chapter.*

1. The vertical limits of Oklahoma City and Tulsa Towers' airspace is _____ and below.
   (A) 5,000 feet MSL   (B) 5,000 feet AGL
   (C) 6,000 feet MSL   (D) 6,000 feet AGL

2. Without coordination with Oklahoma City Approach Control, the lowest cardinal altitude which Aero Center may assign an aircraft overflying the Oklahoma City VORTAC is _____ feet.
   (A) 4,000   (B) 5,000   (C) 5,500   (D) 6,000

3. Aero Center shall transfer control of Oklahoma City IFR arrivals
   (A) at or before the clearance limit.   (B) prior to the clearance limit.
   (C) after the clearance limit.   (D) after established in holding.

4. The normal clearance limit for arrival aircraft to Oklahoma City from over Shawnee on V6 is
   (A) Coyle.   (B) Jones.   (C) Boley.   (D) Moore.

5. Which are the correct frequencies for inbound aircraft to Tulsa and Oklahoma City?
   (A) TUL 116.2 and 256.2; OKC 116.1 and 256.1
   (B) TUL 117.2 and 257.2; OKC 117.1 and 257.1
   (C) TUL 118.2 and 258.2; OKC 118.1 and 258.1
   (D) TUL 119.2 and 259.2; OKC 119.1 and 259.1

6. Without coordination with Tulsa Approach Control, the lowest altitude that Aero Center may clear an inbound to Tulsa, whose clearance limit is Tulsa VORTAC, is _____ feet.
   (A) 4,000   (B) 5,000   (C) 6,000   (D) 7,000

7. Tulsa Tower will not clear a departing IFR aircraft above 5,000 feet until the aircraft is
   (A) established on center assigned route.
   (B) separated from all other departures.
   (C) separated from all arrivals.
   (D) out of Tulsa's area.

8. The normal clearance limit for arrival aircraft to Tulsa Airport is
   (A) an outer fix as depicted on Annex I.   (B) Tulsa VORTAC.
   (C) Tulsa Airport.   (D) Tulsa ILS outer marker.

9. Which radials make up the Tulsa One arrival?
   (A) TUL 360 and MIO 125   (B) TUL 360 and PNC 105
   (C) MLC 360 and TUL 105   (D) MLC 360 and TUL 125

10. Which is the correct Tulsa radial and crossing restriction for the Bolde One departure?
    (A) 070 and cross Flint at or below 5,000
    (B) 090 and cross Bolde at or below 5,000
    (C) 070 and cross Inola at or below 5,000
    (D) 090 and cross Bolde at or above 5,000

11. When should you coordinate with the receiving facility on aircraft departing from a point less than 15 minutes flying time from the transferring facility's boundary?
    (A) Prior to departure
    (B) Prior to issuing clearance
    (C) Before the aircraft is 5 minutes from the boundary
    (D) Before the aircraft is 3 minutes from the boundary

12. When may Aero Center allow an aircraft to enter an adjacent center's area at a wrong altitude for direction of flight?
    (A) When required for separation   (B) After obtaining approval
    (C) When pilot requests   (D) Always

LESSON 14
VERTICAL SEPARATION

In Chapter 1 we covered radio and interphone procedures. Here you were introduced to the language of the air traffic controller, how to communicate with pilots, other controllers, and persons concerned with the control of air traffic. We also covered rules and procedures for collecting, recording, and disseminating flight data using the flight progress strip. These lessons prepared you for the most important phase of your training, which is providing separation between aircraft. Vertical separation is your introduction to the many rules and procedures you will be required to master before you become an air traffic controller.

Objectives

Given **air traffic** situations, without references, and in accordance with 7110.65, you will be **able** to:

1. Select and apply the required minimum vertical separation for aircraft

    A. Up to and including FL 290.

    B. Above FL 290 to FL 600.

    C. Above or below special use and ATC assigned airspace.

    D. When severe turbulence is reported.

    E. When military aerial refueling is in progress.

    F. When aircraft have been cleared to cruise.

    G. When pilot requests discretion descent.

2. Select standard phraseology to

    A. **Assign** altitude/flight levels.

    B. Obtain altitude reports.

Lesson Guide

A. Minimums Between Altitudes

    1.   At or below FL290—1,000 feet separation.

    2.   Above FL290 to FL600—2,000 feet separation.

B. Minimums from Special-Use and ATC-Assigned Airspace

    1.   At or below FL290—Separate nonparticipating aircraft by at least 500 feet above/below the altitude limits of the assigned airspace.

2.   Above FL290—Separate nonparticipating aircraft by at least 1,000 feet above/below the altitude limits of the airspace.

C.   Altitude Assignments

Assign an altitude to an aircraft only after the aircraft previously at that altitude reports leaving it. There are exceptions: when there is severe turbulence, when aircraft are aerial refueling, or when aircraft assigned is a pilot's discretion descent or a cruise clearance. Assign an altitude only after the aircraft previously at that altitude reports at or passing through an altitude that provides minimum separation.

D.   Phraseology

1.   Altitude assignments

a.   "MAINTAIN (altitude)"

b.   "CROSS (number of miles) MILES (direction) OF (fix) AT OR ABOVE/ BELOW (altitude)."

c.   "DESCEND AND MAINTAIN (altitude)."

d.   "CLIMB AND MAINTAIN (altitude)."

e.   "DESCEND NOW TO/THROUGH (altitude) CROSS (fix) AT OR BELOW (altitude)."

2.   Altitude reports

a.   "REPORT LEAVING (altitude)."

b.   "REPORT LEAVING ODD/EVEN ALTITUDES/FLIGHT LEVELS."

c.   "REPORT REACHING (altitude)."

d.   "SAY ALTITUDE."

E.   Altitude Changes

1.   Pilot's discretion descent

2.   Cruise clearance

Clearance to authorize a pilot to conduct flight at any altitude from the minimum IFR altitude up to and including the altitude specified in the clearance. Climb/descent within the block is to be made at the discretion of the pilot. Once the pilot starts descent and verbally reports leaving an altitude in the block, he or she may not return to that altitude without additional ATC clearance.

VERTICAL SEPARATION
PRACTICE EXERCISE

DIRECTIONS: *Using approved strip marking, record the clearance and control information on the flight progress strips for exercise items 1-4, and write the appropriate clearances.*

1. **TIME: 1235**

    Assign A43661 120 and A44321 140.

    "AIR FORCE FOUR FOUR THREE TWO ONE CLIMB AND MAINTAIN ONE FOUR THOUSAND REPORT LEAVING ONE TWO THOUSAND." WHEN A44321 REPORTS LEAVING ONE TWO THOUSAND:
    "AIR FORCE FOUR THREE SIX SIX ONE CLIMB AND MAINTAIN ONE TWO THOUSAND."

A44321	MIO		120√	END	FYV V2 AMA	
	1220	43				
C130/B		12				
		43				
T310		PNC		140	CC	

A43661	MIO		100√	END	FYV V2 AMA	
	1219	42				
C130/B		12				
		42				
T310		PNC		120	CC	

2. **TIME: 1144**

    Assign each aircraft the requested altitude.

    ONE SOLUTION: HAVE EAL20 DESCEND AND MAINTAIN 11,000 TO REPORT LEAVING EVEN ALTITUDES. AS YOU RECEIVE THE EVEN ALTITUDE REPORTS, DESCEND VV72771 TO THOSE ALTITUDES AND REQUEST VV72771 REPORT LEAVING ODD ALTITUDES. AS VV72771

REPORTS LEAVING ODD ALTITUDES, DESCEND AAL341 TO THOSE ALTITUDES.

AAL341	ABI		170√	TUL	LBB V3 V4 TUL	
	1133	46				
B727/B		11				
		46				
T450		OKC	130		CC	

VV72771	ABI		160√	PNC	ELP V4 OKC V3 PNC	
	1134	46				
F14/P		11				
		46				
T480		OKC	120		CC	

EAL20	ABI		150√	TUL	LBB V3 V4 TUL	
	1132	45				
B737/A		11				
		45				
T420		OKC	110		CC	

3.   TIME: 0738

Assign N42P 9,000 feet and N674S 7,000 feet.

ONE SOLUTION: HAVE N42P CLIMB AND MAINTAIN 9,000 TO REPORT LEAVING 7,000. WHEN N42P REPORTS LEAVING 7,000, ASSIGN 7,000 TO N674S.

N674S			↑ ⚓50√	TUL	OKC V4 SGF/~~0053~~	
					0825	
C310/X						D-A
		0732/0732				
T170		OKC P0730	70	50		

N42P			↑ ⚓70√	TUL	OKC V4 SGF/~~0056~~	
					0826	
PA23/U						D-A
		0730/0730				
T160		OKC P0730	90	70		

4. **TIME: 0720**

Describe how to clear these holding aircraft to 6,000, 7,000, and 8,000 feet.

ONE SOLUTION: <u>HAVE A79841 DESCEND AND MAINTAIN TO REPORT LEAVING ODD ALTITUDES. AS YOU RECEIVE THESE REPORTS, DESCEND TWA311 TO THOSE ALTITUDES AND REQUEST TWA311 REPORT LEAVING EVEN ALTITUDES. AS YOU RECEIVE VACATING REPORTS FROM TWA311, ASSIGN TWA209 THOSE ALTITUDES.</u>

TWA209 DC9/B T450	MIO 0712	㉑ 07 / 21 20/ / PNC	↓ 160√ 80		BNA V2 PNC	APCH SW H-210 0740
TWA311 DC9/B T450	MIO 0712	㉑ 07 / 22 20/ / PNC	↓ 140√ 70		MEM V2 PNC	APCH SW H 210 0730
A79841 T43/B T420	MIO 0706	⑰ 07 / 17 17/ / PNC	↓ 120√ 60		SGF V2 PNC	APCH SW H 210 0720

VERTICAL SEPARATION END-OF-LESSON TEST

DIRECTIONS: *Items 1 through 13 are multiple-choice. Indicate your selection by circling the appropriate letter for each test item. Correct answers appear at the end of the chapter.*

1. Aircraft flying below what flight level require 1,000 feet vertical separation?
   (A) FL290   (B) FL310   (C) FL330   (D) FL350

2. The minimum vertical separation required for aircraft between FL290 and FL600 is _____ feet.
   (A) 500   (B) 1,000   (C) 2,000   (D) 5,000

3. Aircraft operating at or below FL290 must be vertically separated from the upper/lower limits of active special-use airspace or ATC-assigned airspace by at least _____ feet.
   (A) 2,000   (B) 1,500   (C) 1,000   (D) 500

4. Aircraft operating above FL290 must be vertically separated from the upper/lower limits of active special-use airspace or ATC-assigned airspace by at least _____ feet.
   (A) 500   (B) 1,000   (C) 1,500   (D) 2,000

5. The rule for providing vertical separation when pilots are **not** executing pilot's discretion descent is to assign an altitude
   (A) only after the aircraft has reported at or passing through another altitude.
   (B) to an aircraft only after the aircraft previously at that altitude has reported leaving it.
   (C) to an aircraft only after the aircraft previously at that altitude has reported another altitude.
   (D) only to an aircraft that has reported at an altitude that provides minimum separation.

6. N1234A has been issued an unrestricted descent from one two thousand to six thousand. N4567B is at one four thousand. N4567B can be assigned one two thousand when N1234A reports leaving
   (A) one two thousand.   (B) one one thousand.
   (C) one zero thousand.   (D) niner thousand.

7. N74Y has been cleared to descend from eight thousand to four thousand at pilot's discretion. A higher aircraft may be assigned eight thousand when N74Y reports
   (A) leaving eight thousand.   (B) leaving seven thousand.
   (C) leaving six thousand.   (D) reaching four thousand.

8. Vertical separation is applied between aircraft experiencing severe turbulence by
   (A) increasing minimums by 500 feet.
   (B) increasing minimums by 1,000 feet.
   (C) assigning altitudes after reports indicate minimum separation exists.
   (D) discontinuing altitude change.

9. The rule for applying vertical separation between aircraft conducting military aerial refueling and other traffic is
   (A) increase minimums 1,000 feet for each aircraft conducting refueling.
   (B) assign altitudes after refueling aircraft reports at or passing an altitude that provides separation.
   (C) assign altitudes when the receiver aircraft reports leaving it.
   (D) assign altitudes when the tanker aircraft reports leaving it.

10. N12B at six thousand, has been cleared for approach. An altitude of six thousand can be assigned to another aircraft as soon as N12B reports
    (A) leaving six thousand.   (B) leaving five thousand.
    (C) leaving four thousand.   (D) on the ground.

11. N1234A has been issued a descent clearance from one two thousand to cross PNC VORTAC at six thousand. N4567B is at one four thousand. N4567B may be assigned one zero thousand when N1234A reports leaving
    (A) one two thousand.   (B) one one thousand.
    (C) one zero thousand.   (D) niner thousand.

12. What is the phraseology used to determine altitude of an aircraft?
    (A) "SAY ALTITUDE."
    (B) "REPORT PRESENT ALTITUDE."
    (C) "WHAT IS YOUR PRESENT ALTITUDE?"
    (D) "VERIFY ALTITUDE."

13. What is the phraseology to obtain altitude reports?
    (A) "CALL LEAVING SEVEN THOUSAND."
    (B) "REPORT LEAVING ODD ALTITUDES."
    (C) "VERIFY LEAVING EVEN ALTITUDES."
    (D) "ADVISE WHEN YOU PASS SIX THOUSAND."

LESSON 15
LATERAL SEPARATION

You have added vertical separation to the previous information on strip marking and clearance formulation. Combined with lateral separation and the use of arcs, covered in this lesson, it will be possible for you to handle larger volumes of traffic and to manage airspace more efficiently.

Objectives

Given air traffic situations, without references, and in accordance with 7110.65, you will be able to:

1. Specify the minimum lateral separation required between

    A. Airways.

    B. Routes other than established airways or routes.

    C. Holding patterns.

    D. DME arcs about a NAVAID.

    E. DME arc and a holding pattern.

    F. Aircraft established on diverging radials of the same NAVAID.

    G. Special use and ATC assigned airspace.

2. Apply the minimum lateral separation required between

    A. Airways.

    B. Restricted areas.

    C. Holding patterns.

    D. DME arcs about a NAVAID.

    E. DME arc and a holding pattern.

    F. Aircraft established on diverging radials of the same NAVAID.

    G. Special use and ATC assigned airspace.

Lesson Guide

A. Lateral Separation Methods

   1. Airways or routes—Clear aircraft via airways or routes whose protected airspace of airways or routes does not overlap.

   2. Geographical locations—Below FL180, have aircraft report over different geographical locations, hold over different locations that may be determined visually or by reference to NAVAIDS.

3. Holding pattern—Protected airspace shall not overlap each other or other airspace to be protected.

4. Departing Aircraft—Departing aircraft that fly specified headings that diverge by at least 45 degrees. (Departure separation will be detailed later).

B. Separation Minima

Protect airspace along other than established airways or routes. Direct courses and course changes of 15 degrees or less:

Via NAVAIDS or radials FL600 and below—Separate aircraft 4 NM either side of the route to a point 51 miles from the NAVAID, then increasing in width on a 4½ degree angle to a width of 10 miles on each side of the route.

Via degree-distance fixes—
Below FL180—4 miles on each side of the route
FL180–FL600—10 miles each side of route

Via degree-distance fixes for RNAV flights above FL450—10 miles each side of the route

When course change is 16 degrees through 90 degrees, protect the airspace on the overflown side, beginning at the point where the course changes, as follows:

Below FL180—(same as above)
FL180–FL230 inclusive—14 miles
Above FL230–FL600 inclusive—17 miles

When course change is 91 degrees through 180 degrees, protect the airspace on the overflown side, beginning at the point where the course changes as follows:

Below FL180—(same as above)
FL180–FL230 inclusive—28 miles
Above FL230–FL600 inclusive—34 miles

After the course changes have been completed and the aircraft is back on course, the appropriate minima may be used.

C. Diverging Radials

Consider separation to exist between aircraft established on radials of the same NAVAID that diverge by at least 15 degrees when either aircraft is clear of the airspace to be protected for the other aircraft.

Use the table to determine the distance required for various divergence angles to clear the airspace to be protected. For divergence that falls between two values, use the lesser divergence value to obtain the distance.

DIVERGENCE-DISTANCE MINIMA

DIVERGENCE DEGREES	DISTANCE (NM) BELOW FL180
15	17
20	13
25	11
30	9
35	8
45	7
55	6
90	5

Separation Minimum at Intersections

Use 10 miles separation at all intersections in Aero Center with the following exception:

East and southeast of tryon intersection on V4N and V11.

V4N—43 miles west of TUL VORTAC
V11—75 miles northwest MLC VORTAC

D.   Holding Pattern

HOLDING PATTERN NO. 8

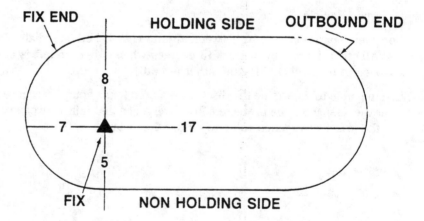

Holding pattern number 8 used in Aero Center holding airspace areas must not overlap.

———————————

NOTE: This table is for DME applications and compensates for DME slant-range error.

OVERLAPPING AIRSPACE

HOLDING PATTERN	AIRWAY	MILEAGE
BOLEY	V4	24
BOLEY	V6S	28
JONES	V4N	32
COYLE	V4N	28
YUKON	V6N	28

E.   DME Arcs

Apply lateral DME separation by requiring aircraft using DME to fly an arc about a NAVAID at a specified distance using the following minima:

Between different arcs about a NAVAID regardless of direction of flight, use 10 miles separation at 35 miles or less from the NAVAID and 20 miles separation more than 35 miles from the NAVAID.

Between an arc about a NAVAID and other airspace to be protected, use 5 miles separation 35 miles or less from the NAVAID, and use 10 miles separation when the aircraft is more than 35 miles from the NAVAID.

Phraseology:

"VIA (number of miles) MILE ARC (direction) OF (name of DME NAVAID)."

At Oklahoma City—The outer fixes holding pattern airspace to be protected, the 30 NM arc from the VORTAC will clear the holding pattern airspace if you utilize 15 degrees divergence on nonmaneuvering side of holding pattern or 20 degrees on maneuvering side.

LATERAL SEPARATION
EXAMPLE

DIRECTIONS: *Use your Aero Center map to answer the questions in this exercise.*

1. What is the required mileage for the following diverging angles?

	BELOW FL180
FIFTEEN DEGREES	17
FORTY-FIVE DEGREES	7

2. What is the minimum distance between two aircraft on different arcs less than 35 miles from the NAVAID?

   10 MILES

3. EAL42 is 40 miles west of Miami VORTAC on V2 at one six thousand. At this position, what airspace must be protected either side of the route?

   4 MILES

4. A12344 is en route AMA direct PNC direct AMA at FL240. How much airspace is to be protected on the overflown side at PNC?

   34 MILES

5. Departing aircraft require specified headings that diverge at least 45 degrees for lateral separation.

6. What is the protected distance between an arcing aircraft and the protected airspace of a holding pattern?

   5 MILES WITHIN 35 MILES OF NAVAID, 10 MILES IF MORE THAN 35 MILES FROM NAVAID.

7. DECAL41 is at one seven thousand, cleared via degree distance fixes. What is the total width of its protected airspace?

   8 MILES

8. A21714 is en route AMA direct PNC direct OKC at FL230. How much airspace is to be protected on the overflown side of the route at PNC?

   28 MILES

9. Aircraft may be cleared to hold over different fixes at the same altitude if

   HOLDING PATTERN AIRSPACES DO NOT OVERLAP.

10. Aircraft established on diverging radials of the same NAVAID are laterally separated when

    EITHER AIRCRAFT IS BEYOND AIRSPACE TO BE PROTECTED FOR THE OTHER.

The following flight progress strip on DAL660 is used to answer questions 11 through 15.

DAL660	MIO		120	END	ATL V2 AMA	
	1247	56				
H/L101/F		12				
T490		PNC				

11. TIME: 1247 RUNWAY: 21

BNF42		T→SW PNC ↑	↑ 150	TUL	PNC V8 FSM	
			×9SE ↕ 110			
B727/A						D-A
		1250/				
T485		PNC P1250		150	C	

BNF42 must be restricted at or below 110 to the PNC __120__ radial __9__ DME to provide lateral separation from DAL660.

12. TIME: 1244

TWA897	MKC		160√ ↓60	MKC V3 PNC	APCH
	1231	(50)	×9NE ↕ 110		
B707/A		12			F
		50			
T480		PNC		CTL	

TWA897 must have a crossing restriction of __9__ NE of PNC VORTAC at or below __110__ thousand to provide separation from DAL660.

13.

AAL529	TUL		140√ ↓60	BNA V8 PNC	APCH
	1249	(59)	×9SE ↕ 110		
B737/A		12			F
		59			
T470		PNC			

AAL529 must have a crossing restriction of __9__ SE of PNC VORTAC at or below __110__ thousand to provide lateral separation from DAL660.

14.

REP751	ICT			140√ ↓100	SNL	DSM V5 DAL	
	1245	59		×5N ↕110			
DC9/A		12					
		59					
T465		PNC					

At what point will lateral separation cease to exist between REP751 and DAL660? _5_ miles __NORTH__ (direction) of __PNC__ VORTAC.

15.   TIME: 1255 RUNWAY: 21

UAL385		T→SW	↑	↑140	OKC	PNC V3 OKC V6 ABQ PHX	
		PNC		×6SW ↕110			
DC10/F							D-A
			1255/				
T490		PNC P1301			140		

UAL385 must be restricted to at or below _110_ thousand until the PNC _210_ radial _6_ DME to provide lateral separation from DL660.

16.   TIME: 1820

N350CC	TUL			140 ↓60	OKC	SGF V4 OKC/1840	
	1803	33 30	↓	×@60	1833		
C500/A		18					F
						C	25 NE
T360		OKC JONES					OKC

UAL21			↑	↑150	TUL	OKC V4N TUL	
				×32NE ↕50			
B727/A							D-A
			1820/				
T410		OKC P1825			150		

UAL21 must be restricted to cross _32_ miles NE of OKC VORTAC on V4N at or below 50 to provide separation from the Jones holding pattern.

17. TIME: 0050

A25817	SLICK 0040	(57)	90√ (↓60)		OKC V4 TUL	
T29/B		00			C	F
		56				
T230		TUL			CTL	20 SW

M256B		↑	↑90 ×7E ↕50	FSM	TUL V8 FSM/0135	
BE65/A						D-A
		0050/				
T160		TUL P0055			90	ZME

Beech 256B must be restricted to cross __7__ miles east of TUL VORTAC at or below __50__ to provide separation from the charted holding pattern at TUL.

18. TIME: 0725

BNF22	SNL 0731	38(35) ↓	160√ ↓(60) ×@60	OKC	MSY V6 OKC	
B727/A		07				F
		35			C	25 E
T410		OKC			CC	OKC

AAL87		↑	↑170 28SE ↕50	MLC	OKC V6S MLC	
B737/A						D-A
		0725/	×46SE ↕90			
T410		OKC P0730			170	

AAL87 must be restricted to cross __28__ miles southeast of OKC VORTAC at or below __50__ to provide separation from the BOLEY holding pattern.

LATERAL SEPARATION
END-OF-LESSON TEST

DIRECTIONS: *Items 1 through 3, 5, 6, 8, 9, and 11 are multiple-choice. Indicate your selection by circling the appropriate letter for each test item. Items 4, 7, and 10 are completion statements. Fill in the blank(s) with the appropriate word or phrases. Correct answers appear at the end of the chapter.*

1. Aircraft may be cleared to proceed to and report over or hold at different geographical locations determined visually or by reference to NAVAIDs
   (A) above 18,000 feet.   (B) below 18,000 feet.
   (C) at pilot's request.   (D) when controller deems it necessary.

2. The lateral separation provided for a degree-distance flight below FL180 is
   (A) 10 miles either side of route.   (B) 8 miles either side of route.
   (C) 5 miles either side of route.   (D) 4 miles either side of route.

3. TIME: 2355

A12345	TUL			180	TUL	MIO TUL MLC TUL MIO	
	2339		57				
T29/B		23					
T220		MLC				RT TURN AT MLC	

How much airspace southwest of MLC, in miles, must you protect for A12345?
(A) 14   (B) 17   (C) 28   (D) 34

4. Aircraft established on diverging radials of the same NAVAID are laterally separated when _____ .

5. TIME: 1135

N76Y	OKC			130	MKC	OKC V3 MKC/1310	
			11				
PAZT/A		12					
T160		PNC					ZKC

N35Z	END			130	TUL	AMA V2 PNC V8	
	1144		11			TUL/1245	
M021/A		12					
T165		PNC					

At what point, in miles, southwest of Ponca City VORTAC, does lateral separation cease to exist between N76Y and N35Z?
(A) 5   (B) 6   (C) 11   (D) 13

6. TIME: 0730

EAL77	CDS			90	SNL	LSV V6 HOT	
	0709		35				
F27/A		07					
T230		OKC					

BNF41					MLC	OKC V6S MLC V6 HOT	
DC9/A							
T410		OKC P0735			110		

At what point, in miles, southeast of OKC VORTAC, will lateral separation exist between EAL77 and BNF41?
(A) 8   (B) 10   (C) 12   (D) 17

7. Identify the **parts** and **dimensions** of holding pattern #8.

8. Aircraft may be cleared to hold over different fixes at the same altitude any time if the
(A) pilot requests it.
(B) controller desires it.
(C) fixes are on established airways.
(D) holding pattern airspace does not overlap.

9. What is the required distance, in miles, between two aircraft on parallel arcs less than 35 miles from the same NAVAID?
(A) 5   (B) 10   (C) 12   (D) 15

10. What is the distance between an arc and the protected airspace of a holding pattern more than 35 miles from the NAVAID?

_____

11. What is the protected distance, in miles, between an arc and the boundary of a holding pattern airspace within 35 miles of the NAVAID?
    (A) 15   (B) 10   (C) 8   (D) 5

LESSON 16
LONGITUDINAL SEPARATION

The number of aircraft operations in the United States is increasing at a rapid pace. How do we keep them all flying? Longitudinal separation is a very important tool used by the air traffic specialist to handle this situation. Separate aircraft on the same route of flight, and at the same altitude, by using time and distance. This is very challenging and requires an extensive knowledge of longitudinal separation rules and of minima. How well you master and apply these rules will affect your future success as a professional air traffic controller.

Objectives

Given air traffic situations, without references, and in accordance with 7110.65, you will:

1. Identify and apply longitudinal separation standards for aircraft

   A. On same courses.

   B. On converging courses.

   C. On crossing courses.

   D. On opposite direction courses.

   E. When climbing or descending through the altitude of another aircraft.

Lesson Guide

A. Longitudinal Separation

   1. Methods

      Four methods to apply longitudinal separation:

      1. Depart at a specified time.

      2. Arrive at a fix at a specified time.

      3. Hold at a fix until a specified time.

      4. Change altitude at a specified time or fix.

   2. Minima on same, converging, or crossing courses

      When applying longitudinal separation, the lead aircraft must be the same speed as or faster than the following aircraft. This will ensure separation is constant or increasing when determining aircraft speed. Aircraft speeds cannot exceed 250 knots below 10,000 feet.

Basic separation minima

Basic separation minima for non-DME aircraft is 10 minutes. To apply the 10-minute rule, both aircraft must estimate over the same NAVAID/Fix. The altitude the aircraft is at must be protected 10 minutes in front of the aircraft. This is called the 10 minute "push."

Basic separation minima for DME aircraft is 20 miles. To apply the DME procedure, direct pilot/controller communications must be maintained, both aircraft must be DME equipped, and the position report of the leading aircraft must be obtained first.

Reduced separation minima

Reduced separation minima may be applied under certain conditions. This allows the controller to apply less than 10 minutes/20 miles.

If the leading aircraft maintains a speed at least 44 knots faster than the following aircraft—5 miles between aircraft using DME and/or RNAV; or 3 minutes between other aircraft if, in either case, one of the following conditions is met: (1) A departing aircraft follows a preceding aircraft that has taken off from the same or adjacent airport; (2) A departing aircraft follows a preceding en route aircraft that has reported over a fix serving the departure airport; (3) An en route aircraft follows a preceding en route aircraft that has reported over the same fix. (This rule is not applicable when the leading aircraft is 44 knots faster and descending through the altitude of the trailing aircraft and the trailing aircraft is at 10,000 feet and the speed is greater than 250 knots.)

When the leading aircraft maintains a speed at least 22 knots faster than the following aircraft—10 miles between aircraft using DME and/or 5 minutes between other aircraft if, in either case, one of the following conditions exists: (1) A departing aircraft follows a preceding aircraft that has taken off from the same or an adjacent airport; (2) A departing aircraft follows a preceding en route aircraft that has reported over a fix serving the departure airport; (3) An en route aircraft follows a preceding en route aircraft that has reported over the same fix.

When an aircraft is climbing or descending through the altitude of another aircraft, use the following minima: (1) Between aircraft using DME—10 miles, if the descending aircraft is leading or the climbing aircraft is following; (2) Between other aircraft—5 minutes, if all of the following conditions are met: (a) the descending aircraft is leading or climbing aircraft is following, (b) the aircrafts were separated by not more than 4,000 feet when the altitude change started, (c) the change is started within 10 minutes after a following aircraft reports over a fix reported by the leading aircraft or has acknowledged a clearance specifying the time to cross the same fix.

Separation between aircraft, when one is using DME and the other is not—30 miles if both the following conditions are met: (1) The aircraft using DME derives distance information by reference to the same NAVAID over which the aircraft not using DME has reported; (2) The aircraft not using DME is within 15 minutes of the NAVAID.

When a climb is required by a faster aircraft overtaking a slower aircraft, you may utilize the "Force 10" rule. The "Force 10" may be applied for a faster overtaking a slower, and the faster will climb through the altitude of the slower—10-mile DME separation must be provided at the time vertical separation is established.

When a descent is required by a faster aircraft overtaking a slower aircraft, you may utilize the "Force 20." You may apply the "Force 20" when an aircraft wants to descend through the altitude of a slower leading aircraft—20-mile DME separation must be provided at the time vertical separation is established.

When an aircraft is making a pilot's discretion descent through the altitude of a following en route aircraft, whether using approved separation—10 minutes/20 miles, 44/22 knot rule, or 5 minutes/10 miles—down in front rule—issue a clearance for a prompt descent to assigned altitude. Ensure vertical separation will exist at or before the approach fix.

Phraseology:

"(aircraft identification) CLEARED FOR APPROACH. CROSS (fix name) AT OR BELOW (altitude)."

"(aircraft identification) CLEARED TO (fix name). CROSS (fix name) AT OR BELOW (altitude), DESCEND AND MAINTAIN (altitude). HOLD (holding instructions)."

"(aircraft identification) DESCEND NOW (to or through) (altitude), CROSS (fix name) AT OR BELOW (altitude). CLEARED FOR APPROACH."

"(aircraft identification), CLEARED TO (fix name). DESCEND NOW (through or to) (altitude). CROSS (fix name) AT OR BELOW (altitude). MAINTAIN (altitude), HOLD (holding instructions)."

3. Minima on opposite courses

    Separate aircraft traveling opposite courses by assigning different altitudes consistent with the approved vertical separation from 10 minutes before, until 10 minutes after they are estimated to pass. Vertical separation may be discontinued after one of the following conditions is met: (1) Both aircraft have reported passing NAVAID's or DME fixes indicating they have passed each other. (2) Both aircraft have reported passing the same intersection and they are at least 3 minutes apart.

    Paper Stop (procedure used in lieu of opposite course minima)

    A clearance to a fix short of the destination, where no delay is expected. The purpose is to stop the protected airspace of an en route aircraft to permit climb/descent of opposite direction traffic.

    The method to use a paper stop is as follows: Clear one aircraft to a clearance limit; clear other aircraft with vertical/lateral restrictions to separate from aircraft cleared to clearance limit, which means you must separate from holding pattern airspace to be protected; then get a report from the aircraft when vertical separation is established. When report is received that vertical separation is established, clear the aircraft through the clearance limit.

Longitudinal Separation
Example 1

DIRECTIONS: *Using longitudinal separation and the flight progress strips provided, answer items 1 through 10.*

1. TIME: 1010   **"FORCE 10"**

AAL16	HOT			120√ ↑ 160	SNL	HOT V6 LAX	
	0955		15	× 15W ↕ 150			
B727/B		10					
		15					
T450		MLC		160		40E/1010	

L85672	HOT			140√	SNL	LIT V6 ABQ	
	0935		05		1020		
CV58/A		10					
		05	05				
T300		MLC				25W/1010	

AAL16 requests climb to 16,000. Using the strips above, how would you handle this request?

ISSUE A CLEARANCE TO AAL16 TO CROSS 15 MILES WEST OF MLC VORTAC AT OR ABOVE 15,000 CLIMBING TO 16,000 L85672 REPORTED 25 MILES WEST OF MLC VORTAC AT 1010

2. TIME: 1511   **"FORCE 20"**

SNAP23	END			170√ ↓ 100		COS AMA V2 LRF	
	1510		21 ↓	× 52W@100			
T38/A		15					
		20					
T420		PNC		100		70W/1511	

G37882	END			110√		MIO	BFK V1 END V2 LRF	
	1500		19					
C131/B		15						
		19						
T240		PNC					32W/1511	

SNAP 23 requested clearance to 10,000 landing at Ponca City. How may 10,000 be assigned?

OBTAIN DME POSITION OF G37882 AND SNAP23 WEST OF PNC VORTAC. THEN CLEAR SNAP23 TO 10,000 WITH A RESTRICTION TO CROSS 20 MILES WEST OF G37882's POSITION AT 10,000 EXAMPLE G37882 IS 32 MILES WEST OF PNC VORTAC AT 1511. HAVE SNAP23 CROSS 52 MILES WEST OF PNC VORTAC AT AND MAINTAIN 10,000.

3. TIME: 1521   5 MINUTES/10 MILES UP IN BACK/DOWN IN FRONT

A33395	FYV			100√		PNC	MEM V2 END V1 DAL	
	1432		10			1530		
T29/A		15						
		09	10					
T230		MIO			160			

N246T	FYV			140√		PNC	MEM V2 AMA	
	1426		04			1524		
M021/X		15						
		03	04					
T230		MIO						

A33395 requests clearance to climb to 16,000. May 16,000 be assigned? Explain you answer.

NO. ALTHOUGH 5 MINUTES' SEPARATION EXISTS, ALTITUDE CHANGE WILL NOT TAKE PLACE WITHIN 10 MINUTES AFTER A33395 REPORTS MIO. DME CANNOT BE USED BECAUSE N246T IS NOT DME EQUIPPED.

4. TIME: 1632   10 MILES ALTITUDE CHANGE

NWA11	MLC			120√		OKC	MLC V6 OKC V3 ABI	
	1620		29			1636		
B727/A		16						
		30	30					
T460		SNL						

EAL80	MLC				170√	OKC	HOT V6 ABQ	
	1617		26			1634		
B727/A		16						
		28	28					
T480	SNL							

A. **EAL80 requests descent to 10,000. How would you handle this request?**

OBTAIN DME POSITION OF EAL80 THEN NWA11. IF 10 MILES EXIST BETWEEN AIRCRAFT, DESCEND EAL80 to 10,000.

B. **If 5 minutes separation existed at SNL and NWA11 was non-DME, may EAL80 be descended to 10,000?**

NO. AIRCRAFT ARE SEPARATED BY MORE THAN 4,000 FEET.

5.   TIME: 1914   PILOT'S DISCRETION DESCENT

A33296	END			90√	MIO	AMA V2 FYV	
	1912		31				
C131/B		19					
		31					
T240	1912	PNC				8E END/1914	

G21568	END			110√ —————	AMA V2 PNC	APCH
	1908	㉗	↓	× ↕ 80		APCH
C131/A		19				
		29		→		1914
T240	1908	PNC			24E END/1914	

G21568 has requested clearance for descent landing at PNC. Explain the procedure for clearing G21568 for approach applying minimum separation with A33296.

FIRST OBTAIN DME POSITION OF G21568, THEN A33296. IF AT LEAST 10 MILES EXIST, ISSUE APPROACH CLEARANCE TO G21568 WITH CLEARANCE FOR PROMPT DESCENT TO 8,000 (DESCEND NOW!) AND TO CROSS PNC VORTAC AT OR BELOW 8,000.

6. TIME: 1849   **20 MILES DME**

AAL5	DAL			150✓ ↓30	PNC	DAL V5 ICT	
	1837		49		1859		
B737/A		18					
		48	49				
T450		SNL		130			

UAL20	DAL			130✓	PNC	DAL V5 ICT	
	1832		44		1854		
B737/A		18					
		43	44				
T450		SNL				38N/1849	

AAL5 is requesting 13,000. Write the DME separation required and the procedure you should use to determine if separation exists.

FIRST OBTAIN DME POSITION OF VA120, THEN AAL5. IF 20 MILES DME EXISTS, DESCEND AAL5 TO 13,000.

7. TIME: 1201   **RUNWAY: 21**

TW5	MIO			120✓	END	MEM V2 AMA	
	1147		00		1210		
B707/A		12					
		01	01				
T490		PNC					

N440		T→SW	↑	↑120	END	PNC V2 AMA/0046	
		PNC					
C310/X		RLS10<N152B					D-A
			1201/				
T240		PNC P1200			120		

N152B		T→SW		↑120	END	PNC V2 AMA/0033	
		PNC					
G159/U		RLS<1204					D-A
			1201/				
T270		PNC P1200		RL100	120		

TW5 reported Ponca City at 1201, N152B requests clearance to Amarillo airport at 12,000. When can N152B depart?

1204—44 KNOT RULE

8. **Using the same strips, what is the minimum longitudinal separation that could be utilized for N440 to depart after N152B?**

5 MINUTES—22 KNOT RULE IF N152B HAS REPORTED LEAVING 10,000 OR 10 MINUTES IF NO REPORT RECEIVED.

9. **TIME: 1903**   **DME/NON-DME SEPARATION**

A11269	OKC			170√		MLC	CDS V6 HOT	
	1859		05					
C135/X		19						
	1859	03						
T470		SNL			150			

UAL5	PNC			150√		MLC	ICT V5 SNL V6 HOT	
	1849		00			1910		
DC8/A		19						
	1849	00	00					
T480		SNL						

A11269 requests descent to 15,000. Write the separation required and the procedure you would use to apply it.

30 MILES—REQUEST DME POSITION FROM VAL5, IF REPORTS INDICATE VAL5 IS 30 MILES FROM SNL VORTAC, ISSUE CLEARANCE FOR DESCENT TO A11269 AS SOON AS A11269 PROGRESSES SNL VORTAC.

10. **TIME: 1709**

AAL20	AMA			120√		PNC	SFO V2 FYV	
	1708		18					
B727/A		17						
		17					62W/1709	
T460		END						

AAL10	AMA			150√ ⌐		LAS V2 END	APCH
	1702		12	× ↕ 110			
B727/A		17					APCH
		13					1709
T490		END				24W/1709	

AAL10, landing at END, is requesting clearance for approach. Explain the procedure for clearing AAL10 for approach using minimum separation with AAL20.

FIRST OBTAIN DME POSITION OF AAL10, THEN AAL20. IF AT LEAST 10 MILES SEPARATION EXISTS, CLEAR AAL10 FOR APPROACH TO CROSS THE END VORTAC AT OR BELOW 11,000. ANOTHER OPTION IS TO VERIFY AIRCRAFT (BOTH) PROGRESS BY AMA AND APPLY TIME PROCEDURE.

LONGITUDINAL SEPARATION EXAMPLE 2

DIRECTIONS: *Answer items 1 through 10. Apply longitudinal separation, using the flight strips provided.*

1. TIME: 1555   OPPOSITE DIRECTION TRAFFIC (TIME)

REP503	CDS			150√		SNL	PHX V6 MLC	
	1545		10					
FA27/A		16						
		10						
T240		OKC			130		60W/1555	

N138T	SNL			140√		CDS	STL V6 PHX/1816	
	1552		04					
BE20/A		16						
		04						
T240		OKC					36E/1555	ZAB

REP503 is requesting 13,000. What time must the aircraft be at 13,000 to ensure vertical separation before passing N138T? Explain.

1557—AIRCRAFT WILL PASS AT 1607. OTHER OPTIONS (1) "PAPER STOP" N138T (2) WAIT TILL THEY HAVE PASSED

2. TIME: 1613   OPPOSITE DIRECTION DME REPORT

N25T	PNC			90√			AMA V2 MIO/1618	
	1553		18 ↓ ↓					
BE90/A		16						
		18						
T195		MIO					15W/1613	

N33Y	FYV			100√ ↓ 80		PNC	JAX V2 AMA/1723	
	1520		10	100/15W		1635		
C310/A		16						
		10	10					
T180		MIO			80		9W/1613	

N33Y reported 9 miles west of MIO requesting 8,000. What procedure should be followed to provide descent and separation from N25T utilizing DME?

REQUEST N25T TO REPORT 9 MILES WEST OF MIO VORTAC. AFTER RECEIVING THE REPORT INDICATING THE TWO AIRCRAFT HAVE PASSED, ISSUE DESCENT CLEARANCE TO N33Y.

OTHER OPTION: REQUEST DME FROM N25T. THEN HAVE N33Y MAINTAIN 10,000 TO THIS POINT, THEN DESCEND TO 8,000.

3. TIME: 1726 OPPOSITE DIRECTION TRAFFIC INTERSECTION REPORT

TWA14	SNL		170√	ICT	DAL V5 ICT	
	1721	31				
B727/A		17				
		30				
T480	1721	PNC	150		TRYON/1726	ZKC

UAL22	ICT		160√	SNL	ICT V5 DAL	
	1702	20		1731		
DC8/A		17				
		20 20				
T480		PNC			TRYON/1725	

UAL22 reported Tryon intersection at 1725. TWA14 reported Tryon at 1726. What is the earliest time TWA14 can descend to 15,000?

1727—DESCENT CLEARANCE CAN BE ISSUED WHEN 3 MINUTES' FLYING TIME EXISTS BETWEEN THE TWO AIRCRAFT

4. TIME: 1929   OPPOSITE DIRECTION TRAFFIC DIVERGING AIRWAYS/ RADIALS OF SAME NAVAID

A33296	MIO		120√	END	FYV V2 AMA	
	1912	31				
T29/A		19				
		31				
T240		PNC			8E/1929	

C21568	OKC				150√ ↓ 90	MKC	ABI V3 MKC	
	1902		27		× 8NE ↕	2000		
C131/A		19			130			
	1904	29	29					
T240		PNC			90			ZKC

C21568 has requested 9,000 at Ponca City. Explain how he or she may be assigned this altitude.

DETERMINE DME POSITION OF A33296 FROM PNC VORTAC. THEN CLEAR C21568 TO CROSS THIS POINT ON V3 NORTHEAST OF PNC VORTAC AT OR ABOVE 13,000, THEN DESCEND AND MAINTAIN 9,000.

5.   TIME: 1625

NWA11	MIO				100√	OKC	MLC V7 TUL V4 CDS	
	1622		28					
B727/A		16						
		28						
T480	1622	TUL					24NE/1625	

AAL80	MIO				160√	OKC	MKC V7 TUL V4 OKC	
	1619		25			1640		
B727/A		16						
		24	25					
T480	1617	TUL			80			

AAL80 is requesting 8,000. Applying minimum longitudinal separation, can 8,000 be assigned? Why/why not?

NO. ALTHOUGH AT LEAST 10 MILES SEPARATION EXISTS, THERE WOULD BE A LOSS OF SEPARATION WHEN AAL80 DESCENDED BELOW 10,000 FEET.

6.   TIME: 1935   10 MILES/5 MINUTES ALTITUDE CHANGE

REP16	CDS				130√	SNL	CDS V6 HOT	
	1910		35					
FA27/A		19						
		35	35					
T240		OKC			90			

EAL15	CDS			110✓		SNL	LAX V6 HOT	
	1903		30					
FA27/A		19						
		29	29					
T240		OKC						

A. At OKC, REP 16 requested descent to 9,000. Using the 10 mile/5 minute altitude change rule, determine if the request can be approved. Why/why not?

NO—THE RULE STATES THE FOLLOWING AIRCRAFT MUST BE CLIMBING.

B. What longitudinal separation rule can be used to assign REP16 9,000?

20 DME

7. TIME: 1459   **20 MILES LONGITUDINAL SEPARATION CONVERGING COURSES**

A33395	FYV			100✓		TUL	MEM V2 MIO V7 MLC	
	1431		10					
T29/B		15						
		09						
T230		MIO					44E/1459	

N246T	MAPLE			130✓ ↓70		TUL	ICT V9 MIO V7 TUL	
	1455		04					
BE90/A		15						
		04						
T230		MIO		70			20NW/1459	

N246T reported 20 NW MIO VORTAC requesting clearance to 7,000. Applying minimum longitudinal separation, determine if this clearance can be issued.

YES—OBTAIN A POSITION REPORT FROM A33395. IF 20 MILES EXIST BETWEEN AIRCRAFT (20 NW − 44 E = 24 MILES), ISSUE DESCENT CLEARANCE TO N246T.

8. **TIME: 1030**   **SEPARATION BETWEEN DME AND NON-DME EQUIPPED AIRCRAFT**

A43176	PRX		120	TUL	HOU V7 MIO	
	1017	31				
C130/X		10				
		31				
T260		MLC	100			

N77T	HOT		100	TUL	MIA V6 MLC V7	
	0950	23		1034	MKC/1104	
CV58/D		10				
		22 23				
T270		MLC				

A43176 requested 10,000. May the 30-mile DME rule be applied?

NO. A43176 HAS NOT REPORTED OVER MCALESTER VORTAC AND N77T HAS NOT REPORTED 30 MILES DME.

9. **TIME: 2018**   **10 MILES/5 MINUTES ALTITUDE CHANGE**

N526L	GCK		70√	OKC	CYS V1 OKC/2039	
	1951	09		2039		
C310/X		20				
		09 09				
T180		END				

N25B	GCK		130√	OKC	SEA V1 OKC/2035	
	1946	03		2033		
BE95/X		20				
		02 03				
T190		END				

N25B requested descent to 6,000. Can clearance for descent be issued?

NO. MORE THAN 4,000 FEET SEPARATE N256L AND N25B. ALL FOUR CONDITIONS HAVE NOT BEEN MET USING TIME.

10. TIME: 1842   10 MINUTES/20 MILES LONGITUDINAL SEPARATION WITH PILOT'S DISCRETION DESCENT

AAL5	SNL		49	130√	HOT	LAX V6 HOT	
	1842						
B737/A		18					
		48					
T450		MLC				56W/1842	

BNF20	SNL	㊽↓	150√——		LAX V6 MLC	APCH
	1837		× ↕120			
B737/A		18				APCH
		43				
T450		MLC			16W/1842	1842

BNF20, landing MLC, is requesting approach clearance. Write the DME separation required and the procedure you would use to issue an approach clearance to BNF20.

20 MILES. REQUEST DME REPORTS FROM BOTH AIRCRAFT. IF 20 MILES SEPARATION EXISTS, CLEAR BNF 20 FOR APPROACH TO CROSS MLC VORTAC AT OR BELOW 12,000.

LONGITUDINAL SEPARATION
END-OF-LESSON TEST

DIRECTIONS: *Items 1 through 14 are multiple-choice. Indicate your selection by circling the appropriate letter for each item. Correct answers appear at end of the chapter.*

1. Choose the statement that indicates the correct application of longitudinal separation.
   (A) Clear at a specified time; arrive at a fix at a specified time; clear aircraft on routes whose widths do **not** overlap; or hold at a fix until a specified time.
   (B) Clear aircraft to fly specified headings that diverge by at least 45 degrees; arrive at a fix at a specified time; hold at a fix until a specified time; or change altitude at a specified time or fix.
   (C) Depart at a specified time; arrive at a fix at a specified time; hold at a fix until a specified time; or change altitude at a specified time or fix.
   (D) Depart on a specified course with at least 30 degrees divergence; hold at a fix until a specified time; change altitude at a specified time or fix; or hold at a fix until a specified time.

2. TIME: 1400   END

N73132	GCK 1412	20	130	OKC	DEN V1 DAL/1450	
L329/A	14					
	END					
T400	END					

N8727R	GCK 1343	05	130	OKC	DEN V1 DAL/1525	
M021/U	14					
	05					
T150	END					

OKC

N8727R	END 1405	45	130	DAL	DEN V1 DAL/1525	
M021/U	14					
	45					
T150	OKC					ZFW

N73132	END			130	DAL	DEN V1 DAL/1450	
	1420		35				
L329/A		14					
T400		OKC					ZFW

With reference to the strips above, select the statement that provides longitudinal separation between N8727R and N73132.

(A) Clear N8727R to cross END at or before 1410, and clear N73132 to cross END at or after 1420, to ensure 10 minutes longitudinal separation at END.

(B) Clear N8727R to cross END VORTAC at or above 140.

(C) Clear N73132 to cross END VORTAC at or below 120.

(D) **No** action required prior to END since 10 minutes still exists between N8727R and N73132 at OKC.

3. TIME: 1400

T38/B	MAPLE			140	OKC	MKC V3 OKC	
	1400		10				
T38/8		14					
		10					
T360		PNC					

TWA5	BLUFF			160	OKC	DEN V8 PNC V3 OKC	
	1357		05				
B707/A		14					
		05					
T490		PNC					

TWA5 is requesting descent to 10,000. With reference to the strips above, choose the correct application of minimum longitudinal separation.

(A) Determine the distance between TWA5 and T38/B. If 20 miles exist, descend TWA5 to 10,000.

(B) TWA5 may be descended now because the 3-minute/44-knot rule is effective.

(C) Determine the distance between TWA5 and T38/B. If 5 miles exist, descend TWA5 to 10,000.

(D) Descent clearance cannot be issued because the 44-knot rule is **not** applicable for aircraft on converging courses.

4. TIME: 1600   RUNWAY: 36

TWA5	HOT 1542	00	160√	SNL 1609	HOT V6 CDS		
B707/A		16					
		00 00					
T490		MLC					

N62Y		T→N MLC	↑ ↑100	SNL	MLC V6 OKC/0035		
CV54/D							D-A
		1001/					
T205		MLC P1601		100			

DAL9		T→N MLC	↑ ↑160	SNL	MLC V6 OKC		
B737/A							D-A
		1000/					
T445		MLC P1600		160			

By using DME separation and applying the 44-knot longitudinal separation standard to the strips above, select the statement that would result in minimum longitudinal separation.

(A) When TWA5 reports 5 miles west of MLC, DAL9 may depart; have DAL9 report 5 miles west of MLC then release N62Y.

(B) TWA5 has reported the MLC VORTAC, which is 5 miles from the airport; therefore, DAL9 can be released immediately. Have DAL9 report passing the MLC VORTAC then release N62Y.

(C) Clear DAL9 to depart turn left heading 315 until intercepting Victor six, report 5 miles west of MLC on Victor six. When you receive the report, clear N62Y to depart north direct to MLC.

(D) The rule **cannot** be applied in this case because the 44-knot rule cannot be used between two en route aircraft.

5. TIME: 1510   RUNWAY: 36

A11859	SNL 1450	09	130	HOT	OKC V6 HOT		
U21/B		15					
T240		MLC					ZME

			110	HOT	CDS V6 HOT	
M31528	SNL 1446	03				
C130/B		15				
T270		MLC				ZME

				HOT	MLC V6 HOT MEM/0133	
N65B						
C310/A						
T190		MLC P1513		90		ZME

				HOT	MLC V6 HOT/0042	
N55Y						
CV54/A						
T215		MLC P1510		110		ZME

A11859 is requesting 11,000.

N55Y and N65B are requesting departure clearance and N55Y will be departing first.

By using DME separation and applying the 22-knot longitudinal separation standard, refer to the strips above and select the statement that would result in minimum longitudinal separation.

(A) The rule **cannot** be applied to A11859 because the leading aircraft will be descending to the altitude of the following. N55Y may be released immediately because M31528 is 31 miles east of MLC. Have N55Y report MLC and release N65B as this will give you the 5 miles needed for separation.

(B) Determine the distance between M31528 and A11859. If 10 miles exist, clear A11859 to 11,000. Release N55Y immediately because M31528 is 6 minutes by MLC. Release N65B 5 minutes after N55Y has departed.

(C) Determine the distance between M31528 and A11859. If 5 miles exist, clear A11859 to 11,000. Release N55Y after you have determined that A11859 is 5 miles east of MLC. Release N65B after N55Y has reported 5 miles east of MLC.

(D) Determine the distance between M31528 and A11859. If 10 miles exist, clear A11859 to 11,000. When A11859 reports 5 miles east of MLC, release N55Y direct to MLC then Victor Six. Obtain a report from N55Y 5 miles east of MLC and release N65B direct to MLC then Victor Six.

6. TIME: 1414

BE95/X	MLC		90√	MIO	PRX V7 MKC/1507	
	1418	33				
BE95		14				
		33				
T195		TUL				

N6245A	FSM		100√	PNC	FSM V8 PNC/1522	
	P1345	20				
AC56/X		14				
		20				
T170		TUL	70			

A31520	FSM		80√	OKC	FSM V8 TUL V4 ABI	
	P1346	16				
T29/X		14				
		16				
T200		TUL				

N6245A is requesting a descent to 7,000. With reference to the strips above, choose the correct statement.

(A) N6245A can be descended now because 10 miles exist between N6245A and A31520.

(B) Separation will exist between N6245A and A31520; a descent clearance can be issued because separation can be ensured between N6245A and BE95/X.

(C) Ten minutes' separation will exist between N6245A and BE95/X. Descent clearance can be issued.

(D) Descent clearance **cannot** be issued.

7. TIME: 1207

TWA6	MIO		160√	MLC	IND V7 MLC	
	1209	14				
B707/A		12				
		14				
T490		TUL				

AAL21	MIO			120√		OKC	IND V7 TUL V4 OKC	
	1205		11					
B727/A		12						
		11						
T490	1206	TUL						

DAL5	MIO			140√		MLC	IND V7 MLC	
	1202		08					
B727/A		12						
		08						
T490	1203	TUL			80			

By using DME separation and the strips above, choose the statement that will result in minimum longitudinal separation if DAL5 is cleared to 8,000 and TWA6 is cleared to 11,000.

Determine the DME distance between DAL5 and AAL21.

(A) If 5 miles exist, clear DAL5 to 8,000. Determine the DME distance between TWA6 and AAL21. If 5 miles exist, descent TWA6 to 11,000.

(B) If 10 miles exist, clear DAL5 to 8,000. Determine the DME distance between TWA6/AAL21 and TWA6/DAL5. If 20 miles exist, descent TWA6 to 11,000.

(C) If 10 miles exist, clear DAL5 to 8,000. Determine the DME distance between TWA6 and AAL21. If 10 miles exist, descent TWA6 to 11,000.

(D) If 20 miles exist, clear DAL5 to 8,000. Determine the DME distance between TWA6 and AAL21. If 10 miles exist, descend TWA6 to 11,000.

8. TIME: 0209

A72155	OKC			70		MLC	CDS V6 HOT	
	0159		09			0225		
C130/X		02						
		09	09					
T280	0159	SNL						

EAL16	OKC			90		MLC	ABI V6 HOT	
	0153		03			0219		
CV58/X		02						
		02	03					
T290	0153	SNL			50			

Refer to the above strips. EAL16 is requesting descent to 5,000. What is the latest time descent may be started?
(A) 0208   (B) 0213   (C) 0214   (D) 0219

9. TIME: 1010   RUNWAY: 21

TOMCAT 8		↑		OKC	PNC V3 OKC V6 LVS	
F14/B						
		1010/				
T480		PNC P1010		160		

N66N	MAPLE		140	OKC	MKC V3 ABI	
	0956	05		1017		
LR36/R		10				
		04 | 05				
T420		PNC				

Using DME separation and the strips above, select the procedure that would result in minimum longitudinal separation.
(A) Release Tomcat 8 immediately since N66N has already progressed the VORTAC.
(B) When N66N reports 5 miles southwest of PNC VORTAC, Tomcat 8 may depart.
(C) Obtain a position report from N66N. Then release Tomcat 8 to cross 10 miles northeast of this position at or above 15,000.
(D) Determine the position of N66N. Then have Tomcat 8 to cross 20 miles northeast of N66N's position at or above 15,000.

10. TIME: 1306

M20133	CDS		150√		LVS V6 OKC	
	1306	2̶0̶ 17 ↓ ↓				
C141/A		13				
T420		O̶K̶C̶ YUKON				

N152B	CDS			130√		TUL	LAX V6 OKC V4 TUL	
	1253		13					
G159/A		13						
		13						
T280		OKC						

M20133, landing OKC, will be cleared to Yukon intersection. Utilizing the strips above, select the answer that would provide minimum longitudinal separation if M20133 was descended to 6,000.

(A) Determine the position of both aircraft. If more than 20 miles exist, clear M20133 to cross 20 miles west of the position of N152B at or below 12,000, cross Yukon at and maintain 6,000.

(B) Obtain a position report on both aircraft. If 20 miles exist, descend M20133 to 6,000, with a restriction to cross Yukon at or below 12,000, report leaving 12,000.

(C) Descend M20133 immediately to 6,000 with a restriction to cross Yukon at or below 12,000.

(D) Descent clearance **cannot** be issued because M20133 is the faster aircraft.

11. TIME: 1700

BONGO45	SNL				80		ABI V4 OKC V6 MLC	
	1655		15	↓				
OV10/A		17						
		15						
T240		MLC						

BONGO44	SNL				100		ABI V3 OKC V6 MLC	
	1650		10	↓				
OV10/A		17						
		09						
T240		MLC						

With reference to the strips above, select the statement that provides minimum longitudinal separation when clearing Bongo44 for approach.

(A) Clear Bongo44 for approach to cross MLC at or below 7,000.

(B) Clear Bongo44 for approach to descend now through 7,000 and cross MLC at or below 7,000.

(C) Since at least 10 miles' separation exists, clear Bongo44 for approach.

(D) Since 20 miles' separation exists, clear Bongo44 for approach.

12. TIME: 1520

A27869	FSM		40		120		PNC	FSM V8 DEN BKF	
T29/A		15							
		40							
T240	P1503	TUL							

AAL35	FSM 1517		30	↓	140			ATL V8 TUL	
B737/A		15							
T400		TUL							

Refer to the strips above. The controller wants to descend AAL35 to 6,000. Applying minimum longitudinal separation, how may this be accomplished?

(A) Determine the position of A27869. Then have AAL35 cross 20 miles east of A27869's position at or below 11,000.

(B) Since 10 minutes longitudinal separation exists at Tulsa, descend AAL35 to 6,000 to cross TUL at or below 11,000.

(C) Determine the position of both aircraft. If 20 miles' separation exists, descend AAL35 to 6,000.

(D) First obtain position of AAL35, then A27869. If 5 miles' separation exists, descend AAL35 to 6,000 to cross TUL at or below 11,000.

13. TIME: 1809

M31008	DAL 1757		10	140√		END	HOU V1 DEN	
C141/X		18						
		10						
T470		OKC			160			

TWA9	DAL 1752		04	160√		END 1815	HOU V1 DEN	
B727/A		18						
		04	04					
T490		OKC						

Utilizing the strips above, indicate which answer will provide approved separation
if M31008 were to request 16,000.

(A) Determine the position of TWA9. If TWA9 is 20 miles from OKC, M31008
can be assigned 16,000.

(B) M31008 can be assigned 16,000 as soon as OKC progress is received,
provided the altitude change is accomplished prior to 1825.

(C) M31008 can be assigned 16,000 now because TWA9 is faster and 6 minutes
exist on estimates at OKC.

(D) Determine the position of TWA9. If TWA9 is 30 miles from OKC, M31008
can be assigned 16,000 as soon as OKC progress is received.

14.

AAL24	END		150√	MIO	AMA V2 FYV	
	1603	12				
B737/A		16				
		12				
T490		PNC				

UAL33	MIO		160√	END	FYV V2 AMA	
	1551	00				
B707/A		16				
		00				
T490		PNC	120			

UAL33 has requested 12,000. Using the opposite direction altitude change procedure, what is the latest time UAL33 must be at or below 14,000 in descent to provide minimum separation?

(A) 1552   (B) 1556   (C) 1603   (D) 1606

LESSONS 13–16 ANSWERS

LETTERS OF AGREEMENT
END-OF-LESSON TEST

1. **A**	3. **B**	5. **D**	7. **A**	9. **C**	11. **A**
2. **D**	4. **C**	6. **C**	8. **B**	10. **C**	12. **B**

VERTICAL SEPARATION
END-OF-LESSON TEST

1. **A**	3. **D**	5. **B**	7. **B**	9. **B**	11. **D**	13. **B**
2. **C**	4. **B**	6. **B**	8. **C**	10. **B**	12. **A**	

LATERAL SEPARATION
END-OF-LESSON TEST

1. **A**
2. **D**
3. **C**

4. **HOLDING PATTERN AIRSPACE TO BE PROTECTED**
5. **B**
6. **D**

7.

HOLDING PATTERN NO. 8

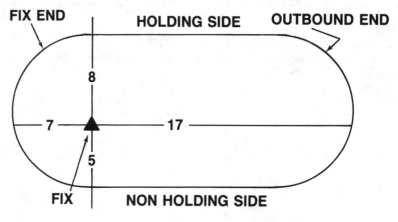

8. **D**   9. **B**   10. **10 MILES**   11. **5**

LONGITUDINAL SEPARATION
END-OF-LESSON TEST

1. **C**	3. **A**	5. **D**	7. **B**	9. **C**	11. **A**	13. **D**
2. **B**	4. **B**	6. **D**	8. **D**	10. **A**	12. **D**	14. **B**

CHAPTER IV

Lessons 17–23

LESSON 17
IFR FLIGHT DIRECTION, ALTITUDE ASSIGNMENT AND ALTIMETER SETTING

As you progress toward your goal of becoming an air traffic controller, you can see that altitude is the most important item you deal with as a controller. At this stage of your training, you must have a thorough knowledge of the rules and procedures for selecting and assigning altitudes. You should also understand the importance of the altimeter and how it is issued.

Objectives

Given air traffic situations, without references, and in accordance with 7110.65, you will:

1. Issue altimeter settings, using approved phraseology.

2. Identify three situations that require altimeter settings to be issued.

3. Determine altitudes for direction of flight.

4. Use standard phraseology to

   a. Assign altitudes for direction of flight.

   b. Assign altitude restrictions.

   c. Verify assigned altitudes.

5. Identify three circumstances that allow controllers to assign altitudes without regard to direction of flight.

Lesson Guide

A.   Altimeter Setting

Obtain altimeter settings from direct reading instruments or weather reporting stations. When issuing the altimeter, identify the source obtained from:

Phraseology:

"THE (facility) ALTIMETER (setting)"

If the altimeter reading is more than an hour old, state the time of the report: Phraseology:

"THE (facility name) (time or report if more than one hour old) ALTIMETER (setting)."

Issue the altimeter setting to en route aircraft at least one time while operating in your area of jurisdiction. Issue the setting of the nearest reporting station along the aircraft's route of flight. Issue the altimeter of the destination airport to arriving aircraft approximately 50 miles from the airport if an approach control facility does not serve the airport.

When issuing a clearance to descend below the lowest usable flight level, advise the pilot of the altimeter setting of the weather reporting station nearest the point at which the aircraft will descend below that flight level. (FL180 is used at Aero Center).

B.   Altitude Direction of Flight

   1.   Altitude Assignments

       Clear aircraft according to the following table.

Aircraft Operating	On course degrees magnetic	Assign	Examples
Below 3,000 feet above surface	Any course	Any altitude	
Below FL 290	0 through 179	Odd cardinal altitudes or flight levels at intervals of 2,000 feet	3,000, 5,000, FL250, FL270
	180 through 359	Even cardinal altitudes or flight levels at intervals of 2,000 feet	4,000, 6,000, FL240, FL260
At or above FL 290	0 through 179	Odd cardinal flight levels at intervals of 4,000 feet beginning with FL 290	FL290, FL330, FL370
	180 through 359	Odd cardinal flight levels at intervals of 4,000 feet beginning with FL 310	FL310, FL350, FL390
Within an ALTRV	Any course	Any altitude or flight level	
In transition to/ from Oceanic airspace where composite separation is authorized	Any course	Any odd or even cardinal flight level including those above FL290	FL280, FL290, FL300, FL310, FL320, FL330, FL340

   Exceptions:

       SAFI Aircraft
       Flight Check
       Meteorological
       Aircraft Limitations

C.   Altitude Information

1.   Phraseology:

"(aircraft ID), CLIMB/DESCEND AND MAINTAIN (altitude)."

a.   Altitude Verification

Phraseology:

"VERIFY AT (altitude)."
"VERIFY ASSIGNED ALTITUDE (altitude)."

IFR FLIGHT DIRECTION, ALTITUDE ASSIGMENT, AND ALTIMETER SETTING
EXAMPLE 1

1.

EA20	PRX			100	TUL	PRX V7 TUL
	1810	19				
B727/A		18				
T410		MLC				

Has EA20 been assigned a correct altitude for direction of flight?
  YES

2.

N123F		↑		MLC	TUL V7 MLC	
PAZT/A						
T160		TUL P0700		70		

Can N123F be assigned the requested altitude?
  YES

3.

N500Y	SGF	↓	80		SGF V4 TUL	
	1000	34				
M021/A		10				
T160		TUL				

Has N500Y been assigned a correct altitude for direction of flight?
  YES

4.

A16234	AMA			280	PRX	AMA J100 MSY	
	2110		38				
T33/B		21					
T360			SNL				

Has A16234 been assigned a correct altitude for direction of flight?
NO

5.

TURQY11		↑	↑		MIO	TUL V7 GVW	
F4/P							
T510		TUL P0030					

What altitudes between 100 and 170 can TURQY11 be assigned?
110, 130, 150, 170

6.

AA44	END			170	DAL	ABQ V2 END V1 DAL	
	1622		35				
B727/A		16					
T430			OKC				ZFW

Has AA44 been assigned a correct altitude for direction of flight?
YES

7.

N121RB			↑		OKC	END V1 DAL	
BE65/B							
T165		END P0600					

What altitudes below 10,000 can be assigned to N121RB?

50, 70, 90

IFR FLIGHT DIRECTION, ALTITUDE ASSIGNMENT AND ALTIMETER SETTING EXAMPLE 2

DIRECTIONS: *Write the phraseology for issuing the clearance marked on the strips.*

1.   TIME: 0050   RUNWAY: 21

N615M		T→SW ↑ PNC	↑ 80 ↓ 60 × COYLE @ 60	OKC	PNC V3 OKC/0050	D- COYLE
C182/A						
		0050/			LV30	
T125		PNC P0050		80		

"CESSNA SIX ONE FIVE MIKE, CLEARED TO COYLE INTERSECTION, VIA DEPART SOUTHWEST DIRECT PONCA CITY VORTAC VICTOR THREE, CLIMB AND MAINTAIN EIGHT THOUUSAND, CROSS COYLE AT AND MAINTAIN SIX THOUSAND, CONTACT AERO CENTER ONE TWO FOUR POINT ZERO LEAVING THREE THOUSAND."

2.   TIME: 1700   SOUTH DEPARTURE

N512Y		T→S ↑ MIO	↑ 90	SGF	MIO V10 SGF V271 CHA/0051	D-A
BE35/B						
					LV30	
T195		MIO P1700		90		ZME

"BONANZA FIVE ONE TWO YANKEE, CLEARED FROM MIAMI AIRPORT TO CHATTANOOGA AIRPORT, VIA DEPART SOUTH DIRECT MIAMI VORTAC VICTOR TEN SPRINGFIELD VICTOR TWO SEVENTY-ONE, CLIMB AND MAINTAIN NINER THOUSAND, CONTACT AERO CENTER ONE TWO FIVE POINT ZERO LEAVING THREE THOUSAND."

3. TIME: 1808

EAL27	GCK	18	18		170 ↓ 150	OKC	GCK V1 OKC	
					170/21 NW			
CV58/A								
			18					
T280	1806			END				

"EASTERN TWENTY-SEVEN, MAINTAIN ONE SEVEN THOUSAND UNTIL TWO ONE MILES NORTHWEST ENID VORTAC, DESCEND AND MAINTAIN ONE FIVE THOUSAND."

4. TIME: 1700

EAL28		↑	↑ 90	TUL	OKC V4 TUL	
			×8NE ↕			
F27/B			60			D-A
		1700/				
T230		OKC P1700		90		

"EASTERN TWENTY-EIGHT, CLEARED TO TULSA AIRPORT VICTOR FOUR, CROSS EIGHT MILES NORTHEAST OKLAHOMA CITY VORTAC AT OR BELOW SIX THOUSAND, CLIMB AND MAINTAIN NINER THOUSAND."

5. TIME: 2007

JOKER06	MLC	12	20		80√ ↑ 100	OKC	HOT V6 CDS	
					80/18E			
C130/A	1957							
			12					
T310				SNL				

"JOKER ZERO SIX, MAINTAIN EIGHT THOUSAND UNTIL ONE EIGHT MILES EAST SHAWNEE VORTAC, CLIMB AND MAINTAIN ONE ZERO THOUSAND."

6. TIME: 1849

UAL57	OKC	56	18		150√ ↑ 170	MLC	CDS V6 HOT	
B727/A	1849							
			56					
T460	1849			SNL				

"UNITED FIFTY-SEVEN, CLIMB AND MAINTAIN ONE SEVEN THOUSAND."

7. TIME: 0205

WAL27	CDS		12	170√ ↓ 150	SNL	LAX V6 HOT	
	0158	02		170/40 E			
B737/A				CDS			
		12					
T420			OKC				

"WESTERN TWENTY-SEVEN, MAINTAIN ONE SEVEN THOUSAND UNTIL FOUR ZERO MILES EAST CHILDRESS VORTAC, DESCEND AND MAINTAIN ONE FIVE THOUSAND."

8. TIME: 0610   DEPART NORTHEAST (NORTH)

KING11		T→N	↑	↑ 120	PNC	MIO V2 END	
		M10		× 5W ↕ 60			
C130/B							D-A
						LV30	
T310		MIO P0610			120		

"KING ONE ONE, CLEARED FROM MIAMI AIRPORT TO ENID AIRPORT, VIA DEPART NORTH DIRECT MIAMI VORTAC VICTOR TWO, CROSS FIVE MILES WEST MIAMI VORTAC AT OR BELOW SIX THOUSAND CLIMB AND MAINTAIN ONE TWO THOUSAND, CONTACT AERO CENTER THREE THREE FIVE POINT ZERO LEAVING THREE THOUSAND."

9. TIME: 1842

UAL33	PNC		47	170√ ↓ 130	FSM	END V8 FSM	
		18		170/7E			
DC8/A	1837						
		47					
T440			TUL				ZME

"UNITED THIRTY-THREE MAINTAIN ONE SEVEN THOUSAND UNTIL SEVEN MILES EAST TULSA VORTAC, DESCEND AND MAINTAIN ONE THREE THOUSAND."

10.   TIME: 0800   RUNWAY: 21

N631C		T→SW ↑ PNC	↑ 140 × 9SW ↕ 40 COYLE	OKC	PNC V3 OKC V6 CDS /0050	D-A
MU2/AA						
			↕ 130		LV30	
T230		PNC P0800		140		

"MITSUBISHI SIX THREE ONE CHARLIE, CLEARED TO CHILDRESS AIR-
PORT VIA DEPART SOUTHWEST DIRECT PONCA CITY VORTAC, VICTOR
THREE OKLAHOMA CITY VORTAC, VICTOR SIX, CROSS NINER MILES
SOUTHWEST PONCA CITY VORTAC AT OR BELOW FOUR THOUSAND,
CROSS COYLE INTERSECTION AT OR ABOVE ONE THREE THOUSAND,
CLIMB AND MAINTAIN ONE FOUR THOUSAND, CONTACT AERO CENTER
ONE TWO FOUR POINT ZERO LEAVING THREE THOUSAND."

11.   TIME: 1220

TWA27	SLICK	25 12	170√ ↓ 150 170/49SW	MIO	ABI V4 TUL V7 MKC
B727/A	1218				
		25			
T460		TUL			

"T-W-A TWENTY-SEVEN, MAINTAIN ONE SEVEN THOUSAND UNTIL FOUR
NINER MILES SOUTHWEST TULSA VORTAC, DESCEND AND MAINTAIN
ONE FIVE THOUSAND."

12.   TIME: 0718

EAL7	MLC	21 07	140√ ↓ 60 140/18E × BOLEY	OKC	HOT V6 OKC	F- BOLEY
B727/A	0710					
			@60			
T410		SNL				

"EASTERN SEVEN, CLEARED TO BOLEY INTERSECTION, MAINTAIN ONE
FOUR THOUSAND UNTIL ONE EIGHT MILES EAST SHAWNEE VORTAC,
CROSS BOLEY AT AND MAINTAIN SIX THOUSAND."

13. TIME: 0929

DAL48	FSM	41	↓	140√ ↓60	MSY V8 TUL	F
		09		140/20 W		
DC9/A	0926	↓		FSM × 7E		
				@60		
T410		TUL				

"DELTA FORTY-EIGHT, CLEARED TO TULSA VORTAC, MAINTAIN ONE FOUR THOUSAND UNTIL TWO ZERO MILES WEST FORT SMITH VORTAC, CROSS SEVEN MILES EAST TULSA VORTAC AT AND MAINTAIN SIX THOUSAND."

IFR FLIGHT DIRECTION, ALTITUDE ASSIGNMENT, AND ALTIMETER SETTING END-OF-LESSON TEST

DIRECTIONS: *Items 1 through 12 are multiple-choice. Indicate your selection by circling the appropriate letter for each test item. Correct answers appear at the end of the chapter.*

1. Current altimeter settings shall be obtained from
   (A) approach control facilities.
   (B) nearest military BASE OPS.
   (C) direct reading instruments or weather reporting stations.
   (D) the flow control position.

2. The phaseology for issuing the Tulsa altimeter of 30.12 is
   (A) "TULSA ALTIMETER THREE ZERO ONE TWO."
   (B) "TULSA ALTIMETER THREE ZERO POINT ONE TWO."
   (C) "ALTIMETER AT TULSA THREE ZERO ONE TWO."
   (D) "ALTIMETER THREE ZERO ONE TWO."

3. When should an altimeter setting be issued to en route aircraft operating below FL 180?
   (A) When altimeter is below 29.92   (B) When the controller is not busy
   (C) Once in your area of jurisdiction   (D) On initial radio contract

4. How far, in miles, from the destination airport should the altimeter setting be issued if approach control service is not provided?
   (A) 125   (B) 100   (C) 75   (D) 50

5. An aircraft operating at FL 220 is cleared to 80. The altimeter setting should be issued for the
   (A) weather reporting station nearest point aircraft will leave FL 180.
   (B) destination airport or next compulsory reporting point.
   (C) weather reporting station nearest point where aircraft was cleared.
   (D) all compulsory reporting points along route to center boundary.

6. An aircraft over OKC requests OKC-TUL. What are the correct flight levels between FL 290 and FL 450, inclusive, for this flight?
   (A) 310, 350, 390, 430   (B) 290, 330, 370, 410, 450
   (C) 290, 330, 350, 370, 410, 450   (D) 290, 310, 350, 390, 430, 450

7. A12468 is requesting clearance from Tulsa to Oklahoma City via V4N. What are the correct altitudes for this flight?
   (A) 30, 50, 70, 90, 110, 130, 150, 170   (B) 20, 40, 60, 80, 100, 120, 140, 160
   (C) 40, 60, 80, 100, 120, 140, 160   (D) 50, 70, 90, 110, 130, 150, 170

8. N281, a Piper Apache, is requesting clearance from McAlester to Tulsa via V7. What are the correct altitudes for this flight?
   (A) 20, 40, 60, 80, 100, 120, 140, 160   (B) 30, 50, 70, 90, 110, 130, 150, 170
   (C) 40, 60, 80, 100, 120, 140, 160   (D) 50, 70, 90, 110, 130, 150, 170

9. Three circumstances that allow controllers to assign the wrong altitude for direction of flight are
   (A) special purpose flight, inoperative NAVAID, and meteorological conditions.
   (B) meteorological conditions, aircraft limitations, and special purpose flight.
   (C) terrain, aircraft limitations, and meteorological conditions.
   (D) meteorological conditions, pilot request, and aircraft limitations.

10. A departure, OKC V4 TUL, is assigned one one thousand. Which phraseology should be used?
    (A) "CLIMB AND MAINTAIN ONE ONE THOUSAND."
    (B) "MAINTAIN ONE ONE THOUSAND."
    (C) "CLIMB TO ONE ONE THOUSAND."
    (D) "AFTER DEPARTURE CLIMB AND MAINTAIN ONE ONE THOUSAND."

11. AAL10 inbound to Tulsa from DEN on V8 at 170 must be cleared to Tulsa VORTAC. D2 has communication but **not** control. You have crossing traffic at TUL VORTAC on V4 at 90. Which clearance is correct phraseology for this situation?
    (A) "AMERICAN TEN, MAINTAIN ONE SEVEN THOUSAND UNTIL ONE ONE MILES SOUTHEAST PONCA CITY VORTAC, CROSS SIX MILES NORTHWEST TULSA VORTAC AT OR BELOW EIGHT THOUSAND, DESCEND AND MAINTAIN SIX THOUSAND."
    (B) "AMERICAN TEN, CLEARED TO TULSA VORTAC, MAINTAIN ONE SEVEN THOUSAND UNTIL ONE ONE MILES SOUTHEAST PONCA CITY VORTAC, CROSS SIX MILES NORTHWEST TULSA VORTAC AT OR BELOW EIGHT THOUSAND, DESCEND AND MAINTAIN SIX THOUSAND."
    (C) "AMERICAN TEN, CLEARED TO TULSA VORTAC, CROSS SIX MILES NORTHWEST TULSA VORTAC AT EIGHT THOUSAND, DESCEND AND MAINTAIN SIX THOUSAND."
    (D) "AMERICAN TEN, CLEARED TO TULSA VORTAC, MAINTAIN ONE SEVEN THOUSAND UNTIL ONE ONE MILES SOUTHEAST PONCA CITY VORTAC, CROSS SIX MILES NORTHWEST TULSA VORTAC AT AND MAINTAIN SEVEN THOUSAND."

12. What is the correct phraseology to verify altitude information for an aircraft in level flight?
    (A) "SAY ALTITUDE."   (B) "VERIFY ALTITUDE."
    (C) "WHAT'S YOUR ALTITUDE?"   (D) "VERIFY AT (altitude)."

LESSON 18
IFR CLEARANCES AND ROUTE ASSIGNMENT

In previous lessons, we covered in detail the different methods employed when separating aircraft. You must know how to formulate the correct clearance and assign the correct route when applying these separation standards. Although route assignment is used primarily to direct aircraft from one point to another, it also plays an important role in separation. It is imperative that you know how to issue IFR clearances and assign different routes in order to achieve the first priority of air traffic control service—the separation of aircraft.

Objectives

Given air traffic situations, without references, and in accordance with 7110.65, you will:

1. Select and issue clearances to

    a. Clear aircraft via airways, routes, or NAVAIDs at the designated altitude.

    b. Amend the route of flight in a previously issued clearance.

    c. Be relayed through non-ATC facilities.

2. Determine and apply procedures to follow when an aircraft requests clearance into

    a. Uncontrolled airspace.

    b. Special use and ATC assigned airspace (ATCAA):
        (1) Prohibited areas.
        (2) Restricted areas.
        (3) Warning areas.
        (4) Military operations area (MOA).

Lesson Guide

A. Clearance Items

    1. Aircraft Identification

    2. Clearance Limit

    3. Departure Procedure or SID

    4. Route of Flight Including POR/PDAR/PAR

    5. Altitude Data in Order Flown

    6. Holding Instructions

    7. Any Special Information

    8. Frequency and Beacon Code Information

B.   Clearance Prefix

Clearance through non-ATC facilities use the phraseology:

"ATC CLEARS," "ATC ADVISES (message)," or "ATC REQUESTS (information)." Omit the prefix "ATC CLEARS/ADVISES/REQUESTS" when issuing clearances directly to aircraft or to an ATC facility.

C.   Route Use

Clear aircraft via designated airways and routes, radials or courses to or from NAVAIDS, DME arcs, radials, courses, headings of departure or arrival routes, and assigned SIDS/STARS.

D.   Route Amendments

Amend route of flight in a previously issued clearance by one of the following: (1) state which portion of the route is being amended and then state the amendment; (2) state the amendment to the route and then state that the rest of the route is unchanged; (3) issue the entire route by stating the amendment.

When route or altitude in a previously issued clearance is amended, restate all applicable altitude restrictions.

E.   Route Structure Transitions

To effect transition within or between route structure, clear an aircraft by one or more of the following methods, based on VOR, VORTAC, or TACAN: (1) Assign a SID/STAR. (2) Clear departing or arriving aircraft to climb or descend via radials, courses, or azimuths of the airway or jet route assigned. (3) Clear departing or arriving aircraft directly to or between the NAVAIDS forming the airway or route assigned. (4) Clear aircraft to climb or descend on specified radials, courses, or azimuths of NAVAIDS.

F.   Minimum En Route Altitudes

Assign altitudes at or above the MEA for the route segment being flown. When a lower MEA for subsequent segments of the route is applicable, issue the lower MEA only after the aircraft is over or past the FIX/NAVAID beyond which the lower MEA applies unless a crossing restriction at or above the higher MEA is used. An aircraft may be cleared below the MEA but not below the MOCA for the route segment being flown if the altitude assigned is at least 300 feet above the floor of controlled airspace and nonradar procedures are used within 22 miles of a VOR, TACAN, or VORTAC.

G.   Uncontrolled Airspace

Include routes through uncontrolled airspace only when requested by the pilot.

H.   Special Use and ATC Assigned Airspace

Includes prohibited, restricted, warning, and military operation areas. Authorize entry only when the pilot states permission has been obtained from the using agency, the using agency states permission granted, and airspace is released to the controlling agency.

To separate nonparticipating aircraft from special-use airspace, clear aircraft below FL290 at an altitude at least 500 feet above or below the upper/lower limit of the airspace. Aircraft above FL290 separate by at least 1,000 feet above/below the upper/lower limit.

To provide lateral separation, clear aircraft on airways/routes whose widths do not overlap protected airspace.

Clear aircraft in/through MOA's/ATCAA's with prior coordination and approved separation between airspace operations and nonparticipating aircraft.

IFR CLEARANCES AND ROUTE ASSIGNMENT END-OF-LESSON TEST

DIRECTIONS: *Items 1 through 11 are multiple-choice. Indicate your selection by circling the appropriate letter for each test item. Correct answers appear at the end of the chapter.*

1. What information is always included in a clearance?
   (A) Aircraft identification   (B) Departure procedure
   (C) Holding instructions   (D) Altitude

2. When should a controller use the prefix phrases "ATC CLEARS," "ATC ADVISES," or "ATC REQUESTS"?
   (A) At the time that a clearance, advisory, or a request is relayed through a tower
   (B) At the time that a clearance, advisory, or a request is relayed through a non-ATC facility
   (C) At all times when issuing a clearance, advisory, or a request
   (D) With general aviation aircraft only

3. How do you amend the route in a previously issued clearance?
   (A) Restate all altitude restrictions.
   (B) Issue the new route and restate the assigned altitude.
   (C) State the change and then state the rest of route unchanged.
   (D) Restate the amendment and state that all altitude restrictions remain the same.

4. If an aircraft is recleared, but altitude restrictions remain the same, what is the correct way to amend the clearance?
   (A) Amend the route and state "ALTITUDE RESTRICTIONS SAME."
   (B) Amend the route and restate the altitude restrictions.
   (C) Amend the route only if desired by the pilot.
   (D) Amend the route only.

5. When may a SID/STAR be assigned?
   (A) As a substitute for en route aircraft
   (B) As a route of flight only
   (C) During route structure transitions only
   (D) During route structure transition or as a route of flight

6. TIME: 0950

N785T	END 0947		06		50√	MKC	AMA V2 PNC V3 MKC	
BE90/A		10						
		07						
T220			PNC					ZKC

C22410	ICT 0937		05		60√	SNL	OFF ICT V5 DAL	
T29/X		10						
		05						
T240			PNC					

N77AY	END 0945		04		70√	MIO	LAS V2 FYV	
CV54/A		10						
		04						
T240			PNC					

Refer to the flight progress strips above. Which clearance will provide separation and terrain clearance?

(A) N785T - Maintain 5,000 until 9 miles northeast Ponca City VORTAC, climb and maintain 7,000.

(B) C22410 - Cross 5 miles north Ponca City at or above 8,000, climb and maintain 10,000.

(C) N785T - Cross 9 miles northeast Ponca City VORTAC at or below 6,000, climb and maintain 7,000.

(D) N77AY - Climb and maintain 9,000, report leaving 7,000.

7. When may an aircraft be cleared below the MEA, but **not** below the MOCA?

(A) Pilot is operating in VFR conditions

(B) Within 22 NM of a VOR, VORTAC, or TACAN

(C) When requested by the pilot

(D) Never

8. When may aircraft be cleared through uncontrolled airspace?

(A) At the controller's discretion

(B) During adverse weather conditions

(C) When requested by the pilot

(D) When traffic conditions require it

9. A12715 is on an approved ALTRV and is operating at FL 180 through FL 190. R-3426A is in use from 5,000 through FL 210. A12715's route of flight is through R-3426A. What action should you take?
   (A) Clear A12715 via a route that will keep the aircraft clear of R-3426A.
   (B) Clear A12715 at an altitude that will keep the aircraft 1,000 feet above or below the altitudes in use in R-3426A.
   (C) Take no action. ALTRV operations within restricted airspace are the responsibility of mission project officers.
   (D) Coordinate with the controlling facility for approval for A12715 to operate in R-3426A.

10. B0B015's route of flight at FL 180 will transit a warning area. What action should be taken?
    (A) Advise pilot to file an amended route clear of the warning area.
    (B) Assign B0B015 an altitude at least 500 feet above the warning area.
    (C) Take no action. Restrictions do **not** apply to military aircraft.
    (D) Assign any altitude above the area if aircraft operations are **not** involved.

11. When may a nonparticipating aircraft be cleared through a MOA?
    (A) At any time that the clearance is covered by a letter of agreement and approved separation is applied
    (B) When the pilot requests the clearance
    (C) If MOA is outside controlled airspace
    (D) At any time the nonparticipating aircraft is a military aircraft

LESSON 19
DEPARTURE PROCEDURES

Having been exposed to basic separation rules in Chapter 2, you are about to venture into the more complex areas of control. The first is the departure phase of flight. Prior to an aircraft's departure, a clearance must be issued that will provide separation from en route aircraft. In order to issue these clearances, procedures, rules, and techniques must be covered and practiced.

Objectives

Given air traffic situations, without references, and in accordance with 7110.65, you will identify and issue:

1. Initial departure instructions.

2. SIDs.

3. Abbreviated clearances.

4. Departure clearances without restrictions.

5. Sequencing delays.

6. Receiving facility coordination.

7. Information to be forwarded.

8. VFR release of IFR departures.

Lesson Guide

A. Clearances

1. Departure Airport — Always include the airport of departure when issuing a departure clearance for relay to an aircraft by an FAA, dispatcher, etc.

2. Clearance Limit — Specify the destination airport when practicable, even though it is outside controlled airspace. Issue short-range clearances as provided for in any procedures established for their use.

3. Direction of Takeoff/Turn or Initial Heading/Azimuth—Specify direction of takeoff/turn or initial heading/azimuth to be flown after takeoff as follows: (1) Locations with Airport Traffic Control Service—specify these items as necessary. (2) Locations without Airport Traffic Control Service, but within a control zone—specify these items if necessary. Obtain/solicit the pilot's concurrence concerning items before issuing them in a clearance. (3) At all other airports—Do not specify direction of takeoff/turn after takeoff. If necessary to specify an initial heading/azimuth to be flown after takeoff, issue the initial heading/azimuth so as to apply only within controlled airspace.

4.   Published Departure Procedures

When IFR departure procedures are published for a location and pilot compliance is necessary to ensure separation, include the published departure procedure as part of the ATC clearance.

5.   Compatibility Verification

Compatibility with a procedure issued may be verified by asking the pilot if terms obtained/solicited will allow him or her to comply with local traffic patterns, terrain, or obstruction avoidance.

6.   SID/PDR Routes

Assign a SID (including transition, if necessary). Assign a Preferential Departure Route (PDR) or the route filed by the pilot only when a SID is not established for the departure route to be flown or the pilot has indicated that he or she does not wish to use a SID.

7.   Route of Flight

Specify one or more of the following: (1) Airway, route, course, heading, azimuth, arc, or vector. (2) The routing a pilot can expect if any part of the route beyond a short-range clearance limit differs from that filed.

8.   Altitude Assignment

Use one of the following, in order of preference listed: (1) Assign the altitude filed by the aircraft. (2) Assign an altitude within the highest route stratum filed or as near as possible to the altitude filed by the aircraft. Interim altitude assignments shall not be used to satisfy this order of preference.

Assign an interim altitude within the highest route stratum filed or as near as possible to the highest route stratum filed, and inform the aircraft when to expect clearance to filed altitude.

B.   Abbreviated Departure Clearance

Issue an abbreviated departure clearance if its use reduces verbiage and the following conditions are met: (1) The route of flight filed with ATC has not been changed by the pilot, company, operations officer, input officer, or in the stored flight program prior to departure. (2) All ATC facilities concerned have sufficient route of flight information to exercise their control responsibilities. (3) When the flight will depart IFR, destination airport information is relayed between the facilities concerned prior to departure. (4) The assigned altitude is stated in the clearance.

C.   Departure Restrictions

Assign departure restrictions, clearance vocal times, hold for release, or release times, when necessary to separate departures from other traffic or to restrict or regulate the departure flow. When issuing clearance void times at airports not served by control towers, provide alternative instructions requiring the pilots to advise ATC of their intentions no later than 30 minutes after the clearance void time if not airborne. The facility delivering a clearance void time to a pilot shall issue a time check.

"Hold for release" instructions shall be used when necessary to inform a pilot or a controller that a departure clearance is not valid until additional instructions are received. When issuing hold for release instructions, include departure delay information. When conditions allow, release the aircraft as soon as possible.

Release times shall be issued to pilots when necessary to specify the earliest time an aircraft may depart. The facility issuing a release time to a pilot shall include a time check.

D. Sequencing Delays

When aircraft elect to take delay on the ground before departure, issue departure clearances to them in the order in which the requests for clearance were originally made if practicable.

E. Departure Coordination

The transferring facility shall coordinate prior to the departure of an aircraft if the departure point is less than 15 minutes' flying time from the boundary of the airspace of the transferring aircraft. If multiple clearances are given, coordination must be completed within 3 minutes of the last clearance issued. If automated systems are used, the time may be reduced to 5 minutes.

F. Information to be forwarded to the receiving facility

   1. Aircraft identification

   2. Point of departure

   3. Assumed or subsequent departure time

   4. Altitude data

   5. Applicable restrictions

   6. Forward actual departure when time differs by more than 3 minutes from assumed departure time.

G. VFR Release of IFR Departure

If traffic permits, inform the pilot of the frequency and where and/or when to contact center. If unable to issue clearance due to traffic, inform the pilot and suggest the delay be taken on the ground. If the pilot insists on departing IFR, the terminal facility informs the center of the pilot's intentions and departure time.

DEPARTURE PROCEDURES EXAMPLE 1

1. TIME: 1200   RUNWAY: 3

REP891		T → NE	↑ 150	MIO	PNC V2 FYV	
		TR 120/				
B727/A		⇒ V2				D-A
		1200/			LV30	
T480		PNC P1200		150		

Write the phraseology and mark the strip to issue a clearance for REP891 to FYV airport that will *not* permit REP891 to proceed over the PNC VORTAC.

<u>"REPUBLIC EIGHT NINETY-ONE CLEARED TO FAYETTEVILLE AIRPORT, VIA DEPART NORTHEAST, TURN RIGHT FLY HEADING ONE TWO ZERO UNTIL JOINING VICTOR TWO, VICTOR TWO, CLIMB AND MAINTAIN ONE FIVE THOUSAND, CONTACT AERO CENTER ONE TWO FOUR POINT ZERO LEAVING THREE THOUSAND."</u>

2. TIME: 1200

EAL628		T → SW	↑ 100	AMA	END V2 AMA	
		TR 300/				
CV58/B		⇒ V2				D-A
		1200/			LV30	
T280		END P1200		110		ZAB

Write the phraseology and mark the strip to issue a clearance to EAL628. Due to traffic, you need the aircraft to take off southwest and to make a right turn without proceeding to the END VORTAC.

Obtain pilot concurrence for direction of takeoff and turn.

<u>"EASTERN SIX TWENTY-EIGHT CLEARED FROM ENID AIRPORT TO AMARILLO AIRPORT VIA DEPART SOUTHWEST, TURN RIGHT FLY HEADING THREE ZERO ZERO UNTIL JOINING VICTOR TWO, VICTOR TWO, CLIMB AND MAINTAIN ONE ZERO THOUSAND, CONTACT AERO CENTER ONE TWO FOUR POINT ZERO LEAVING THREE THOUSAND."</u>

3. TIME: 1200

N265Q		T → S – MIO ↑	↑ 80 × 6 W ↕ 50	PNC	MIO V2 ABQ/0123	
BE65/B						D-A
		1200/			LV30	
T175		MIO P1200		80		

Write the phraseology and mark the strip to issue a clearance to Miami radio for N265Q. Due to en route traffic on V7 you need the aircraft to be at or below 5,000 feet six west of MIO VORTAC.

First obtain/solicit the direction of takeoff from the pilot.

"QUEEN AIR TWO SIX FIVE QUEBEC CLEARED FROM MIAMI AIRPORT TO ALBUQUERQUE AIRPORT, VIA DEPART SOUTH DIRECT MIAMI VORTAC VICTOR TWO, CROSS SIX MILES WEST MIAMI VORTAC AT OR BELOW FIVE THOUSAND, CLIMB AND MAINTAIN EIGHT THOUSAND, CONTACT AERO CENTER ONE TWO FIVE POINT ZERO LEAVING THREE THOUSAND."

DEPARTURE PROCEDURES
EXAMPLE 2

TIME: 1200

N1578Y		T → S – MIO ↑	↑ 100	MLC	MIO V9 MLC	
BE55/B						D- PRYOR
		1200/				
T180		MIO P1200		100		

Write the phraseology and mark the strip to issue a clearance to MIO radio for N1578Y. Due to traffic you *cannot* clear the aircraft as filed and decide you must clear the aircraft to prior and later clear the aircraft via V9. Also, you wish to have the aircraft depart south direct M1O.

Obtain concurrence for direction of takeoff from pilot.

"BARON ONE FIVE SEVEN EIGHT YANKEE CLEARED FROM MIAMI AIRPORT TO PRIOR INTERSECTION VIA DEPART SOUTH DIRECT MIAMI VORTAC VICTOR NINER, CLIMB AND MAINTAIN ONE ZERO THOUSAND, EXPECT FURTHER CLEARANCE VIA VICTOR NINE MCALESTER."

DEPARTURE PROCEDURES
END-OF-LESSON TEST

DIRECTIONS: *Items 1, 2, and 4 through 10 are multiple-choice. Indicate your selection by circling the appropriate letter for each test item. Item 3 is a completion statement. Fill in the blanks with the appropriate words or phrases. Correct answers appear at the end of the chapter.*

1. The normal clearance limit specified in a departure clearance is
   (A) the approach fix serving destination airport.
   (B) a short-range fix to expedite traffic.
   (C) the point at which the aircraft leaves controlled airspace.
   (D) the destination airport.

2. What departure clearance item(s) may be specified at airports in a control zone that do **not** have a tower?
   (A) Direction of takeoff, turn, heading
   (B) Departure restrictions
   (C) Standard instrument departure
   (D) SIDs, departure restrictions, and direction of takeoff, turn, or heading

3. IFR departure clearance compatibility may be verified by asking the pilot if items obtained/solicited will allow the pilot to comply with

   _____ or

   _____

4. The controller may assign a SID when
   (A) requested by the tower.   (B) necessary.
   (C) traffic is moderate to heavy.   (D) weather is below VFR.

5. What is necessary in order to use an abbreviated departure clearance?
   (A) The pilot must request it.
   (B) It must be issued through a tower.
   (C) The procedure must be covered by a letter of agreement.
   (D) The route of flight must not have been changed.

6. What must always be stated in an abbreviated clearance?
   (A) Route of flight   (B) En route altitude
   (C) Transition   (D) SID and transition

7. When delays are in progress at the destination airports and aircraft elect to take their delays on the ground at the departure airport, you should issue departure clearances
   (A) based upon proposed departure times.
   (B) in the order requests were made, if practicable.
   (C) to jets before piston-driven aircraft.
   (D) in the following order: air carrier, military, and general aviation.

8. Unless automated transfer of data will occur, you must coordinate proposed departures within _____ flying minutes of a receiving facility's boundary.
   (A) 5   (B) 10   (C) 15   (D) 30

9. Actual departure time need **not** be forwarded if within _____ minutes of assumed departure time.
   (A) 2   (B) 3   (C) 5   (D) 15

10. If you are unable to authorize a VFR release for an IFR aircraft because of traffic conditions, what information should you relay to the pilot?
    (A) Give an estimated departure clearance time.
    (B) Advise the pilot you cannot issue a clearance, and give traffic information.
    (C) Advise flight plan is cancelled.
    (D) Advise you cannot issue a clearance, and suggest the pilot delay on the ground.

DEPARTURE SEPARATION CHART

MIN		DME
1	COURSES DIVERGE (BY AT LEAST 45 DEGREES) IMMEDIATELY AFTER TAKEOFF	✕
2	COURSES DIVERGE (BY AT LEAST 45 DEGREES) WITHIN 5 MIN. AFTER TAKEOFF	✕
✕	COURSES DIVERGE (BY AT LEAST 45 DEGREES) WITHIN 13 N.M. AFTER TAKEOFF	**3**
3	SECOND AIRCRAFT CLIMBS THRU ALTITUDE OF FIRST AIRCRAFT	**5**
3	LEAD AIRCRAFT AT LEAST 44 KNOTS FASTER	**5**
5	LEAD AIRCRAFT AT LEAST 22 KNOTS FASTER	**10**
10	LEAD AIRCRAFT LESS THAN 22 KNOTS FASTER	**20**

COURSE

ALTITUDE

TAS

SAME OR ADJACENT AIRPORT

DIRECT PILOT-CONTROLLER COMM

LESSON 20
ARRIVAL AND APPROACH PROCEDURES

Having completed departure procedures, we continue adding to the separation rules. You are now ready for the methods of handling arrival aircraft. To be an effective air traffic controller, you must be able to handle arriving aircraft as well as departure and en route aircraft.

Objectives

Given air traffic situations, without references, and in accordance with 7110.65, you will:

1. Select terminology associated with instrument approach procedures.

2. List conditions that must be met to issue an approach clearance.

3. Issue arrival/approach clearances, using standard phraseology.

4. Select and issue

    a. Arrival information to
        (1) Approach controls.
        (2) VFR towers.
        (3) FSS's.

    b. Advance descent clearances, using standard phraseology and procedures.

Lesson Guide

A. Definitions

    1.   Approach Clearance

        Authorization by air traffic control for a pilot to make an instrument approach.

    2.   Instrument Approach

        A series of predetermined maneuvers for the orderly transfer of an aircraft under instrument flight conditions from the beginning of initial approach to a landing or to a point from which a landing may be made visually.

    3.   Approach Chart

        A portrayal of aeronautical data that is required to make an instrument approach to an airport.

B. Arrival Information

    1.   Clearance Information

        a.   Name of fix or airport.

b.   Route of flight including STAR and STAR transition, if appropriate.

c.   Assigned altitude if different.

d.   Holding information, EFC, and additional delay information as required.

e.   Further communications instructions.

2.   Destination Airport

Specify the destination airport as a clearance limit when airport traffic control service is not provided.

3.   Forwarding Information—Arrival Information to Approach Control

a.   Aircraft identification.

b.   Type aircraft including heavy, if appropriate.

c.   Equipment suffix.

d.   Clearance limit and estimate at clearance limit.

e.   Altitude data, including restrictions inside the transfer control point.

f.   Destination airport if other than primary airport.

g.   Pertinent remarks.

h.   Transfer control point.

Forward this information to approach control prior to the transfer of control point.

4.   Forwarding Information—VFR Towers and FSS

a.   Aircraft identification.

b.   Type aircraft.

c.   NAVAID and center estimate of NAVAID serving the airport.

d.   Destination airport if other than primary airport.

e.   Pertinent remarks

Forward this information soon enough to permit adjustment of the traffic flow.

C.   Arrival Procedures

Indicate arriving aircraft by down arrow in space 16 of the flight progress strip.

D.   Approach Clearance

1.   When to Issue

Issue approach clearance after preceding aircraft has landed. (It takes 7 minutes to make approach from estimate over fix.) You must receive landing time from tower or FSS, or been told to contact tower control by approach.

Clearance is issued by the controller only if approved separation is established and maintained.

2. Conditions

   If the arrival is 3 minutes or more from the approach fix, hold the arrival and issue the departure clearance with vertical/lateral restrictions. Obtain a position report from the departure establishing lateral separation, then issue the approach clearance to the arrival.

   If the arrival is less than 3 minutes from the approach fix, issue the approach clearance and hold the departure. At a VFR tower location, release the departure with visual separation approved. At the FSS locations, hold the departure until the arrival lands.

E. Issuing Approach Clearance

   1. Pilot's Choice—Authorize pilots to execute approach of their choice.

      Phraseology:

      "CLEARED FOR APPROACH."

   2. Non-ATC Service Airports

      At airports without air traffic control services, include the destination airport with approach clearance.

   3. Approach Control Location

      At approach control locations the en route facility clears the arriving aircraft to the clearance limit. The approach control facility issues approach clearance and provides separation for aircraft under their control.

F. Particular Approach Requirements

   To require a particular approach, specify in the approach clearance the name of the approach as published on the approach chart.

G. Unpublished Routes

   Issue approach clearances for aircraft on unpublished routes after the aircraft is established on a published route or established on a segment of the approach procedure. Assign an altitude with the approach clearance until the aircraft is established on the published route or segment of approach procedure. The assigned altitude must ensure terrain and obstruction clearance.

H. Advance Descent—For Arrival Near Common Boundary

   Coordinate with the receiving facility a lower altitude to allow normal descent and speed reduction.

ARRIVAL AND APPROACH PROCEDURES
EXAMPLE 1

DIRECTIONS: *Mark each strip and write the phraseology specifying the transfer of control point for passing each inbound in exercise items 1 through 3.*

1. TIME: 1410

TW421	PNC			170√↓60		LAX GCK V8 TUL	
			㉑ ↓ ↓	×17NW ↕			F
B727/A	1412	14		100			
		22					
T450		TUL					20NW

INBOUND: "TWA FOUR TWENTY-ONE BOEING SEVEN TWENTY-SEVEN SLANT ALFA ESTIMATED TULSA VORTAC ONE FOUR TWO ONE DESCENDING TO SIX THOUSAND WITH RESTRICTION TO CROSS ONE SEVEN MILES NORTHWEST TULSA VORTAC AT OR BELOW ONE ZERO THOUSAND. YOUR CONTROL TWO ZERO MILES NORTHWEST TULSA VORTAC."

2. TIME: 0913

AA241	CDS		26 ㉓ ↓	170√↓⑥⓪	OKC	LAX V6 OKC	
				170/40E			F
B727/A	0913	09		CDS×@60			
		23					25W
T450		YUKON					OKC

INBOUND: "AMERICAN TWO FORTY-ONE BOEING SEVEN TWENTY-SEVEN SLANT ALFA ESTIMATED YUKON ZERO NINER TWO THREE AT SIX THOUSAND. YOUR CONTROL TWO FIVE MILES WEST OF OKLAHOMA CITY VORTAC."

3. TIME: 0944

N242P	AFTON		⑥⓪√		STL V4 TUL/1002	
		⓪⓪				F
BE20/A	0948	10				
		01				
T240		TUL				PRYOR

INBOUND: "SUPER KING AIR TWO FOUR TWO PAPA B-E TWENTY SLANT ALFA ESTIMATED TULSA VORTAC ONE ZERO ZERO ZERO AT SIX THOUSAND YOUR CONTROL PRIOR."

ARRIVAL AND APPROACH PROCEDURES EXAMPLE 2

DIRECTIONS: *Write the phraseology for passing each inbound and for issuing the arrival clearance to the aircraft. Mark strips as appropriate.*

1. TIME: 1545

N234	GCK 1540	⑤⑨ 15 59	70✓ ↓	DEN GCK V1 END	APCH
C310/A					APCH
T180		END		PT CC	1545

INBOUND: "ENID RADIO, AERO CENTER, INBOUND, CESSNA TWO THREE FOUR, CESSNA THREE TEN SLANT ALFA, ESTIMATED ENID VORTAC ONE FIVE FIVE NINER FOR APPROACH, GD."

ARRIVAL CLEARANCE: "CESSNA TWO THREE FOUR, CLEARED FOR APPROACH TO ENID AIRPORT, CONTACT ENID RADIO PROCEDURE TURN."

2. TIME: 1610

A67850	CDS 1614	~~34~~ ③① 16 34	150✓ ↓ 60 ✕ @60	SRF V6 OKC	
C130/A					F
T310		OKC YUKON	60		25W OKC

INBOUND: "OKLAHOMA CITY APPROACH, AERO CENTER, INBOUND, AIR FORCE SIX SEVEN EIGHT FIVE ZERO, C-ONE THIRTY SLANT ALFA, ESTIMATED YUKON ONE SIX THREE ONE AT SIX THOUSAND, YOUR CONTROL TWO FIVE MILES WEST OKLAHOMA CITY VORTAC."

ARRIVAL CLEARANCE: "ACTIVE AT CHILDRESS, AIR FORCE SIX SEVEN EIGHT FIVE ZERO, CLEARED TO YUKON INTERSECTION, CROSS YUKON AT AND MAINTAIN SIX THOUSAND, GD." (REQ. CC)
WHEN AIRCRAFT CALLS: "AIR FORCE SIX SEVEN EIGHT FIVE ZERO, AERO CENTER, OKLAHOMA CITY ALTIMETER TWO NINER NINER TWO, CONTACT OKLAHOMA CITY APPROACH TWO FIVE NINER POINT ONE THREE ZERO MILES WEST OKLAHOMA CITY VORTAC."

3. TIME: 1615

A16850	SNL 1618	(30) 16 30 PNC	170✓ ×10S SNL ↑90	SAT V5 PNC	APCH
H/C141/A					APCH
T420				PT	1615

INBOUND: "AIR FORCE ONE SIX EIGHT FIVE ZERO, HEAVY C-ONE FORTY-ONE, ESTIMATED PONCA CITY VORTAC ONE SIX THREE ZERO, FOR APPROACH, GD."

ARRIVAL CLEARANCE: "AIR FORCE ONE SIX EIGHT FIVE ZERO, CLEARED FOR APPROACH, CROSS ONE ZERO MILES SOUTH OF SHAWNEE VORTAC AT OR ABOVE NINER THOUSAND, CONTACT PONCA CITY TOWER TWO FIVE EIGHT POINT ONE PROCEDURE TURN."

4. TIME: 1600

N456	PNC 1600	(25) 16 MIO	70	AMA V2 MIO	APCH
C310/A					APCH
T180			PT		1600

INBOUND: "... CESSNA FOUR FIVE SIX, CESSNA THREE TEN, ESTIMATED MIAMI VORTAC ONE SIX TWO FIVE, FOR APPROACH, GD."

CLEARANCE THRU D1: "ACTIVE AT PONCA CITY: CESSNA FOUR FIVE SIX CLEARED FOR APPROACH TO MIAMI AIRPORT."

AFTER AIRCRAFT CONTACTS D2: "CESSNA FOUR FIVE SIX, MIAMI ALTIM-ETER TWO NINER NINER TWO, CONTACT MIAMI RADIO PROCEDURE TURN."

ARRIVAL AND APPROACH PROCEDURES
EXAMPLE 3

DIRECTIONS: *Mark each strip and write the phraseology specifying the transfer of control point for passing each inbound in exercise items 1 through 4.*

1. TIME: 0940   Runway: 07

N78A	BLUFF	⑤④	↓	80		ICT V13 END	APCH
	0941	09					NE
C310/A							H 070
							1004
T180		END				CC	

N356N	AMA	㊿	↓	90√ ───		AMA V2 END	APCH
		09		×8W ↕ 70 ↘			APCH
C320/A							0940
		50					PT
T190	D0928	END				CTL	

A. N356N was cleared for approach as shown. Write the phraseology used when clearing N356N for approach.

"CESSNA THREE FIVE SIX NOVEMBER, CROSS EIGHT MILES WEST OF ENID VORTAC AT OR BELOW SEVEN THOUSAND, CLEARED FOR APPROACH TO THE ENID AIRPORT, CONTACT ENID RADIO PROCEDURE TURN.

B. What condition(s) must exist before N78A may be cleared for approach?

N356N MUST HAVE LANDED OR CANCELED IFR.

2. TIME: 1501   RUNWAY: 36

EAL93	SNL	⓪⑤	↓	70√		OKC V6 MLC	APCH
	1450	15					N
CV58/B							H 360
		05					
T300		MLC				CTL	1015

EAL 41		T→N MLC	↑ 90	HOT	MLC V6 ATL	D-A
			×5E ↕ 60		LV30	
CV58/B						
		1500/			RP5E/	
T300		MLC P1500		90		ZME

EAL41 has been issued a departure clearance as shown. Under what condition may EAL93 be cleared for approach? Record the clearance on the flight progress strip.

WHEN EAL41 REPORTS PASSING 5 MILES EAST OF MCALESTER VORTAC

3.   TIME: 1001   RUNWAY: 21

N422X	MIO	17	60✓	END	MIO V2 END	SW
	0952	10				H 210
M021/A						
		16				
T190		PNC				1026

AAL 25	END	10	310		DEN AMA V2 PNC	APCH
	1000	10	×17W ↕ 50			APCH
B727/A						1001
	1000				PT	
T450		PNC	RL50			

AAL25, landing Ponca City, is requesting descent clearance. Write the procedure and record the information on the flight progress strips for issuing approach clearance to AAL25 and maintaining separation with N422X.

" PAPER STOP" N422X, THEN ISSUE APPROACH CLEARANCE TO AAL25 TO CROSS 17 WEST OF PNC VORTAC AT OR BELOW 5,000, TO REPORT LEAVING 5,000.

4.   TIME: 1700   RUNWAY:18

AAL25	PNC	⑤05	110✓		AMA V2 MIO	APCH
	1655	17	×5W ↕ 70			H ^{5}180
B727/A						1715
		06				APCH
T450	1655	MIO			CTL	1702

N422X	FYV		03		60√		PNC	FYV V2 AMA	
	1613	17					1725		
M021/A									
		00	00						
T190	1611		MIO					RP 5W/1702	

A. What conditions are required for clearing AAL25 for approach at Miami Airport and maintaining separation with N422X? Record required information on the strips, using approved strip marking.

REQUEST N422X REPORT CLEAR OF HOLDING PATTERN AIRSPACE, PASSING 5 MILES WEST OF MIO VORTAC, OR OBTAIN DME PASSAGE. WHEN N422X REPORTS, CLEAR AAL25 FOR APPROACH TO CROSS 5 WEST MIO VORTAC AT OR ABOVE 7,000.

B. The time is now 1702, and the required conditions have been met. Write the approach clearance phraseology and record the information on the flight progress strips.

"AMERICAN TWENTY-FIVE, CROSS FIVE MILES WEST OF MIAMI VORTAC AT OR ABOVE SEVEN THOUSAND, CLEARED FOR APPROACH TO MIAMI AIRPORT, CONTACT MIAMI RADIO PROCEDURE TURN."

5. TIME: 1026   RUNWAY: 36

M41376	PRX		㉛		120⌐			HOU V7 MLC	APCH
	1022	10							APCH
C141/A									
									1026
T400			MLC					CC	

N77T	PRX		23		100√		TUL	MSY V11 MLC V7 MKC/	
	1010	10					1033	1059	
CV58/D									
		22	22						
T270			MLC					17NW/1026	

A. When may M41376 be cleared for approach:

WHEN N77T REPORTS PASSING 17 MILES NORTHWEST OF MLC VORTAC (COULD USE FORCE 20).

B. **Write the phraseology for the procedure to clear M41376 for approach. Record appropriate information on flight progress strips.**

"CONVAIR SEVEN SEVEN TANGO REPORT PASSING ONE SEVEN MILES NORTHWEST OF MCALESTER VORTAC. (AFTER N77T REPORTS) MAC ONE SEVEN SIX CLEARED FOR APPROACH CONTACT MCALESTER TOWER (ONE ONE EIGHT POINT TWO) PROCEDURE TURN."

ARRIVAL AND APPROACH PROCEDURES END-OF-LESSON TEST

DIRECTIONS: *Items 1 through 16 are multiple-choice. Indicate your selection by circling the appropriate letter for each test item. Correct answers appear at the end of the chapter.*

1. Authorization by ATC for a pilot to make an instrument approach is the definition of
   (A) instrument approach.
   (B) approach clearance.
   (C) approach chart.
   (D) pilot's choice of approach.

2. Arrival information must be forwarded to approach control facilities
   (A) before issuing descent clearance.
   (B) in time to provide airport advisory service.
   (C) prior to transfer of control.
   (D) in time to permit adjustment of traffic flow.

3. TIME: 1620

UAL 80	MLC			100 ↓ 60	PRX V7 MLC TUL 1 TUL	
			30	↓		
DC8/A	1622	16				F
						30N
T480			TUL			MLC

The phraseology to forward the above arrival estimate is
   (A) "UNITED EIGHTY D-C EIGHT ESTIMATED TULSA ONE SIX THREE ZERO DESCENDING TO SIX THOUSAND, YOUR CONTROL THREE ZERO MILES NORTH MCALESTER."
   (B) "UNITED EIGHTY D-C EIGHT SLANT ALFA ESTIMATED TULSA ONE SIX THREE ZERO SIX THOUSAND, YOUR CONTROL THREE ZERO NORTH OF MCALESTER VORTAC."
   (C) "UNITED EIGHTY D-C EIGHT SLANT ALFA ESTIMATED TULSA ONE SIX THREE ZERO DESCENDING TO SIX THOUSAND, YOUR CONTROL MCALESTER."
   (D) "UNITED EIGHTY D-C EIGHT SLANT ALFA ESTIMATED TULSA VORTAC ONE SIX THREE ZERO DESCENDING TO SIX THOUSAND, YOUR CONTROL THREE ZERO MILES NORTH OF MCALESTER VORTAC."

4. What arrival information would be forwarded to a nonapproach control tower?
   (A) Appropriate equipment suffix and ETA
   (B) ETA, type of approach, and control point

(C) Type of approach, ETA, and EFC
(D) Aircraft ID, type of aircraft, estimate for NAVAID serving destination airport, and type of approach

5. When an aircraft is landing at an airport served by a nonapproach control tower, coordination must be accomplished
   (A) 15 minutes prior to arrival.
   (B) at least 3 minutes prior to arrival.
   (C) in time to permit adjustment of traffic flow.
   (D) in time to permit traffic advisory service.

6. TIME: 1537

N456	GCK			90	DEN V1 END	
		50	↓			
C310/A	1632	16				
T180		END				

The phraseology to forward the above arrival estimate is
(A) "CESSNA FOUR FIVE SIX SLANT ALFA, ESTIMATED ENID ONE SIX FIVE ZERO FOR APPROACH."
(B) "CESSNA FOUR FIVE SIX CESSNA THREE TEN, ESTIMATE ENID ONE SIX FIVE ZERO DESCENDING TO SIX THOUSAND FOR APPROACH."
(C) "CESSNA FOUR FIVE SIX CESSNA THREE TEN, ESTIMATED ENID VORTAC ONE SIX FIVE ZERO FOR APPROACH."
(D) "CESSNA FOUR FIVE SIX CESSNA THREE TEN, ESTIMATED ONE SIX FIVE ZERO FOR APPROACH."

7. When issuing holding instructions to an arriving aircraft, the controller shall
   (A) advise the aircraft when to contact the next facility.
   (B) issue current weather.
   (C) issue approach sequence.
   (D) issue an EFC.

8. When an arriving aircraft is cleared to an outer fix at a facility served by an approach control, transfer of communications should be accomplished
   (A) early enough to allow approach control to clear the aircraft beyond the fix before it reaches the fix.
   (B) prior to descent clearance.
   (C) at the clearance limit.
   (D) with the approval of approach control.

9. An aircraft can be cleared for an approach
   (A) any time it is requested.
   (B) when the preceding aircraft has departed.
   (C) any time, if it has canceled IFR flight plan.
   (D) when the preceding aircraft has landed.

10. In determining the operational priority between an arrival and a departure, the arrival has priority when the departure clearance is requested and the
    (A) arrival is less than 3 minutes from the approach fix.
    (B) departure follows a preceding en route aircraft over the fix.
    (C) arrival is 3 minutes or more from the approach fix.
    (D) arrival will take 7 minutes to make the approach using visual separation.

11. Approach clearance can be issued by a controller
    (A) whenever it is deemed necessary.
    (B) only if approved separation is established and maintained.
    (C) if the aircraft involved is in contact with the tower.
    (D) only when the preceding aircraft has canceled.

12. TIME: 1710   RUNWAY: 36

N124N	TUL		70✓	PNC V7 MLC	APCH
		⑳			
C310/A	1702	17			APCH
				PT	
T180		MLC		30NE/1710	1710

The phraseology to issue approach clearance marked on the above strip is "CESSNA ONE TWO FOUR NOVEMBER CLEARED FOR
    (A) APPROACH."
    (B) V-O-R APPROACH."
    (C) STRAIGHT-IN APPROACH TO MCALESTER."
    (D) APPROACH TO THE MCALESTER AIRPORT."

13. What is required to clear an aircraft for approach at an FSS location?
    (A) The runway must be specified.
    (B) The phrase "ATC clears" is used.
    (C) The airport name must be specified in the clearance.
    (D) The pilot must execute a special instrument approach.

14. At an approach control location, approach clearance is the responsibility of the
    (A) FSS located at the airport involved.
    (B) VFR control tower.
    (C) en route controller working the aircraft.
    (D) approach control facility.

15. The phraseology used to clear a pilot for a particular approach is
    (A) "CLEARED FOR APPROACH."
    (B) "CLEARED FOR (type) APPROACH."
    (C) "CLEARED FOR (specific procedure to be flown) APPROACH."
    (D) "CLEARED FOR STANDARD INSTRUMENT APPROACH PROCEDURE."

16. When an aircraft is landing at an airport near the common boundary in an adjacent center's airspace, the controller shall
    (A) forward the flight data at least 1 hour in advance.
    (B) coordinate and issue clearances that will allow for normal descent and speed reduction.
    (C) ask if the pilot will accept a lower altitude.
    (D) issue an approach clearance and advise the receiving controller.

LESSON 21
HOLDING AIRCRAFT

In previous exercises you have issued clearances for en route and departing aircraft using the prescribed format and phraseology. You must also ensure the orderly sequence of en route and arriving aircraft. The issuance of holding instructions is one means of doing this.

Objectives

Given air traffic situations, without references, and in accordance with 7110.65, you will:

1. Identify when to issue

   a. Holding instructions.

   b. Clearance beyond a clearance limit.

2. Select and use designated phraseology and strip marking when

   a. Issuing holding instructions to aircraft in charted and uncharted holding patterns.

   b. Clearing aircraft beyond a clearance limit.

Lesson Guide

A. Holding

A predetermined maneuver that keeps aircraft within a specified airspace while awaiting further clearance from air traffic control.

B. Holding Fix

A specified fix identifiable to a pilot by NAVAIDs or visual reference to the ground. Used as a reference to the ground, and also as a reference point in establishing and maintaining the position of an aircraft while holding.

C. EFC—Expect Further Clearance (time)

The time a pilot can expect to receive clearance beyond a clearance limit.

D. Standard Holding Pattern

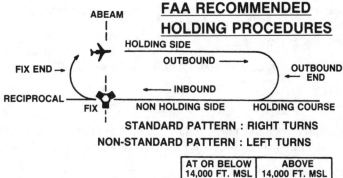

E. ZAE Holding Pattern

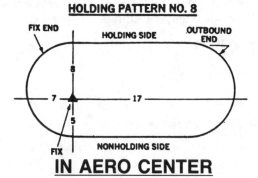

F. Clearance to Holding Fix

Issue clearances to a holding fix at least 5 minutes before clearance limit estimate to allow the pilot to start a speed reduction. When issuing holding instructions, notify the pilot of the delay expected.

G. Noncharted Holding

When issuing holding instructions to a noncharted holding pattern, include these items as necessary:

1. Clearance limit.

2. Route change, if applicable.

3. Direction of hold from fix.

4. Holding fix.

5. Airway, radial, course, or bearing on which aircraft is to hold.

6. Leg length in miles.

7. Direction of turns (if left turns are made or pilot requests).

8. EFC (Expect Further Clearance).

H.   Charted Holding

Only one in Aero Center is at Tulsa. Clearance items issued:

1.   Clearance limit.

2.   Direction of hold and statement "as published."

3.   EFC.

Issue complete holding when requested by the pilot. When direction of hold is omitted, aircraft will comply with charted hold.

I.   Clearance Beyond the Fix

When no delay is expected and an aircraft is cleared to holding for separation purposes, inform the pilot no delay is expected. You may eliminate holding instructions and an EFC but must issue a clearance limit.

To issue a clearance beyond the fix issue: (1) New clearance limit or approach clearance; (2) Route of flight; (3) Altitude, if changed.

J.   Clearance Items to Issue

1.   Clearance limit/approach.

2.   Route of flight.

3.   Altitude, if different from present.

HOLDING AIRCRAFT EXERCISE

DIRECTIONS: *Write the phraseology and mark strips accordingly.*

1. TIME: 1620

N76332	FYV			80√	PNC	STL V2 LAX/2305	
	1549						S
CV58/D		16²⁵					180
		26					1030
T250		MIO					

Clear N76332 to the Los Angeles airport.

"CONVAIR THREE THREE TWO, CLEARED TO LOS ANGELES AIRPORT VIA VICTOR TWO."

2. TIME: 1603

A31725	CDS			150√	LSV V6 OKC V4 TUL	
	1543					JONES
T 33/N		16¹⁰				-NE
		10				V4
T355	OKC				JONES 1614	1624

Issue holding instructions at Jones NE on V4.

"AIR FORCE THREE ONE SEVEN TWO FIVE CLEARED TO JONES INTER-SECTION, HOLD NORTHEAST ON VICTOR FOUR, EXPECT FURTHER CLEARANCE ONE SIX TWO FOUR."

3. TIME: 0950

AAL47	MLC			170√	MIO	PRX V7 MKC	
	0950						
H/B747/A		09⁵⁵					-NW
		55					
T490		TUL					1005

Issue holding as charted at TUL.

"AMERICAN FORTY-SEVEN HEAVY CLEARED TO TULSA VORTAC, HOLD NORTHWEST AS PUBLISHED, EXPECT FURTHER CLEARANCE ONE ZERO ZERO FIVE."

4. TIME: 1012

BNF705	PRX 1010			160√	TUL	HOU PRX V7 TUL	N
H/B747/A		10¹⁸				TUL 1	360
			18				
T480		MLC				EFC VIA TUL 1	1028

Issue holding at MLC with EFC as TUL #1.

"BRANIFF SEVEN OH FIVE HEAVY CLEARED TO MCALESTER VORTAC, HOLD NORTH ON THREE SIX ZERO RADIAL, EXPECT FURTHER CLEARANCE VIA TULSA ONE ARRIVAL, EXPECT FURTHER CLEARANCE ONE ZERO TWO EIGHT."

HOLDING AIRCRAFT
END-OF-LESSON TEST

DIRECTIONS: *Items 1, 2, 3, 4, 5, 6, 7, 8, and 10 are multiple-choice. Indicate your selection by circling the appropriate letter for each test item. For item 9, fill in blanks with correct phraseology and mark spaces on strip correctly. Correct answers appear at the end of the chapter.*

1. You anticipate a delay. When should holding be issued?
   (A) Before the aircraft reaches the clearance limit
   (B) At least 5 minutes before the aircraft reaches the clearance limit
   (C) At least 10 minutes before the aircraft reaches the clearance limit
   (D) In time for the pilot to slow the aircraft

2. An aircraft is estimating Tulsa VORTAC at 0826. If you are anticipating a delay, holding instructions should be issued no later than
   (A) 0816.   (B) 0821.   (C) 0823.   (D) 0826.

   For questions 3, 4, and 6, select the correct phraseology to issue the clearance indicated on each strip.

3.

DAL99	AMA 1816		↓	170√	LAS V2 END .	NE 070
B727/A		18^{27}				
		26				
T410	END					1840

   (A) "DELTA NINETY-NINE, HOLD NORTHEAST OF ENID VORTAC, EXPECT FURTHER CLEARANCE ONE EIGHT FOUR ZERO."
   (B) "DELTA NINETY-NINE, HOLD NORTHEAST ON THE ZERO SEVEN ZERO RADIAL, EXPECT FURTHER CLEARANCE ONE EIGHT FOUR ZERO."
   (C) "DELTA NINETY-NINE, CLEARED TO ENID VORTAC, HOLD NORTHEAST ON THE ZERO SEVEN ZERO RADIAL, EXPECT FURTHER CLEARANCE ONE EIGHT FOUR ZERO."
   (D) "DELTA NINETY-NINE, CLEARED TO ENID VORTAC, HOLD NORTHEAST, EXPECT FURTHER CLEARANCE ONE EIGHT FOUR ZERO."

4.

N2150K	PRX			100√		MSY V7 MLC/0655		
			↓					N
BE90/A	0620	06⁴³						360
			41					LT
T190		MLC						0645

(A) "KING AIR FIVE ZERO KILO, CLEARED TO MCALESTER VORTAC, HOLD NORTH, LEFT TURNS, EXPECT FURTHER CLEARANCE ZERO SIX FOUR FIVE."

(B) "KING AIR FIVE ZERO KILO, HOLD NORTH ON MCALESTER THREE SIX ZERO RADIAL, LEFT TURNS, EXPECT FURTHER CLEARANCE ZERO SIX FOUR FIVE."

(C) "KING AIR FIVE ZERO KILO, CLEARED TO MCALESTER VORTAC, HOLD NORTH ON THE THREE SIX ZERO RADIAL, LEFT TURNS, EXPECT FURTHER CLEARANCE ZERO SIX FOUR FIVE."

(D) "KING AIR FIVE ZERO KILO, CLEARED TO MCALESTER VORTAC, HOLD NORTH ON THE THREE SIX ZERO RADIAL, EXPECT FURTHER CLEARANCE ZERO SIX FOUR FIVE."

5. When holding instructions are issued, the direction of turns is always issued
   (A) if right turns are to be made.
   (B) at the controller's discretion.
   (C) if left turns are to be made.
   (D) if the aircraft is to be issued an indefinite delay.

6.

A25817	SLICK			130√	MIO	ABQ V4 TUL V7 MKC		
	2113							NW
T29/B		21³⁰						
			30					
T210		TUL						2135

(A) "AIR FORCE TWO FIVE EIGHT ONE SEVEN, HOLD NORTHWEST OF TULSA VORTAC, AS PUBLISHED, EXPECT FURTHER CLEARANCE TWO ONE THREE FIVE."

(B) "AIR FORCE TWO FIVE EIGHT ONE SEVEN, CLEARED TO TULSA VORTAC, HOLD NORTHWEST, AS PUBLISHED, EXPECT FURTHER CLEARANCE TWO ONE THREE FIVE."

(C) "AIR FORCE TWO FIVE EIGHT ONE SEVEN, HOLD NORTHWEST OF TULSA VORTAC, ON TULSA TWO EIGHT FIVE RADIAL, EXPECT FURTHER CLEARANCE TWO ONE THREE FIVE."

(D) "AIR FORCE TWO FIVE EIGHT ONE SEVEN, CLEARED TO TULSA VORTAC, HOLD IN THE CHARTED HOLDING PATTERN, NORTHWEST OF TULSA VORTAC, EXPECT FURTHER CLEARANCE TWO ONE THREE FIVE."

7. What is the correct phraseology for issuing holding instructions when the holding pattern is charted?
   (A) "CLEARED TO TULSA VORTAC, HOLD NORTHWEST, AS PUBLISHED, EXPECT FURTHER CLEARANCE (time)."
   (B) "CLEARED TO TULSA VORTAC, HOLD NORTHWEST, AS CHARTED, EXPECT FURTHER CLEARANCE (time)."
   (C) "CLEARED TO TULSA VORTAC, EXPECT FURTHER CLEARANCE (time)."
   (D) "CLEARED TO TULSA VORTAC, HOLD NORTHWEST. LEFT TURNS. EXPECT FURTHER CLEARANCE (time)."

8. Holding instructions may be omitted when
   (A) the holding pattern is charted.
   (B) no delay is expected.
   (C) the aircraft is more than 10 minutes from the clearance limit.
   (D) a standard pattern is flown.

9. TIME: 1023
   Clear EAL24 to DEN Airport and mark the strip.

EAL24	PRX		160√	PNC	HOU V7 MLC V11 PNC V8 DEN	
DC9/A	1020	10²⁸				
		29				
T480		MLC				

_____

_____

_____

10. Select the phraseology to reduce verbiage and clear an aircraft beyond a holding fix.
    (A) "CLEARED AS FILED" (B) "VIA LAST ROUTING CLEARED"
    (C) "VIA LAST ASSIGNED ROUTING" (D) "VIA LAST FILED ROUTE"

LESSON 22
INITIAL SEPARATION OF DEPARTURES/ARRIVALS AND VISUAL SEPARATION

In Chapter 3 we discussed en route separation. So far in Chapter 4, you have covered procedures for departing and arriving aircraft. As a controller, you will be required to handle aircraft in all three phases of flight. Now we will deal with the initial separation of arrivals and departures and how to authorize visual separation.

Objectives

Given air traffic situations, without references, and in accordance with 7110.65, you will select and apply standard phraseology and procedures for applying:

1. Initial separation between departing aircraft.

2. Visual separation within a control zone between arriving and departing aircraft.

Lesson Guide

A. General Information on Diverging Courses

Separate aircraft that will fly courses diverging by 45 degrees or more after separating the same or adjacent airports by use of one of the following minima: (1) When aircraft will fly diverging courses immediately after takeoff—1 minute until courses diverge. (2) Within 5 minutes after takeoff—2 minutes until courses diverge. (3) Within 13 miles DME after takeoff—3 miles until courses diverge.

Consider aircraft performance characteristics when applying initial separation to successive departing aircraft.

Flyback—A flyback exists when a departure aircraft will climb to or through the altitude of another aircraft (en route or previous departure) that is on an airway in the same quadrant as the airport. Flybacks are resolved either vertically or longitudinally; time does not clear up flybacks.

B. Departures on Same Course

Separate aircraft that will fly the same course when the following aircraft will climb through the altitude assigned to the leading aircraft by using a minimum of 3 minutes until the following aircraft passes through the assigned altitude of the leading aircraft, or 5 miles if both aircraft are using DME. The aircraft must be the same speed, or the trailing aircraft is slower. Neither aircraft is assigned an at or below crossing restriction.

C. Arrival/Departure Priority

If the arrival is 3 minutes or more from the approach fix, hold the arrival and issue departure clearance with vertical/lateral separation from the arrival.

Obtain a position report from the departure establishing lateral separation from the arrival. When that report is received, clear the arrival for approach.

If the arrival is less than 3 minutes from the approach fix, issue an approach clearance and hold the departure. At VFR tower locations release the departure with visual separation from the arrival. At FSS locations delay the departure until an arrival time is received.

D.   Visual Separation

Authorize a nonapproach control tower, within a control zone between an arrival and departure, approval to provide visual separation, provided other separation is approved before and after visual separation.

INITIAL SEPARATION OF DEPARTURES/ARRIVALS AND VISUAL SEPARATION EXERCISE 1

DIRECTIONS: *Complete exercise items 1 through 3, using the information given on the flight strips.*

1.   TIME: 1340   RUNWAY: 36

N795K		T→N ↑	↑ 100	MIO	MLC V9 MIO/0032	
		360/⇒V9				D-MIO
BE90/A		RLS1'<N34V				
		1340/				
T190		MLC P1345		100	LV30	

N34V		T→N ↑	↑ 100	OKC	MLC V6 OKC/0042	
		360/⇒V6				D-A
BE80/A						
		1340/				
T190		MLC P1345		100	LV 30	

Using the one minute rule, write the phraseology to clear both aircraft and mark the strips.

"KING AIR SEVEN NINER FIVE KILO, CLEARED TO MIAMI VORTAC VIA DEPART NORTH, FLY HEADING THREE SIX ZERO UNTIL JOINING VICTOR NINE, VICTOR NINE, CLIMB AND MAINTAIN ONE ZERO THOUSAND, CONTACT AERO CENTER ONE TWO FIVE POINT ZERO LEAVING THREE THOUSAND." RELEASE KING AIR SEVEN NINER FIVE KILO ONE MINUTE AFTER QUEEN AIR THREE FOUR VICTOR DEPARTS.

"QUEEN AIR THREE FOUR VICTOR, CLEARED TO OKLAHOMA CITY AIRPORT VIA DEPART NORTH, TURN LEFT, FLY HEADING THREE SIX ZERO UNTIL JOINING VICTOR SIX, VICTOR SIX, CLIMB AND MAINTAIN ONE ZERO THOUSAND, CONTACT AERO CENTER ONE TWO FIVE POINT ZERO LEAVING THREE THOUSAND."

2.   TIME: 1340   RUNWAY: 36

N795K		T→N -MLC RLS 2LN34V	↑100	MIO	MLC V9 MIO/0032	
BE90/A						D-MIO
		1842/				
T190		MLC P1345		100	LV 30	

N34V		↑	↑100	OKC	MLC V6 OKC/0042	
BE80/A						D-A
		1340/				
T190		MLC P1345		100	LV 30	

Using the two-minute rule, write the phraseology to clear both aircraft and mark the strips.

"KING AIR SEVEN NINER FIVE KILO, CLEARED TO MIAMI VORTAC VIA DEPART NORTH, DIRECT MCALESTER VORTAC, VICTOR NINE, CLIMB AND MAINTAIN ONE ZERO THOUSAND, CONTACT AERO CENTER ONE TWO FIVE POINT ZERO LEAVING THREE THOUSAND." RELEASE KING AIR SEVEN NINER FIVE KILO TWO MINUTES AFTER QUEEN AIR THREE FOUR VICTOR DEPARTS.

"QUEEN AIR THREE FOUR VICTOR, CLEARED TO OKLAHOMA CITY AIRPORT VIA DEPART NORTH, DIRECT MCALESTER VORTAC, VICTOR SIX, CLIMB AND MAINTAIN ONE ZERO THOUSAND, CONTACT AERO CENTER ONE TWO FIVE POINT ZERO LEAVING THREE THOUSAND."

3.   TIME: 0955   RUNWAY: 21

CO321		T→SW-PNC RLS<UAL617 RP 2NE	↑160 ↓60	OKC	PNC V3 OKC	
DC8/A			X COYLE			D-
		0956/	@60			COYLE
T450		PNC P1000		160	LV 30	

UA617		T→SW -PNC	↑170	TUL	PNC V8 TUL	
B727/A						D-A
		0955/			@ PNC	
T450		PNC P1000		170	RP 2NE	

Using the three-minute rule, write the phraseology to clear both aircraft and mark the strips.

"CONTINENTAL THREE TWENTY-ONE, CLEARED TO COYLE INTERSEC-TION VIA DEPART SOUTHWEST, DIRECT PONCA CITY VORTAC VICTOR THREE, CLIMB AND MAINTAIN ONE SIX THOUSAND CROSS COYLE AT AND MAINTAIN SIX THOUSAND CONTACT AERO CENTER ONE TWO FOUR POINT ZERO LEAVING THREE THOUSAND." RELEASE CONTINENTAL THREE TWENTY-ONE WHEN UNITED SIX SEVENTEEN REPORTS TWO MILES NORTHEAST OF PONCA CITY VORTAC.

"UNITED SIX SEVENTEEN, CLEARED TO TULSA AIRPORT VIA DEPART SOUTHWEST, DIRECT PONCA CITY VORTAC VICTOR EIGHT CLIMB AND MAINTAIN ONE SEVEN THOUSAND. REPORT TWO MILES NORTHEAST OF PONCA CITY VORTAC TO PONCA CITY TOWER. CONTACT AERO CENTER ONE TWO FOUR POINT ZERO AT PONCA CITY VORTAC."

INITIAL SEPARATION OF DEPARTURES/ARRIVALS AND VISUAL SEPARATION EXERCISE 2

DIRECTIONS: *Complete exercise items 1 through 5, using the information on the strips.*

1. TIME: 0055   RUNWAY: 36

N36Q		T→N TL ↑	↑ 100	DAL	MLC V9 DAL/0105	
		270⇒V9				D-A
BE90/D		RLS 1'<N45C				
		0055/				
T190		MLC P0100		100	LV 30	ZFW

N45C		T→N ↑	↑ 90	HOT	MLC V6 HOT/0048	
		360/⇒V6				D-A
BE80/X						
		0055/			LV 30	
T190		MLC P0100		90		ZME

Using the one-minute rule, write the phraseology to clear both aircraft and mark the strips.

"KING AIR THREE SIX QUEBEC, CLEARED TO DALLAS AIRPORT VIA DEPART NORTH, TURN LEFT, FLY HEADING TWO SEVEN ZERO UNTIL JOINING VICTOR NINE, VICTOR NINE, CLIMB AND MAINTAIN ONE ZERO THOUSAND, CONTACT AERO CENTER ONE TWO FIVE POINT ZERO LEAVING THREE THOUSAND." RELEASE KING AIR THREE SIX QUEBEC ONE MINUTE AFTER QUEEN AIR FOUR FIVE CHARLIE DEPARTS.

"QUEEN AIR FOUR FIVE CHARLIE CLEARED TO HOT SPRINGS AIRPORT VIA DEPART NORTH, TURN RIGHT, FLY HEADING THREE SIX ZERO UNTIL JOINING VICTOR SIX, VICTOR SIX, CLIMB AND MAINTAIN NINER THOUSAND, CONTACT AERO CENTER ONE TWO FIVE POINT ZERO LEAVING THREE THOUSAND."

2.   TIME: 1700   RUNWAY: 21

N23N		T→SW -PNC RLS 2'<BNF61	↑150	TUL	PNC V8 TUL/0012	
LR25/A						D-A
		1702/				
T450		PNC P1705		160	LV 30	

BN611		T→SW -PNC	↑120 X 20 NE OKC ↑60	OKC	PNC V3 OKC V1 DAL	
B720/A						D-A
		1700/				
T450		PNC P1705		120	LV 30	

Using the two-minute rule, write the phraseology to clear both aircraft and mark the strips.

"LEARJET TWO THREE NOVEMBER, CLEARED TO TULSA AIRPORT VIA DEPART SOUTHWEST, DIRECT PONCA CITY VORTAC, VICTOR EIGHT, CLIMB AND MAINTAIN ONE FIVE THOUSAND, CONTACT AERO CENTER ONE TWO FOUR POINT ZERO LEAVING THREE THOUSAND." RELEASE LEARJET TWO THREE NOVEMBER TWO MINUTES AFTER BRANIFF SIX ELEVEN DEPARTS.

"BRANIFF SIX ELEVEN, CLEARED TO DALLAS AIRPORT VIA DEPART SOUTHWEST, DIRECT PONCA CITY VORTAC, VICTOR THREE OKLAHOMA CITY, VICTOR ONE. CROSS TWO ZERO MILES NORTHEAST OF OKLA-HOMA CITY VORTAC AT OR ABOUT SIX THOUSAND, CLIMB AND MAINTAIN ONE THREE THOUSAND, CONTACT AERO CENTER ONE TWO FOUR POINT ZERO LEAVING THREE THOUSAND."

3.   TIME: 1455   RUNWAY: 21

AA476		T→SW- PNC RLS 2'<TW56	↑160 ×20NE OKC ↕60	OKC	PNC V3 ABI	
B707/A						D-A
		1457/				
T450		PNC P1500		160	LV 30	

TW56		T→SW ↑ -PNC	↑ 150	TUL	PNC V8 TUL	
B707/A						D-A
		1455/				
T450		PNC P1500		160	LV 30	

Using the two-minute rule, write the phraseology to clear both aircraft and mark the strips.

"AMERICAN FOUR SEVENTY-SIX, CLEARED TO ABILENE AIRPORT VIA DEPART SOUTHWEST, DIRECT PONCA CITY VORTAC, VICTOR THREE. CROSS TWO ZERO MILES NORTHEAST OF OKLAHOMA CITY VORTAC AT OR ABOUT SIX THOUSAND, CLIMB AND MAINTAIN ONE SIX THOUSAND. CONTACT AERO CENTER ONE TWO FOUR POINT ZERO LEAVING THREE THOUSAND." RELEASE AMERICAN FOUR SEVENTY-SIX TWO MINUTES AFTER TWA FIFTYSIX DEPARTS.

"TWA FIFTY-SIX, CLEARED TO TULSA AIRPORT VIA DEPART SOUTHWEST, DIRECT PONCA CITY VORTAC VICTOR EIGHT. CLIMB AND MAINTAIN ONE FIVE THOUSAND, CONTACT AERO CENTER ONE TWO FOUR POINT ZERO LEAVING THREE THOUSAND."

4.   TIME: 1455   RUNWAY: 18

N107B		T→S TL ↑	↑ 130	PRX	MLC V7 PRX/0022	
		120/⇒V7				
BE90/A		RLS 1'<N23Y				D-A
		1455/				
T200		MLC P1500		130	LV 30	ZFW

N23Y		T→S TR ↑	↑ 140	DAL	MLC V9 DAL/0100	
		250/⇒V9				
BE90/A						D-A
		1455/				
T210		MLC P1500		140	LV 30	ZFW

Using the one-minute rule, write the phraseology to clear both aircraft and mark the strips.

"TRAVEL AIR ONE ZERO SEVEN BRAVO, CLEARED TO PARIS AIRPORT VIA DEPART SOUTH, TURN LEFT, FLY HEADING ONE TWO ZERO UNTIL JOINING VICTOR SEVEN, VICTOR SEVEN, CLIMB AND MAINTAIN ONE THREE THOUSAND, CONTACT AERO CENTER ONE TWO FIVE POINT ZERO LEAVING THREE THOUSAND." RELEASE TRAVEL AIR ONE ZERO SEVEN BRAVO ONE MINUTE AFTER KING AIR TWO THREE YANKEE DEPARTS.

"KING AIR TWO THREE YANKEE, CLEARED TO DALLAS AIRPORT VIA DEPART SOUTH, TURN RIGHT, FLY HEADING TWO FIVE ZERO UNTIL JOINING VICTOR NINE, VICTOR NINE, CLIMB AND MAINTAIN ONE FOUR THOUSAND, CONTACT AERO CENTER ONE TWO FIVE POINT ZERO LEAVING THREE THOUSAND."

5. TIME: 1248   RUNWAY: 21

CO410 DC9/A T450	TUL 1231	㊺ 12 45 45 PNC	60✓— 60/11 SE	TUL V8 PNC PT	APCH APCH 1241

| N23Y BE95/A T195 | | T→SW -PNC SYD COA 410 1250/ PNC P1250 | ↑80 | END PNC V2 END/0025 80 | LV 30 | D-END |

Write the phraseology to clear N23Y and authorize tower to separate C0410 and N23Y. Mark strips accordingly.

"TRAVEL AIR TWO THREE YANKEE, CLEARED TO ENID VORTAC VIA DEPART SOUTHWEST DIRECT PNC VORTAC VICTOR TWO CLIMB AND MAINTAIN EIGHT THOUSAND CONTACT AERO CENTER ONE TWO FOUR POINT ZERO LEAVING THREE THOUSAND." VISUAL SEPARATION APPROVED BETWEEN TRAVEL AIR TWO THREE YANKEE AND CONTINENTAL FOUR TEN. TRAVEL AIR TWO THREE YANKEE RELEASED YOUR DISCRETION.

INITIAL SEPARATION OF DEPARTURES/ARRIVALS AND VISUAL SEPARATION END-OF-LESSON TEST

DIRECTIONS: *Items 1 through 6 and 8 are multiple-choice. Indicate your selection by circling the appropriate letter for each test item. For item 7, fill in the blanks with the correct answer. Answers appear at the end of the chapter.*

1. When using initial separation minima for departures, what is the minimum degree divergence?
   (A) 15 degrees   (B) 30 degrees   (C) 45 degrees   (D) 60 degrees

2. TIME: 1501   RUNWAY: 36

N795K		T→N TR		PRX	MLC V7 HOU/0200	
		070/⇒V7				
C172/D		HFR				D-A
		1501/				
T120		MLC P1500		70	LV 30	ZFW

N45C		T→N360	↑80	TUL	MLC V7 MKC/1613	
		⇒V7	×21SE		1613	
BE18/B			TUL ↕60			D-A
		1501/1501			LV30	
T140		MLC P1500		80		

Refer to the above strips.
What is the earliest time Cessna 795K may depart McAlester airport?
(A) 1501   (B) 1502   (C) 1503   (D) 1504

3.

N64019		T→SW72	↑90	TUL	PNC V8 TUL/1766	
		170/⇒V8			1755	
C182						D-A
		1730/			LV30	
T180		PNC P1730		90		

N3571W			↑		GCK	PNC V8 GCK/0040	
M021/A							D-A
			1730/				
T180			PNC P1730		80		

What is the phraseology to clear N3571W, using the one-minute rule?

"MOONEY THREE FIVE SEVEN ONE WHISKEY, CLEARED TO GARDEN CITY AIRPORT VIA

(A) DEPART SOUTHWEST, HEADING TWO ONE ZERO UNTIL JOINING VICTOR EIGHT, VICTOR EIGHT, MAINTAIN ..."

(B) DEPART SOUTHWEST, HEADING TWO SEVEN ZERO UNTIL JOINING VICTOR EIGHT, VICTOR EIGHT, MAINTAIN ..."

(C) DEPART SOUTHWEST, TURN RIGHT, HEADING ONE SEVEN ZERO UNTIL JOINING VICTOR EIGHT, VICTOR EIGHT, MAINTAIN ..."

(D) TURN RIGHT, HEADING TWO ONE FIVE UNTIL JOINING VICTOR EIGHT, VICTOR EIGHT, MAINTAIN ..."

4. When departing aircraft will fly the same course initially, but will fly courses that diverge by at least 45 degrees within 5 minutes after takeoff, the approved minimum separation to be maintained is

(A) 1 minute   (B) 2 minutes   (C) 3 minutes   (D) 4 minutes

5. TIME: 1711   RUNWAY: 36

EA730		T→N- MLC	↑	↑ 150	MIO	MLC V9 ICT	
DC9/A		HFR					D-A
			1710/			LV 30	
T450		MLC P1710			150		

AA493		T→N -MLC	↑	↑ 160	SNL	MLC V6 ABQ	
DC9/A							D-A
		1710/1711					
T450		MLC P1710			160	LV30	

Refer to the above strips.

Using minimum DME separation, EA 730 may be released when AA493 reports
(A) McAlester VORTAC.
(B) 2 miles south of McAlester VORTAC.
(C) 3 miles south of McAlester VORTAC.
(D) 5 miles south of McAlester VORTAC.

6. Visual separation may be applied between an arriving and departing IFR aircraft
   (A) anytime, if pilots concur.
   (B) only if the airport is served by approach control and pilots concur.
   (C) at airports served by nonapproach towers.
   (D) when the arriving aircraft has reported over the VOR inbound.

7. You may authorize a tower to provide visual separation between two aircraft within a control zone provided

   _____

   _____

   _____

8. What is the phraseology used to authorize a nonapproach control tower to provide visual separation between arriving and departing IFR aircraft?
   (A) "RELEASE WHEN (ID) IN SIGHT AND LANDING ASSURED."
   (B) "RELEASE SUBJECT YOUR DISCRETION (ID)."
   (C) "RELEASE SUBJECT YOUR DISCRETION WHEN (ID) IN SIGHT, LANDING ASSURED."
   (D) "VISUAL SEPARATION APPROVED BETWEEN (ID) AND (ID), (departing aircraft) RELEASED, YOUR DISCRETION."

LESSON 23
RECOGNIZING AIR TRAFFIC SITUATIONS

You have covered the rules and procedures that you will use in the lab. In a previous lesson you were told that you must have instant recall of these to control traffic. Not only must you recall the rules and procedures, now you must show that you can apply them. You must first recognize which rule or procedure will be best for a situation, then correctly apply it. We will now review and practice recognizing situations. Remember, there is often more than one solution to a problem.

Objectives

Given air traffic situations, and in accordance with 7110.65, you will:

1. Analyze traffic situations to determine if separation exists and will continue to exist.

2. Establish a priority of control actions.

3. Formulate preplanned clearances that will provide separation.

RECOGNIZING AIR TRAFFIC SITUATIONS EXERCISE

DIRECTIONS: *Refer to the following strips to answer items 1 through 10.*

AA590 N/B727/A T485	TRYON 1137	↓ 11⁴⁵ TUL	170	ABQ V4N TUL	

BN808 B707/A T475	MLC 1137 11	 11⁴⁴ MAYES	140	MIO DFW V9 ICT	

RC164 CD9/A T460	MIO 1137	 11⁴² TUL	100	MLC MSP V7 HOU	 ZFW

UA656 B737/A T450	MLC 1132	 11⁴¹ DEPEW	120	PNC MSY V11 ICT	

EA122 B727/A T480	OKC 1122	↓ 11⁴¹ TUL	120	ELP V4 TUL	 ZME

DL232	PNC 1127			140	FSM	DEN V8 ATL	
DC9/A			11^{40}				
T460			TUL				ZME

1. On which flight progress strips would it be necessary to record intersection times?

   DAL 232, EAL122, UAL656

2. Are DL232 and BN308 separated? Explain your answer.

   N0—COMPUTING A MAYES TIME WILL SHOW THAT LESS THAN 10 MINUTES EXISTS AT MAYES

3. Are any aircraft wrong altitude for direction of flight? If so, which ones?

   DAL 232, EAL122, REP164

4. Which aircraft are considered arriving aircraft?

   EAL122 AND AAL590

5. Which aircraft are considered traffic for AA590?

   DAL232, EAL122, UAL656, REP164

6. Which aircraft are traffic for EA122?

   UAL656, REP164, AAL590

7. Are there any opposite direction traffic situations?

   NO

8. What is the next posted fix on BN808?

   MIAMI

9. Is UA656 considered traffic for AA590? Why/Why not?

   YES—AAL590, LANDING TULSA, MUST BE DESCENDED THROUGH THE ALTITUDE OF UAL656. LESS THAN 10 MINUTES' SEPARATION EXISTS AT TRYON.

10. What is the next posted fix on RC164?

    MCALESTER

RECOGNIZING AIR TRAFFIC SITUATIONS END-OF-LESSON TEST

DIRECTIONS: *Items 1 through 5, 7 through 9, and 11 through 13 are multiple-choice. Indicate your selection by circling the appropriate letter for each test item. Items 6 and 10 are completion statements. Fill in the blanks with the appropriate words or phrases.*

Use the clearances and information on the following flight progress strips to answer items 1–5.

C0515	PNC 2122		110	MLC	SLC V8 PNC V11 MLC
DC9/A		21^{30}			
T460		DEPEW			

FL251	MIO 2120		120	MLC	ICT V9 MIO V10 TUL V7 PRX
CV48/B		21^{28}			
T280		TUL			

UA57	SGF 2116	↓	150		SGF V4 TUL
B737/A		21^{27}			
T450		TUL			

DL312	TRYON 2117	↓	130		OKC V4N TUL
DC9/A		21^{25}			
T460		TUL			

TW133	MIO			130	MLC	ORD V10 MIO V9 DFW	
	2114						
B707/B		21²⁰					
T470		MAYES					

1. On which aircraft should intersection times be recorded?
   (A) COA515, UAL57, and DAL312   (B) UAL57, DAL312, and EAL251
   (C) TWA133, DAL312, and COA515   (D) TWA133, COA515, and UAL57

2. Which aircraft need to be separated?
   (A) DAL312 from TWA133, UAL57 from DAL312
   (B) DAL312 from UAL57, UAL57 from TWA133 and EAL251
   (C) TWA133 from DAL312 and UAL57, UAL57 from EAL251
   (D) UAL57 from TWA133 and EAL251, DAL312 from EAL251, COA515, and
        UAL57

3. Which aircraft are WAFDOF?
   (A) UAL57, TWA133, and EAL251   (B) UAL57, DAL312, and COA515
   (C) TWA133, EAL251, and DAL312   (D) COA515, UAL57, and TWA133

4. Which clearance will guarantee separation for DAL312, assuming you have
   control?
   (A) $\underline{130 \downarrow 60}$ (B) $\underline{130 \downarrow 60}$
        X43W $\updownarrow$ 100   X43W $\uparrow$ 120
        X17W @ 60   X17W @ 60

   (C) $\underline{130 \downarrow 60}$ (D) 130 $\downarrow$ 60
        X17W @ 60

5. Which clearance guarantees separation for UAL57, assuming you have control?
   (A) $\underline{150 \downarrow 70}$ (B) $\underline{150 \downarrow 70}$
        X40NE $\updownarrow$ 120   X30NE $\updownarrow$ 110
        X9NE $\updownarrow$ 110

   (C) $\underline{150 \downarrow 70}$ (D) $\underline{150 \downarrow 70}$
        X40NE $\updownarrow$ 120   X30NE $\updownarrow$ 140
        X8NE $\updownarrow$ 110

6. TIME: 1321   RUNWAY: 18

WAL160	TUL		↓	90		OKC V4 TUL V7 MIO	
	1325						
L188/A		13³³					
		33					
T280		MIO					

N45GA	PNC			110		END V2 MIO	
	1314		↓				
N265/A		13²⁵					
		25					
T420		MIO					

N12242			↑		PNC	MIO V2 PNC V8 DEN	
BE10/A							
		1320/					
T240		MIO P1320			80		

A. MIO radio requested a clearance on N12242 at 1320. Between N12242 and N45GA, which aircraft has operational priority?

_____

B. Write the procedure for issuing clearance to N12242 that provides approved separation.

_____

_____

_____

7. TIME: 0547

RC134	CDS			100√	SNL	ABQ V6 HOT	
	0539						
CV44/P		06⁰⁴					
		04					
T240		OKC					

UA232	CDS			140√		LAX V6 OKC	
	0541		↓				
DC9/A		05⁵⁴					
		54					
T480		OKC					

Which procedure is correct for establishing an arrival sequence for UA232?
(A) Clear UA232 to Minco via a 30-mile arc SW to cross OKC 255R at or above 11,000 to cross Minco at 6,000.
(B) Establish 5 miles between UA232 and RC134, then clear UA232 to Yukon to cross Yukon at 6,000.

(C) Establish 10 miles between aircraft, then clear UA232 to Yukon to descend now through 9,000 to cross Yukon at 6,000.

(D) Clear UA232 to Yukon to descend and maintain 6,000.

8. TIME: 0957

N824A	DAL 0948		70√	HOT	DAL V9 MLC V6 HOT	
BE100/A		10¹⁷				
		17				
T220		MLC				ZME

N2864A	SNL 0956		90√	HOT	CDS V6 HOT	
C421/A		10¹⁵			CC	
		15				
T205		MLC			3E SNL/0957	ZME

TN33AA	SNL 0951	↓	110√		CDS V6 MLC	APCH
C421/A		10⑩				APCH
		10				0957
T205		MLC			18E SNL/0957	

Complete the following clearance for TN33AA after establishing longitudinal separation with N2864A: "CESSNA THREE ALFA ALFA CLEARED FOR APPROACH

(A) CROSS SEVEN MILES WEST OF MCALESTER VORTAC AT OR BELOW SIX THOUSAND."

(B) DESCEND NOW THROUGH EIGHT THOUSAND CROSS MCALESTER VORTAC AT OR BELOW SIX THOUSAND."

(C) CROSS MCALESTER VORTAC AT OR BELOW SIX THOUSAND CONTACT MCALESTER TOWER ONE ONE EIGHT POINT TWO."

(D) DESCEND NOW THROUGH EIGHT THOUSAND CROSS SEVEN MILES WEST OF MCALESTER VORTAC AT OR BELOW SIX THOUSAND."

9. TIME: 0401

N645G	PNC		120√	ABI	ICT V5 PNC V3 ABI	
	0400					
N265/A		04¹⁵				
		15				
T400	00	OKC				ZAB

N73JD	PNG		140√		MKC V3 OKC	
	0358					
LR36/A		04¹¹				
		11				
T460		OKC				

Which is the correct procedure to effect separation between N73JD and N645G?
(A) Establish 20 miles between N73JD and N645G; then clear N73JD to Coyle to cross Coyle at 6,000.
(B) Establish 10 miles between N73JD and N645G to descend and maintain 6,000.
(C) Clear N73JD to Jones via 30 mile arc NE to cross OKC 045R at or above 13,000 to cross Jones at 6,000.
(D) Establish 5 miles between N73JD and N645G; then clear N73JD to Coyle to cross Coyle at 6,000.

10. TIME: 0358

TW69	DAL		150W	HOT	ELP V9 MLC V6 MEM	
	0410					
H/B747/A		04²⁵				
T480		MLC				ZME

VV6K17	PRX		150W	MIO	MSY V11 MLC V9 ICT	
	0410					
A4/P		04¹⁹				
T420		MLC				

N824D	DAL			150√/W	HOT	CRP V9 MLC V6 HOT	
	0349					LIT	
G159/B		04^{12}					
			12				
T300		MLC				CTL	ZME

Write the Phraseology for solving the above situation.

N824D _____

_____

_____

VV6K17 _____

_____

_____

11. TIME: 2024   RUNWAY: 36

OZ811	MLC					MLC V11 PNC V2 LAX	
B727/B							
T480	+8	DEPEW					

N8166	MIO			100√	OKC	SGF V4 OKC V6 CDS	
	2003				2055		
BE100/A		20^{15}					
			15 15				
T190		TUL					

N200Y	HOT		↓	100 ↓ 60		HOT V6 MLC	APCH
	2005						N
C500/A		20^{30}					H360
							2040
T360		MLC				CC	

OZ811		T→N ↑		PNC	MLC V11 PNC V2 LAX	
B727/B		MLC				D-A
		2024/				
T480		MLC P2024		160		

Which restriction for 0Z811 guarantees separation?

(A) $\underline{\quad \uparrow 160 \quad}$
X17BW $\updownarrow$ 50
X52NW $\updownarrow$ 110

(B) $\underline{\quad \uparrow 160 \quad}$
X17NW $\updownarrow$ 50

(C) $\underline{\quad \uparrow 160 \quad}$
X52NW $\updownarrow$ 110

(D) $\underline{\quad \uparrow 160 \quad}$
X9NW $\updownarrow$ 50
X62NW $\updownarrow$ 110

12. TIME: 0219

N645G	MLC 0211	↑	150$\sqrt{}$ ↓60 ×6N MLC	DAL V9 MLC V7 TUL TUL 1	
N265/A		02②⓪	$\updownarrow$ 110		F
					30N
T360		TUL		30N MLC	MLC

N111MH	MLC 0205		100$\sqrt{}$	PNC 0238	MSY V11 ICT	
C210/D		02²⁰				
		19 19				
T250		DEPEW				

AL160		↑		OKC	TUL V4 ABI	
L188/A						D-A
		0219/				
T300		TUL P0218		120		

Which clearance for AL160 will effect separation with N111MH and N645G?

(A) "... CROSS TWO NINER MILES SOUTHWEST OF TULSA VORTAC AT OR ABOVE ONE ONE THOUSAND, MAINTAIN ONE TWO THOUSAND."

(B) "... CROSS ONE SEVEN MILES SOUTHWEST OF TULSA VORTAC AT OR BELOW FIVE THOUSAND, CROSS TWO NINER MILES SOUTHWEST OF TULSA VORTAC AT OR ABOVE ONE ONE THOUSAND, MAINTAIN ONE TWO THOUSAND."

(C) "... CROSS ONE SEVEN MILES SOUTHWEST OF TULSA VORTAC AT OR BELOW FIVE THOUSAND, MAINTAIN ONE TWO THOUSAND."

(D) "... MAINTAIN ONE TWO THOUSAND."

13. TIME: 0035

N967K	OKC 0030			70√W	TUL	ABI V4 TUL	
C310/U		00⁴⁵					
T180		SLICK					

N98324	MLC 0018			80√	OKC	MLC V6 CDS	
PA31/A		00⁴³					
		43					
T180		SNL					

TN34721	DAL 0011			70√√	PNC	DAL V5 ICT	
PAZT/B		00⁴⁰					
		40					
T180		SNL					

Which clearance is correct for TN34721?

(A) $\frac{70 \uparrow 90}{70/5N}$ (B) $\frac{70 \uparrow 90}{X13N \updownarrow 80}$

X13N ↕ 80

(C) $\frac{70 \uparrow 90}{X5S @ 90}$ (D) 70 ↑ 90

LESSONS 17–23 ANSWERS

IFR FLIGHT DIRECTION, ALTITUDE ASSIGNMENT AND ALTIMETER SETTING
END-OF-LESSON TEST

1. C	4. D	7. C	10. A
2. A	5. A	8. C	11. B
3. C	6. B	9. B	12. D

IFR CLEARANCE AND ROUTE ASSIGNMENT
END-OF-LESSON TEST

1. A	4. B	7. B	10. B
2. B	5. D	8. C	11. A
3. A	6. A	9. C	

DEPARTURE PROCEDURE
END-OF-LESSON TEST

1. D	6. B
2. B	7. B
3. LOCAL TRAFFIC PATTERN, TERRAIN, OBSTRUCTION AVOIDANCE	8. C
	9. B
4. B	10. D
5. D	

ARRIVAL AND APPROACH PROCEDURES
END-OF-LESSON TEST

1. B	5. C	9. D	13. C
2. C	6. C	10. A	14. D
3. D	7. D	11. B	15. B
4. D	8. A	12. A	16. B

HOLDING AIRCRAFT
END-OF-LESSON TEST

1. B	4. C	7. A
2. B	5. C	8. B
3. C	6. B	9. B

INITIAL SEPARATION OF DEPARTURES/ARRIVALS AND VISUAL SEPARATION
END-OF-LESSON TEST

1. C
2. B
3. C
4. B
5. B

6. C
7. OTHER SEPARATION IS ENSURED AND TOWER HAS ARRIVAL IN SIGHT.
8. D

RECOGNIZING AIR TRAFFIC SITUATIONS
END-OF-LESSON TEST

1. D
2. D
3. A
4. B
5. A
6. a. N12242
   b. ISSUE WAL 160 @ 90 WITH AN EFC
      N45GA: X 6 W MIO @ 80
      N12242: ISSUE DEPARTURE CLEARANCE CLIMBING TO 70—GET TAIL TO TAIL WITH N45GA OR HAVE N45GA SAY DME THEN ISSUE RESTRICTIONS TO N12242 REFERENCE THE DME REPORT.
7. C
8. D
9. D
10. N824D—CROSS 6 MILES SOUTHWEST OF MCALESTER VORTAC AT OR ABOVE 160 CLIMB AND MAINTAIN 170.
    VV6K17—CROSS 6 MILES SOUTHEAST MCALESTER VORTAC AT AND MAINTAIN 140.
11. A
12. B
13. A

ZAE MAP INSTRUCTIONS

The following two pages show the ZAE map to be used with the exercises in this book (see Lesson 2: Aero Center Map Study, starting on page 33). To use the map properly, carefully follow these instructions:

1. Remove both pages from the book by cutting carefully along the dotted line.
2. Align the pages carefully so that all map features line up <u>exactly</u>.
3. Tape the two pages together.
4. Make several photocopies of the complete map. Do not enlarge it or reduce it in size.
5. To create an unlabeled version, use white-out to remove all numbers and letter codes. Make full-size photocopies of the unlabeled map.

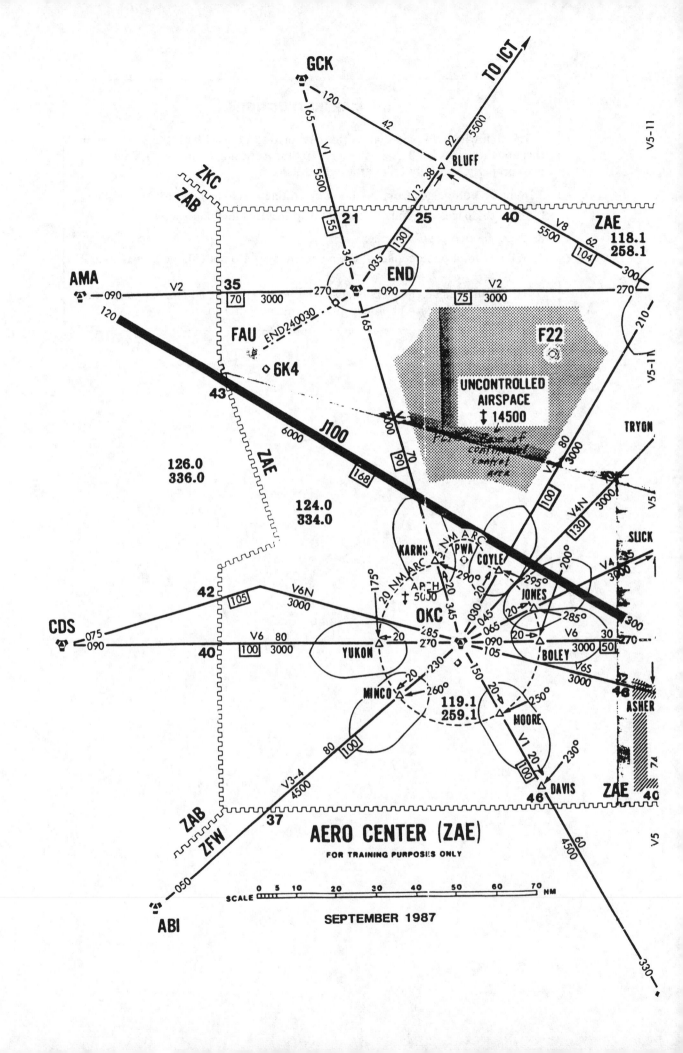

AERO CENTER (ZAE)

FOR TRAINING PURPOSES ONLY

SCALE 0 5 10 20 30 40 50 60 70 NM

SEPTEMBER 1987

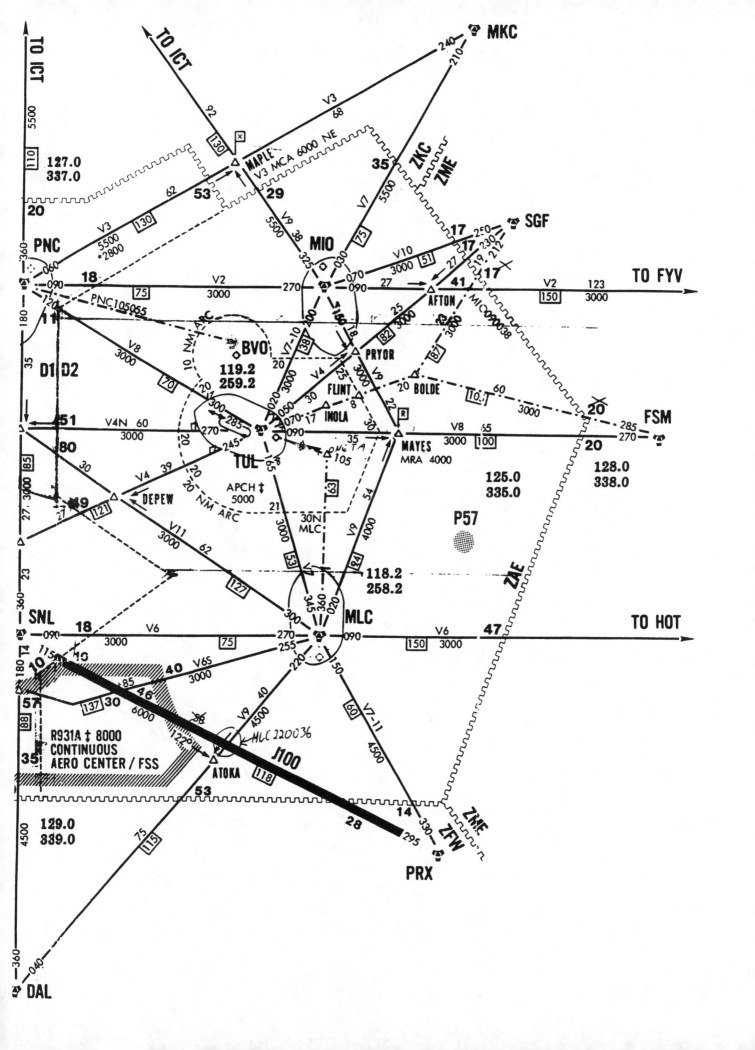